Bloom's Modern Critical Interpretations

The Adventures of
Huckleberry Finn
The Age of Innocence
Alice's Adventures in
Wonderland
All Quiet on the
Western Front
Animal Farm
The Ballad of the Sad
Café
Beloved
Beowulf
Black Boy
The Bluest Eye
The Canterbury Tales
Cat on a Hot Tin
Roof
Catch-22
The Catcher in the
Rye
The Chronicles of
Narnia
The Color Purple
Crime and
Punishment
The Crucible
Cry, the Beloved
Country
Darkness at Noon
Death of a Salesman
The Death of Artemio
Cruz
The Diary of Anne
Frank
Don Quixote
Emerson's Essays
Emma
Fahrenheit 451
A Farewell to Arms
Frankenstein
The Glass Menagerie
The Grapes of Wrath

Great Expectations
The Great Gatsby
Gulliver's Travels
Hamlet
Heart of Darkness
The House on Mango
Street
I Know Why the
Caged Bird Sings
The Iliad
Invisible Man
Jane Eyre
The Joy Luck Club
Julius Caesar
The Jungle
King Lear
Long Day's Journey
into Night
Lord of the Flies
The Lord of the Rings
Love in the Time of
Cholera
Macbeth
The Man Without
Qualities
The Merchant of
Venice
The Metamorphosis
A Midsummer Night's
Dream
Miss Lonelyhearts
Moby-Dick
My Ántonia
Native Son
Night
1984
The Odyssey
Oedipus Rex
The Old Man and the
Sea
On the Road

One Flew over the
Cuckoo's Nest
One Hundred Years of
Solitude
Othello
Persuasion
Portnoy's Complaint
Pride and Prejudice
Ragtime
The Red Badge of
Courage
Romeo and Juliet
The Rubáiyát of Omar
Khayyám
The Scarlet Letter
A Separate Peace
Silas Marner
Slaughterhouse-Five
Song of Solomon
The Sound and the
Fury
The Stranger
A Streetcar Named
Desire
Sula
The Sun Also Rises
The Tale of Genji
A Tale of Two Cities
"The Tell-Tale Heart"
and Other Stories
Their Eyes Were
Watching God
Things Fall Apart
The Things They
Carried
To Kill a Mockingbird
Ulysses
Waiting for Godot
The Waste Land
Wuthering Heights
Young Goodman
Brown

William Shakespeare's
King Lear
New Edition

Edited and with an introduction by
Harold Bloom
Sterling Professor of the Humanities
Yale University

BLOOM'S
LITERARY CRITICISM
An imprint of Infobase Publishing

Bloom's Modern Critical Interpretations: King Lear—New Edition

Copyright © 2010 by Infobase Publishing
Introduction © 2010 by Harold Bloom

Bloom's Literary Criticism
An imprint of Infobase Publishing
132 West 31st Street
New York NY 10001

Library of Congress Cataloging-in-Publication Data
William Shakespeare's King Lear / edited and with an introduction by Harold Bloom.
— New ed.
    p. cm. — (Bloom's modern critical interpretations)
    Includes bibliographical references and index.
    ISBN 978-1-60413-886-3 (hardcover)
    1. Shakespeare, William, 1564–1616. King Lear.   2. Lear, King (Legendary character), in literature. I. Bloom, Harold.
    PR2819.W55 2010
    822.3'3—dc22

                                    2010006131

Bloom's Literary Criticism books are available at special discounts when purchased in bulk quantities for businesses, associations, institutions, or sales promotions. Please call our Special Sales Department in New York at (212)967-8800 or (800)322-8755.

You can find Bloom's Literary Criticism on the World Wide Web at
http://www.chelseahouse.com

Contributing editor: Pamela Loos
Cover design by Takeshi Takahashi
Composition by IBT Global, Troy NY
Cover printed by IBT Global, Troy NY
Book printed and bound by IBT Global, Troy NY
Date printed: July 2010
Printed in the United States of America

10 9 8 7 6 5 4 3 2 1

This book is printed on acid-free paper.

Contents

Editor's Note   vii

Introduction   1
    Harold Bloom

King Lear   13
    Northrop Frye

The Emotional Landscape of *King Lear*   31
    Arthur Kirsch

"Is This the Promised End?"
    Death and Dying in *King Lear*   53
    David Bevington

King Lear: The Tragic Disjunction
    of Wisdom and Power   67
    Paul A. Cantor

Lear's System   85
    Ralph Berry

King Lear   97
    Frank Kermode

Lear's Three Shamings   113
    Robert Lanier Reid

Naked Lear   137
    Millicent Bell

Performance and Text: *King Lear*   151
        R. A. Foakes

Chronology   165

Contributors   167

Bibliography   169

Acknowledgments   173

Index   175

Editor's Note

My introduction centers on the chaotic cosmos of *King Lear* with its Jobean intensities. The volume begins with Northrop Frye's discussion of the ways the language of prophesy and madness inform the play. Arthur Kirsch then connects the universality of the tragedy to its portrayal of the primacy of anguish.

David Bevington traces the play's preoccupation with mortality and all things final, after which Paul A. Cantor locates the work's tragic vision in Shakespeare's understanding of the limitations and demands of political life.

Ralph Berry sees the work as a tragedy of identity, linked to Lear's rigid conception of systems of power. Frank Kermode also notes the play's Jobean dimensions in its preoccupation with notions of suffering and justice.

Robert Lanier Reid contends that the characters are ultimately exalted by the cycles of abasement they undergo, after which Millicent Bell explores nudity in the play and the metaphysics of Elizabethan fashion. R. A. Foakes then concludes the volume with a consideration of the interpretive gaps that are opened between the text and its performance.

HAROLD BLOOM

Introduction

King Lear is cosmos falling into chaos. So are *Othello, Macbeth,* and *Paradise Lost,* but they do not match *King Lear,* the unique eminence in the Earth's literary art.

Like Charles Lamb, I have learned not to attend performances of Shakespeare's most sublime work. A dramatic poem that ultimately reveals all familial joy to be delusional purchases the heights at dumbfoundering cost.

Beyond all other instances of *materia poetica,* what Freud termed the "family romance" is the matrix of profoundest sorrow, in literature as in life.

Freud quested for a release from escapable sorrow and tried to impart that quest to others. Psychoanalysis is now waning, if only because it could make no contribution to biology but only to discursive literature. And yet Freud was the Montaigne of the twentieth century and so one of the age's great writers, comparable to Joyce, Proust, Beckett, Mann, and Faulkner. Unlike those five peers, Freud resented Shakespeare for having gotten there first and taken up all the human space. This may account for Freud's weak misreading of *King Lear:* Both Cordelia and her father suffer a repressed incestuous desire and hence the catastrophe.

One of Freud's insights is that thought can be freed from its sexual past, in each child's early curiosity, only by a disciplined mode of recollection. Alas, it does not seem to me that thinking *can* be freed from its sexual foregrounding. *King Lear,* most comprehensive of dramas, shows us only one character so free, and he is anything but a great soul. Edmund the Bastard is the most frightening of Shakespearean villains because he is the coldest, transcending even Iago. And yet is even he utterly emancipated from the family romance?

1

Where Falstaff and Hamlet remain free—if only to fall—no one can be free in the cosmos of *King Lear* and *Macbeth*.

Of Shakespeare's own inwardness we know nothing, and yet the heterocosms he created persuade us pragmatically that his was the freest of spirits, like Falstaff's and Hamlet's before they fall into time. One of the most perplexing persons in all Shakespeare is Lear's godson, Edgar. It startles me when Stanley Cavell calls Edgar "a weak and murderous character" and when the late A. D. Nuttall says that "Edgar is partly the loving son, partly devilish." Between them, Cavell and Nuttall divide the palm as Shakespeare's best philosophical critic. And yet, Edgar is anything but weak or murderous, and there is nothing devilish in him. Perhaps a philosophically guided criticism of Shakespeare touches its limits with Edgar?

We have no adequate vocabulary for describing Shakespeare's tragic art. No one else in the world's literature thinks so powerfully and originally as Shakespeare does, but "thinks" may be a misleading word for his movements of mind.

Among the philosophers, Hume and Wittgenstein disliked Shakespeare, while Hegel exactly praised Shakespeare for creating characters who are "free artists of themselves." But if there is no freedom in the Lear-cosmos, how can anyone be a free artist of herself or himself? That is Edgar's dilemma: His enemy half-brother, Edmund, designs the entire drama. How is Edmund to be defeated? With a genius for negativity, the outcast Edgar goes downward and outward to become Tom O'Bedlam, and then a discarded serving man, and finally a black knight without a name, to avenge himself and his father on Edmund and his cohorts. Edgar's quest, like Hamlet's, is to sustain the honor of the father and of the god-father, Lear. It can be said that Edgar does a better job than Hamlet does, but at a very high price, for himself and for his father, Gloucester.

At the close of Shakespeare's revised *King Lear*, a reluctant Edgar becomes king of Britain, accepting his destiny but in the accents of despair. Nuttall speculates that Edgar, like Shakespeare himself, usurps the power of manipulating the audience by deceiving poor Gloucester. The speculation is brilliant, and no more than Nuttall does would I make the error of judging Edgar to be Shakespeare's surrogate. Negation is central to Shakespeare's mediation between the sublime and the grotesque, and Edgar is that mediation.

What is called thinking by the ontologist Heidegger does have its affinities with the Pindaric odes of Hölderlin, as Heidegger insisted, but is irrelevant to Shakespearean negativity. Hegel thought he saw something of his own dialectics of negation in Shakespeare's art.

The poet who created *The Tragedy of King Lear* was no more a theologian than a philosopher. My late friend the scholar William Elton said of *King*

Lear that it was "a pagan play for a Christian audience." "Christian poetry" is an oxymoron; poetry in a deep sense is always pagan. Shakespeare was not interested either in solving problems or in finding God. Nothing is solved in or by *King Lear*, and Lear loses his old gods without finding new ones. Shakespeare was larger than Plato and than St. Augustine. He *encloses* us, because we *see* with his fundamental perceptions.

I

Lear is so grand a literary character that he tends to defy direct description; nearly everything worth saying about him needs to be balanced by an antithetical statement. Like my mentor, the late and much-lamented Northrop Frye, I tend to find Lear's precursor in the Yahweh of the J Writer, as mediated for Shakespeare by the Geneva Bible. As Frye remarked, that Yahweh "is not a theological god at all but an intensely human character as violent and unpredictable as King Lear." Lear's sudden furies indeed are as startling as Yahweh's, and like Yahweh, Lear remains somehow incommensurate with us. Beyond the scale of everyone else in his drama, Lear is as much a fallen, mortal god as he is a king. And unlike the J Writer's Yahweh, Lear is loved as well as feared by everyone in the play who is at all morally admirable: Cordelia, Kent, Gloucester, Edgar, Albany. Those who hate the king are monsters of the deep: Goneril, Regan, Cornwall. That leaves Lear's Fool, who loves the king, yet also manifests an uncanny ambivalence toward his master. The Fool, at once Lear's fourth child and his tormentor, is one of the two great reflectors of the king in the play. The other is Edmund, who never speaks to Lear or is spoken to by him, but who illuminates Lear by being his total antithesis, as nihilistically devoid of authentic, strong emotions as Lear is engulfed by them. I propose in this introduction a twofold experiment, to analyze the Fool and Edmund in themselves, and then to consider Lear in their dark aura as well as in his own sublimity. The Fool I see as a displaced spirit, and even after having abdicated Lear cannot be that, since he remains massively in what always must be his place. Edmund, so dangerously attractive to Goneril and Regan, and to something in ourselves as well, is loved by the fatal sisters precisely because he incarnates every quality alien to their father, whom they at once loathe and dread.

II

Why call Lear's Fool a displaced spirit, since his sublimely bitter wit catches up so much of the wisdom to be learned from Lear's tragedy? Do we ever sense that the Fool has wandered in from some other play, as it were? Love, Dr. Johnson remarks, is the wisdom of fools, and the folly of the wise. He presumably was not thinking of Lear and the Fool, but as with Lear and

Cordelia, the bond and torment of that relationship certainly is authentic and mutual love. William R. Elton shrewdly says of the Fool that "his Machiavellian realism [is] defeated by his own foolish sympathy," his love for Lear. As Coleridge noted, the Fool joins himself to the pathos or suffering of the drama; he does not stand apart in a jester's role. Yet Shakespeare excludes the Fool from the tragedy of Lear and Cordelia; the Fool simply drops out of the play, notoriously without explanation. I take it that he wanders off to another drama, which Shakespeare unfortunately did not choose to write, except perhaps for certain moments in *Timon of Athens*.

Elton also observes that the Fool is "at once more than a character and less," which seems to me just right. Shylock, Barnardine (despite his brevity), Malvolio, Caliban; these all are grand characters, but the Fool's dramatic function, like Horatio's, is partly to be a surrogate for the audience, mediating Lear's sublimity for us even as Horatio mediates the sublime aspects of Hamlet. The Fool and Horatio are floating presences, rather than proper characters in themselves. Horatio's only affect, besides his love for Hamlet, is his capacity for wonder, while the Fool's love for Lear is accompanied by a capacity for terror, on Lear's behalf as on his own. Perhaps it is fitting that the Fool's last sentence (act 2, scene 6, line 84) is the hugely enigmatic "And I'll go to bed at noon" in response to Lear's pathetic: "So, so. We'll go to supper i' th' morning." Like Falstaff, the Fool has little to do with the time of day; the wisdom of his folly indeed is timeless. As with nearly everything uttered by Falstaff, each outburst of the Fool seems endless to our meditation, yet Falstaff enlightens us; a great teacher, he makes us wittier and more vital, or at least more aware of the pathos of a heroic vitality. The Fool drives us a little mad, even as perversely he punishes Lear by helping Lear along to madness. To instruct in folly, even in the Erasmian sense, is to practice a dark profession, since one is teaching unreason as the pragmatic alternative to knavery. Folly is a kind of Renaissance version of Freud's death drive, beyond the pleasure principle. Blake's Proverb of Hell, that if the Fool would persist in his folly, he would become wise, is perfectly exemplified by Lear's Fool, except that this Fool is uncannier even than that. Lear lovingly regards him as a child, and he is or seems to be a preternaturally wise child, but a child who cannot grow up, almost as though he were more sprite than human. He does not enter the play until its fourth scene, and before his entrance we are told that he has been pining away for Cordelia, with whom Lear famously confuses him at the tragedy's close: "And my poor fool is hanged." Unlike Cordelia, who more than Edgar is the play's idealized, natural Christian in a pre-Christian cosmos, the Fool exacts a kind of exasperated vengeance on Lear, who both courts and winces at the Fool's truthtelling. In one rather subtle way, the relationship between Lear and his Fool parallels the problematic relationship between Falstaff and Hal, since both Lear and Falstaff are in the position of loving fathers somewhat bewildered by the ambivalence shown toward them by their adopted "sons," the Fool and the future Henry V.

Criticism has tended to underestimate the Fool's responsibility for the actual onset and intense nature of Lear's madness. Hal knows that he will reject Falstaff: The Fool knows that he cannot reject Lear, but he also cannot accept a Lear who has unkinged himself, who indeed has abdicated fatherhood. To teach Lear wisdom so belatedly is one thing; to madden the bewildered old monarch is quite another. On some level of purposiveness, however repressed, the Fool does labor to destroy Lear's sanity. Hal labors, quite consciously, to destroy Falstaff's insouciance, which is why the prince so desperately needs to convince himself, and Falstaff, that Falstaff is a coward. He has convinced some moralizing scholars but not any audience or readership of any wit or vitality whatsoever. The Fool belongs to another world, where "fool" means at once "beloved one," "mad person," "child," and "victim." Lear's Fool is all of those but something much stranger also.

When the newly crowned Henry V brutally rejects Falstaff, he rather nastily observes: "How ill white hairs become a fool and jester!" We wince (unless we are moralizing scholars) both at the reduction of Falstaff's role as Hal's educator to the status of "fool and jester" and also because that unkind line fuses Lear and Lear's Fool together, and for an instant the crushed Falstaff embodies such a fusion. Desperately wistful in his broken-heartedness, Falstaff falls out of comic supremacy into a pathos tragic enough to accommodate Lear's Fool, if not quite Lear. It is as though, in that terrible moment, he leaves the company of the heroic wits—of Rosalind and Hamlet—and joins Shylock and Lear's Fool, Barnardine and Malvolio, and even Caliban as a displaced spirit. Suddenly the great and vital wit finds himself in the wrong play, soon enough to be Henry V, where all he can do is waste away into a pathetic death. Lear's Fool vanishes from Lear's tragedy because its terrible climax would be inappropriate for him. Dr. Johnson could not bear the vision of Lear carrying the dead Cordelia in his arms. How much more unbearable it would have been had Lear carried the dead Fool in his arms! Mercutio dies, and a joyous if obscene exuberance departs from *Romeo and Juliet*. Lear's Fool vanishes, but the displaced wisdom of his folly lingers in the king's final return to a sublime madness. We do not resent or even wonder at the Fool's tormenting of Lear, but the torment itself is wisdom, however bitter. Yet a wisdom that is madness returns us to the uncanny, to a sublime that is beyond our capacity to apprehend.

We cannot love Lear's Fool, but then we are not Lear. Feste, that marvelous contrast to Malvolio, is the best of Shakespearean fools, because he is so superbly humanized, unlike the rancid Touchstone, who is human—all too human. Lear's Fool stands apart; he does not quite seem a representation of a merely human being. He is a spirit who has wandered in from some other realm, only to be enthralled by the patriarchal, flawed greatness of Lear. Perhaps Lear's Fool, more even than Shakespeare's other displaced spirits, incarnates what Nietzsche thought was the motive for all metaphor, and so for all high literature: the desire to be elsewhere, the desire to be different.

III

One need not be a Goneril or a Regan to find Edmund dangerously attractive, in ways that perpetually surprise the unwary reader or playgoer. With authentic learning, William R. Elton makes the suggestion that Edmund is a Shakespearean anticipation of the seventeenth-century Don Juan tradition, which culminates in Molière's great play (1665). Elton also notes the crucial difference between Edmund and Iago, which is that Edmund paradoxically sees himself as overdetermined by his bastardy even as he fiercely affirms his freedom, whereas Iago is totally free. Consider how odd we would find it had Shakespeare decided to present Iago as a bastard or indeed given us any information at all about Iago's father. But Edmund's status as natural son is crucial, though even here Shakespeare confounds his age's expectations. Elton cites a Renaissance proverb that bastards by chance are good but by nature bad. Faulconbridge the Bastard, magnificent hero of *The Life and Death of King John*, is good not by chance, but because he is very nearly the reincarnation of his father, Richard Lionheart, whereas the dreadful Don John, in *Much Ado about Nothing*, has a natural badness clearly founded on his illegitimacy. Edmund astonishingly combines aspects of the personalities of Faulconbridge and of Don John, though he is even more attractive than Faulconbridge and far more vicious than Don John of Aragon.

Though Edmund, unlike Iago, cannot reinvent himself wholly, he takes great pride in assuming responsibility for his own amorality, his pure opportunism. Don John in *Much Ado* says, "I cannot hide what I am," while Faulconbridge the Bastard affirms, "And I am I, how'er I was begot." Faulconbridge's "And I am I" plays against Iago's "I am not what I am." Edmund cheerfully proclaims: "I should have been that I am, had the maidenl'est star in the firmament twinkled on my bastardizing." The great "I am" remains a positive pronouncement in Edmund, and yet he is as grand a negation, in some other ways, as even Iago is. But because of that one positive stance toward his own being, Edmund will change at the very end, whereas Iago's final act of freedom will be to pledge an absolute muteness as he is led away to death by torture. Everything, according to Iago, lies in the will, and in his case everything does.

In act 5, scene 3, Edmund enters with Lear and Cordelia as his prisoners. It is only the second time he shares the stage with Lear, and it will be the last. We might expect that he would speak to Lear (or to Cordelia), but he avoids doing so, referring to them only in the third person in his commands. Shakespeare, in this vast, indeed cosmological tragedy, gives us the highly deliberate puzzle that the two crucial figures, the tragic hero Lear, and the brilliant villain Edmund, never speak a single word to one another. Clearly Edmund, in act 5, scene 3, does not wish to speak to Lear, because he is actively plotting the murder of Cordelia and perhaps of Lear as well. Yet all the intricacies of the double plot do not in themselves explain away this remarkable gap in the play, and I wonder why Shakespeare avoided the confrontation. You can say he had no need of it, but this drama tells us to reason not the need. Shakespeare is our Scripture, replacing Scripture itself, and one should learn to read him the way the Kabbalists read the Bible, interpreting every absence as being significant. What can it tell us about Edmund and also about Lear that Shakespeare found nothing for them to say to each other?

These days, paternal love and filial love are not exactly in critical fashion, and most younger Shakespeareans do not seem to love Lear (or Shakespeare, for that matter). And yet it is difficult to find another Shakespearean protagonist as deeply loved by other figures in his or her play as Lear is loved by Kent, Cordelia, Gloucester, and the Fool, and by Edgar and Albany as well. Goneril, Regan, Cornwall, Edmund, and the wretched Oswald do not love the king, but they are all monsters, except for the subtly amoral Edmund. Lear may seem as violent, irascible, and unpredictable as the Biblical J Writer's Yahweh, on whom he is based, but clearly he has been a loving father to his people, unlike the original Yahweh. Edmund, for all his sophisticated and charismatic charm, inspires no one's love, except for the deadly and parallel voracious passions of Goneril and Regan, those monsters of the deep. And Edmund does not love them, or anyone else, or even himself. Perhaps Lear and Edmund cannot speak to each other because Lear is bewildered by the thwarting of his excess of love for Cordelia and by the hatred for him of Goneril and Regan, unnatural daughters, as he must call them. Edmund, in total contrast, hardly regards love as natural, even as he grimly exults in being the natural son of Gloucester. But even that contrast hardly accounts for the curious sense we have that Edmund somehow is not in the same play as Lear and Cordelia.

When Goneril kisses Edmund (act 4, scene 2, line 22), he gallantly accepts it as a kind of literal kiss of death, since he is too grand an ironist not to appreciate his own pledge: "Yours in the ranks of death." Still more remarkable is his soliloquy that closes act 5, scene 1:

To both these sisters have I sworn my love;
Each jealous of the other, as the stung
Are of the adder. Which of them shall I take?
Both? one? or neither? Neither can be enjoy'd
If both remain alive: to take the widow
Exasperates, makes mad her sister Goneril;
And hardly shall I carry out my side,
Her husband being alive. Now then, we'll use
His countenance for the battle: which being done,
Let her who would be rid of him devise
His speedy taking off, As for the mercy
Which he intends to Lear and to Cordelia,
The battle done, and they within our power
Shall never see his pardon; for my state
Stands on me to defend, not to debate.

So cool a negativity is unique, even in Shakespeare. Edmund is superbly sincere when he asks the absolutely open questions: "Which of them shall I take? / Both? one? or neither?" His insouciance is sublime, the questions being tossed off in the spirit of a light event, as though a modern young nobleman might ask whether he should take two princesses, one, or none out to dinner? A double date with Goneril and Regan should daunt any libertine, but the negation named Edmund is something very enigmatic. Iago's negative theology is predicated on an initial worship of Othello, but Edmund is amazingly free of all connection, all affect, whether toward his two adder- or shark-like royal princesses, or toward his half-brother, or toward Gloucester, in particular. Gloucester is in the way, in rather the same sense that Lear and Cordelia are in the way. Edmund evidently would just as soon not watch his father's eyes put out, but this delicacy does not mean that he cares at all about the event, one way or another. Yet, as Hazlitt pointed out, Edmund does not share in the hypocrisy of Goneril and Regan: His Machiavellianism is absolutely pure and lacks an Oedipal motive. Freud's vision of family romances simply does not apply to Edmund. Iago is free to reinvent himself every minute, yet Iago has strong passions, however negative. Edmund has no passions whatsoever; he has never loved anyone, and he never will. In that respect, he is Shakespeare's most original character.

There remains the enigma of why this cold negation is so attractive, which returns us usefully to his absolute contrast with Lear and with Lear's uncanny Fool. Edmund's desire is only for power, and yet one wonders if desire is at all the right word in connection with Edmund. Richard II lusts for power; Iago quests for it over Othello, so as to uncreate Othello, to reduce the mortal god of war into a chaos. Ulysses certainly seeks power over Achilles, in order to get on with the destruction of Troy. Edmund is the most Marlovian of these grand negations, since the soldier Macbeth does not so much will to usurp power, as he is overcome by his own imagination of usurpation. Edmund accepts the overdetermination of being a bastard, indeed he overaccepts it and glorifies in it, but he accepts nothing else. He is convinced of his natural superiority, which extends to his command of manipulative language, and yet he is not a Marlovian rhetorician, like Tamburlaine, nor is he intoxicated with his own villainy, like Richard II and Barabas. He is a Marlovian figure not in that he resembles a character in a play by Marlowe, but because I suspect he was intended to resemble Christopher Marlowe himself. Marlowe died, aged 29, in 1593, at about the time that Shakespeare composed *Richard III*, with its Marlovian protagonist, and just before the writing of *Titus Andronicus* with its Marlovian parody in Aaron the Moor. By 1605, when *King Lear* was written, Marlowe had been dead for 12 years, but *As You Like It*, composed in 1599, is curiously replete with wry allusions to Marlowe. We have no contemporary anecdotes connecting Shakespeare to Marlowe, but it seems quite unlikely that Shakespeare never met his exact contemporary and nearest precursor, the inventor of English blank-verse tragedy. Edmund, in the pre-Christian context of *King Lear*, is certainly a pagan atheist and libertine naturalist, as Elton emphasizes, and these are the roles that Marlowe's life exemplified for his contemporaries. Marlowe the man, or rather Shakespeare's memory of him, may be the clue to Edmund's strange glamour, the charismatic qualities that make it so difficult for us not to like him.

Whether or not an identification of Marlowe and Edmund is purely my critical trope, even as trope it suggests that Edmund's driving force is Marlovian nihilism, revolt against authority and tradition for revolt's own sake, since revolt and nature are thus made one. Revolt is heroic for Edmund, and he works his plots so that his natural superiority will make him king, whether as consort either to Regan or to Goneril, or as a solitary figure, should they slay each other. After Goneril first has murdered Regan and then killed herself, Edmund undergoes his radical transformation. What is exposed first is his acute overdetermination by his status as bastard. On knowing that his death wound is from Edgar, at least his social equal, he begins to be reconciled to the life being left behind him, the great line of acceptance being the famous:

The wheel is come full circle: I am here.

"I am here" reverberates with the dark undertone that here I started originally, that to have been born a bastard was to start with a death wound. Edmund is quite dispassionate about his own dying, but he is not doom-eager, unlike Goneril and Regan, both of whom seem to have been in love with him precisely because they sought a death wound. Nowhere else even in Shakespeare are we racked by the Hitchcockian suspense that attends Edmund's slow change as he dies, a change that comes too late to save Cordelia. Edmund, reacting to Edgar's extraordinary account of their father's death, confesses to being moved and hesitates on the verge of reprieving Cordelia. He does not get past that hesitation until the bodies of Goneril and Regan are brought in, and then his reaction constitutes the paradigmatic moment of change in all of Shakespeare:

> Yet Edmund was beloved:
> The one the other poisoned for my sake,
> And after slew herself.

Out of context this is outrageous enough to be hilarious. The dying nihilist reminds himself that in spite of all he was and did, he was beloved, albeit by these two monsters of the deep. He does not say that he cared for either or for anyone else, and yet this evidence of connection moves him. In context, its mimetic form is enormous. An intellect as cold, powerful, and triumphant as Iago's is suddenly startled by overhearing itself, and the will to change comes over Edmund. The good he means to do will be "despite of mine own nature," he tells us, so that his final judgment must be that he has not changed, more a Marlovian than a Shakespearean stance. And yet he is finally mistaken, for his nature has altered, too late to avoid the play's tragic catastrophe. Unlike Iago, Edmund has ceased to be a pure or grand negation. It is an irony of Shakespearean representation that we like Edmund least when he turns so belatedly toward the good. The change is persuasive, but by it Edmund ceases to be Edmund. Hamlet dies into apotheosis; Iago will die stubbornly Iago, in silence. We do not know who Edmund is, as he dies, and he does not know either.

IV

No other tragedy by Shakespeare risks a final pathos as terrible as Lear's. His entrance with the dead Cordelia in his arms is a spectacle scarcely to be borne; Dr. Samuel Johnson could not tolerate it. We are not given any finality in regard to the Fool; he vanishes from the play, almost as though Shakespeare has forgotten him. Edmund's enormous transformation has no pragmatic consequences; his change of orders comes too late, and his death affects no one. Lear's death is something like an apocalypse for Edgar, Albany, and Kent and scarcely less than that for us. Hamlet's death has elements in it of a transcendental release, while Lear's offers us no solace, aesthetic or metaphysical. The three survivors—Albany, Kent, and Edgar—are left standing onstage like so many waifs, lamenting a father-god lost forever to them. Albany, astonishingly but persuasively, attempts to yield rule to Kent and Edgar, but Kent indicates that he expects to follow Lear into death soon enough, while Edgar concludes with a plangent couplet that intimates a universal decline:

> The oldest hath borne most: we that are young
> Shall never see so much, nor live so long.

It is as if the death of the father-king-god has removed the only figuration that participated neither in origin nor in end. William R. Elton persuasively sees the tragedy as non-Christian, in harmony with its pre-Christian paganism, set as it is in a Britain contemporaneous with the Book of Job. Lear dies in despair of the pagan gods, and his survivors echo his despair, but in that echo Shakespeare blends overtones of biblical apocalypse. Nothing becomes the Creation, in the Bible, and never can be reduced to nothing again, even in apocalypse. But in Lear's tragedy, nothing does come of nothing, and so nothing is at last both origin and end. Had Lear not abdicated, a middle ground might have been kept for a while longer, but even in the opening scene the center must give way. The greatness of Lear's nature is always beheld by us, since his rages, his opacities, his blindnesses are on a cosmological scale. He derives from the Yahweh of the Sinai theophany but also from the half-mad Yahweh who leads a half-mad rabblement through the wilderness in Numbers. I return to the ways in which his qualities are exposed by his Fool and by Edmund, since they are the nothings of origin and of end that he ought to have labored to keep back, to fend off from his kingdom.

The Fool's ambivalence toward Lear may not be primal, but pragmatically it becomes so. Edmund, beyond all affect until his dying change, seems indifferent to the king and never expresses any reaction to Lear. We need expect none, since Edmund is so passionless in regard to his own father, Gloucester. Yet Edmund's whole being is a critique of Lear's passionate being, of a kingly father who cannot control any element whatsoever in his own self. Perfectly controlled to a preternatural degree, Edmund represents a nature that is precisely a knowing nothingness. We never would believe that Lear incarnates nothing and represents nothing, inadequate as he is in self-knowledge. He is the image of authentic authority, and though he himself will mock that image, we agree with Kent, who always seeks out and serves that authority.

Edmund cannot love anyone. The Fool loves Cordelia and, more ambivalently, Lear. What the uncanniness of both figures highlight in the king is his furious, hyperbolical capacity to love and to be loved. Lear's love for the Fool is a shadow of his thwarted love for Cordelia, thwarted not so much by her reticence as by his own excess, his bewilderment at the burden of something inexpressible in his love for her. Despite Lear's enormous eloquence, his very sublimity perpetually places him on the frontiers of what cannot be said. Again, the contrast both to the Fool and to Edmund is overwhelming. The Fool strikes home with every phrase, and Edmund surpasses even Iago as a manipulative rhetorician, invariably enabled by nature to say exactly what he intends to say. But Lear is always beyond his own intentions, always beyond the sayable. He persuades us of his Jobean dilemmas even though they are not truly Jobean. His rashness is matched by his furious sincerity and over-matched only by his mysterious authority, an eminence that survives madness and petulance and every error of his palpable bad judgments. The Fool is uncannily accurate; Edmund cannot make a mistake; Lear is gigantically wrong but never less than titanic, at least a daemon and sometimes a hint of something larger, a man who is also a god.

The gods, in this play, are nothing admirable, and yet they are the only gods in existence. What Edmund helps us see in Lear's character is that the king's elements of greatness are subdued neither by their antitheses in the bastard's analytical nihilism or by the monarch's own developing skepticism as to divine justice. What the Fool helps us see is that wisdom, however bitter, also does not diminish Lear's greatness, even when that is manifested only as a great unwisdom. Except for the Yahweh of the original portions of what are now called Genesis, Exodus, and Numbers, Lear remains the largest Western instance of a literary character raised to the heights, to the sublime.

NORTHROP FRYE

King Lear

The story of Lear is one of a series of legends about the ancient history of Britain, legends that in Shakespeare's day were thought to be genuine history. How they got to be that makes a curious story, but we just have time for its main point. A Welsh priest living in the twelfth century, called Geoffrey of Monmouth, concocted a fictional history of early Britain modelled on Virgil, and according to this Britain was settled by Trojan refugees led by one Brutus, after whom Britain was named. There follows a long chronicle of kings and their adventures, mostly, so far as we can see, gathered out of Welsh legend and historical reminiscence. This is where the story of Lear and his three daughters came from: Lear was supposed to have lived somewhere around the seventh or eighth century before Christ. So, except for *Troilus and Cressida*, which is a very medievalized version of the Trojan War, *King Lear* is the earliest in historical setting of all Shakespeare's plays. It's true that we notice a tendency to mix up various historical periods increasing as Shakespeare goes on. In *Hamlet*, for instance, we seem to be most of the time in Denmark of the Dark Ages, but Hamlet is a student at Wittenberg, a university founded around 1500, and Laertes appears to be going off to a kind of Renaissance Paris. In *King Lear* we find Anglo-Saxon names (Edmund, Edgar, Kent) and Roman ones (Gloucester), and we also have contemporary allusions, including religious ones, of a type that the audience

From *Northrop Frye on Shakespeare*, edited by Robert Sandler, pp. 101–21. Copyright © 1986 by Fitzhenry and Whiteside.

was accustomed to. But still there does seem to be a roughly consistent effort to keep the setting pre-Christian.

There are a lot of advantages for what is perhaps Shakespeare's biggest dramatic design. First, with a setting so far back in time, the sense of the historical blurs into the sense of the mythical and legendary. The main characters expand into a gigantic, even titanic, dimension that simply wouldn't be possible in a historical context like that of *Henry IV*. Then again, there are certain tensions between a tragic structure and a framework of assumptions derived from Christianity. Christianity is based on a myth (story) which is comic in shape, its theme being the salvation and redemption of man. You can see what I mean by comic: when Dante wrote his poem about hell, purgatory and paradise he called it a *commedia* because it followed the central Christian story, which ends happily for all the people who matter. Tragedy needs a hero of outsize dimensions: you can get this easily in Greek tragedy, where some men can really be descended from gods, and where there's very little distinction between history and legend anyway, but in Christianity there's no hero except Christ who has a divine dimension of any kind. Also, tragedy raises some disturbing questions about what kind of power is in charge of the universe. Christianity has prompt and confident answers, but the more emotionally convincing the tragedy, the more we may feel that the answers sometimes are a bit too pat. We can see this feeling reflected in what people say who are assumed to be living before the coming of Christ.

The very little evidence we have seems to indicate that Shakespeare took more time over *King Lear* than over most of his plays, and the freedom with which he handled a story familiar to his audience is extraordinary. No previous account of Lear suggests that he went mad, or that Cordelia was hanged by her enemies; and the incorporating of the Gloucester–Edgar subplot, as a counterpoint to the main, Lear–Cordelia one, is entirely Shakespeare's. The material seems to have come from Sir Philip Sidney's *Arcadia*, but the source doesn't seem significant. Neither do the books he consulted for the names of the devils inhabiting Poor Tom and the like. There's a Quarto text as well as a Folio one, but the relations between them that an editor has to deal with are just too complex to go into.

When you start to read or listen to *King Lear*, try to pretend that you've never heard the story before, and forget that you know how bad Goneril and Regan and Edmund are going to be. That way, you'll see more clearly how Shakespeare is building up our sympathies in the opposite direction. The opening scene presents first Gloucester and then Lear as a couple of incredibly foolish and gullible dodderers (Gloucester's gullibility comes out in a slightly later scene). Gloucester boasts about how he begot Edmund in a way that embarrasses us as well as Kent, and we feel that Edmund's treachery, whatever we think of it, is at any rate credibly motivated. Even at the end of the play, his simple phrase "Yet Edmund was beloved," meaning that Goneril and Regan loved him at least, reminds us how intensely we can feel dramatic sympathy where we don't necessarily feel moral sympathy.

As for Lear and his dreary love test, it's true that Goneril and Regan are being hypocrites when they patter glibly through the declarations of love they are required to make, but we shouldn't forget that it's a genuine humiliation, even for them, to have to make such speeches. At no time in the play does Lear ever express any real affection or tenderness for Goneril or Regan. Of course loving Goneril and Regan would be uphill work, but Lear never really thinks in terms of love: he talks about his kindness and generosity and how much he's given them and how grateful they ought to feel. He does say (publicly) that Cordelia was always his favourite, and that certainly registers with the other two, as their dialogue afterward shows. But they don't feel grateful, and nobody with Shakespeare's knowledge of human nature would expect them to. Then again, while they're not surprised that Lear acts like an old fool, even they are startled by how big a fool he is, and they realize that they have to be on their guard to stop him from ever having the power to do to them what he's just done to Cordelia. The hundred knights Lear insists on could easily start a palace revolution in such a society, so the hundred knights will have to go.

In the first two acts, all Lear's collisions with his daughters steadily diminish his dignity and leave them with the dramatic honours. They never lose their cool: they are certainly harsh and unattractive women, but they have a kind of brusque common sense that bears him down every time. A hundred knights would make quite a hole in any housekeeper's budget, and we have only Lear's word for it that they're invariably well behaved. If we look at the matter impartially, we may find ourselves asking, with the daughters, what all the fuss is about, and why Lear must have all these knights. When Regan says:

This house is little: the old man and 's people
Cannot be well bestow'd. (II.iv.290–91)

what she says could have a ring of truth in it, if we forget for the moment that she's talking about Gloucester's house, which she and Cornwall have commandeered. Every move that Lear makes is dramatically a flop, as when he kneels to Regan, intending irony, and she says "these are unsightly tricks," which they assuredly are. The same thing is true of some of Lear's allies, like Kent and his quarrel with Oswald that lands him in the stocks. It is not hard to understand Kent's feelings about Oswald, or his exasperation with the fact that Goneril's messenger is treated with more consideration than the king's, but still he does seem to be asking for something, almost as though he were a kind of *agent provocateur*, adopting the strategy of Goneril's "I'd have it come to question."

It is not until the scene at the end of the second act, with its repeated "shut up your doors," that our sympathies definitely shift over to Lear. Regan says, "He is attended with a desperate train," meaning his fifty (or whatever their present number) knights, but they seem to have sloped off pretty promptly as soon as they realized that they were unlikely to get their next meal there, and Lear's "desperate train" actually consists only of the Fool. When we catch her out in a lie of that size we begin to see what has not emerged before, and has perhaps not yet occurred to them: that "his daughters seek his death," as Gloucester says. It is during and after the storm that the characters of the play begin to show their real nature, and from then on we have something unique in Shakespeare: a dramatic world in which the characters are, like chess pieces, definitely black or white: black with Edmund, Goneril, Regan and Cornwall; white with Lear, Cordelia, Edgar, Gloucester, Kent and eventually Albany.

Perhaps the best way of finding our bearings in this mammoth structure is to look for clues in the words that are so constantly repeated that it seems clear they're being deliberately impressed on us. I'd like to look at three of these words in particular: the words "nature," "nothing" and "fool."

To understand the word "nature," we have to look at the kind of world view that's being assumed, first by Shakespeare's audience, then by the characters in the play. The opening words of Edmund's first soliloquy are "Thou, Nature, art my goddess," and later in the first act Lear, beginning his curse on Goneril, says: "Hear, Nature, hear; dear goddess, hear." It seems clear that Edmund and Lear don't mean quite the same thing by the goddess Nature, but I think Shakespeare's audience would find this less confusing than we do.

At that time most people assumed that the universe was a hierarchy in which the good was "up" and the bad "down." These ups and downs might be simply metaphors, but that didn't affect their force or usefulness. At the top of the cosmos was the God of Christianity, whose abode is in heaven; that is, the place where his presence is. The lower heaven or sky is not this heaven, but it's the clearest visible symbol of it. The stars, made, as was then believed, out of a purer substance than this world, keep reminding us in their circling of the planning and intelligence that went into the Creator's original construction.

God made a home for man in the garden of Eden, which, like the stars, was a pure world without any death or corruption in it. But Adam and Eve fell out of this garden into a lower or "fallen" world, a third level into which man now is born but feels alienated from. Below this, a fourth level, is the demonic world. The heaven of God is above nature; the demonic world of the devils is below it; but the important thing to keep in mind is that the two middle levels both form part of the order of nature, and that consequently "nature" has two levels and two standards. The upper level, the world symbolized by the stars and by the story of the garden of Eden, was man's original home, the place God intended him to live in. The lower level, the one we're born into now, is a world to which animals and plants seem to be fairly well adjusted: man is not adjusted to it. He must either sink below it into sin, a level the animals can't reach, or try to raise himself as near as he can to the second level he really belongs to. I say "try to raise himself," but he can't really do that: the initiative must come from above or from social institutions. Certain things—morality, virtue, education, social discipline, religious sacraments—all help him to raise his status. He won't get back to the garden of Eden: that's disappeared as a place, but it can be recovered in part as an inner state of mind. The whole picture looks like this to the audience:

1. Heaven (the place of the presence of God), symbolized by the sun and moon, which are all that's left of the original creation.

2. Higher or human order of nature, originally the "unfallen" world or garden of Eden, now the level of nature on which man is intended to live as continuously as possible with the aid of religion, morality and the civilized arts.

3. Lower or "fallen" order of physical nature, our present environment, a world seemingly indifferent to man and his concerns, though the wise can see many traces of its original splendour.

4. The demonic world, whatever or wherever it is, often associated with the destructive aspects of nature, such as the storm on the heath.

When we speak of "nature" it makes a crucial difference whether we mean the upper, human level of nature or the environment around us that we actually do live in. Many things are "natural" to man that are not natural to anything else on this lower level, such as living under authority and obedience, wearing clothes, using reason, and the like. Such things show that the proper "natural" environment for man is something different from that of animals. But when Edmund commits himself to *his* goddess Nature, he means only the lower, physical level of nature, where human life, like animal life, is a jungle in which the predators are the aristocracy. When Lear appeals to the goddess Nature to curse Goneril, he means a nature that includes what is peculiarly natural to man, an order of existence in which love, obedience, authority, loyalty are natural because they are genuinely human; an order in which "art," in all its Elizabethan senses, is practically indistinguishable from nature. Goneril is being cursed because her treatment of her father is "unnatural" in this context.

But we shouldn't assume that Edmund knows clearly that he is talking about a lower aspect of Nature, or that Lear knows clearly that he is talking about a higher one. Such categories aren't clear yet in a pre-Christian world. In the Lear world there is no actual God, because there is only the Christian God, and he has not revealed himself yet. Very early, when Kent stands out against Lear's foolish decision, Lear says, "Now, by Apollo—" and Kent answers:

> Now, by Apollo, King
> Thou swear'st thy Gods in vain. (I.i.160–61)

Lear retorts by calling him "miscreant," unbeliever. A parody of this discussion occurs later, when Kent is in the stocks. And just as the divine world is hazy and mysterious, so is the demonic world. *King Lear* is in many respects the spookiest of all the great tragedies, and yet nothing explicitly supernatural or superhuman occurs in it: there is nothing to correspond to the Ghost in *Hamlet* or the witches in *Macbeth*. Five fiends inhabit Poor Tom, but we don't believe in his devils, and wouldn't even if we didn't know that Poor Tom is really Edgar. To Shakespeare's audience, the Lear world would look something like this:

1. World of impotent or nonexistent gods, which tend to collapse into deified personifications of Nature or Fortune.

2. Social or human world with the elements the more enlightened can see to be essential to a human world, such as love, loyalty and authority. In particular, the world represented by Cordelia's and Edgar's love, Kent's loyalty, Albany's conscience, etc.

3. World of physical nature in which man is born an animal and has to follow the animal pattern of existence, i.e., join the lions and eat well, or the sheep and get eaten.

4. A hell-world glimpsed in moments of madness or horror.

As an example of what I'm talking about, notice that one of the first points established about Edmund is his contempt for astrology. If we ignore the question of "belief" in astrology, for ourselves or for Shakespeare or his audience, and think of it simply as a dramatic image revealing character, we can see that of course Edmund would dismiss astrology: it has no place in his conception of nature. Astrology was taken seriously in Shakespeare's day because of the assumption that God had made the world primarily for the benefit of man, and although the original creation is in ruins, we can still see many evidences of design in it with a human reference. The stars in the sky are not just there: they've been put there for a purpose, and that's why the configurations of stars can spell out the destinies of men and women.

Similarly, there are links, however mysterious and fitful, between natural and human events, at least on the top social level. Comets, earthquakes and other natural disturbances don't just happen: they happen at crucial times in human life, such as the death of a ruler. Not necessarily a Christian ruler: there were, as we saw, such portents at the time of the murder of Julius Caesar. So Lear has some ground for expecting that the order of nature around him might take some notice of his plight and of his daughters' ingratitude, considering that he's a king. But one thing the storm symbolizes is that he's moving into an order of nature that's indifferent to human affairs. His madness brings him the insight: "They told me I was everything: 'tis a lie; I am not ague-proof." With his abdication, whatever links there may be between the civilized human world and the one above it have been severed.

It should be clear from all this that the question "What is a natural man?" has two answers. On his own proper human level it is natural to man to be clothed, sociable and reasonable. When Goneril and Regan keep asking Lear why he needs all those knights, the first part of his answer, in the speech beginning "Oh, reason not the need," is a quite coherent statement of the fact that civilized life is not based simply on needs. But in this storm world that Lear is descending into, what is natural man like? Lear has hardly begun to formulate the question when Poor Tom appears as the answer to it. "Didst thou give all to thy two daughters?" Lear asks, still preoccupied with his own concerns. But we're getting down now to the underside of the Goneril–Regan world:

Poor Tom, that eats the swimming frog, the toad, the tadpole, the
wall-newt and the water; that in the fury of his heart, when the
foul fiend rages, eats cow-dung for sallets, swallows the old rat
and the ditch-dog; drinks the green mantle of the standing pool
... (III.iv.132ff.)

The imagery creates a world more nauseating than Hamlet ever dreamed of. "Is man no more than this?", Lear asks. In a way Poor Tom is a kind of ghastly parody of a free man, because he owes nothing to the amenities of civilization. Lear is reminded that he still has at least clothes, and starts tearing them off to be level with Poor Tom, but he is distracted from this. He says in a miracle of condensed verbal power: "Thou art the thing itself." He has started at one end of nature and ended at the other, and now his downward journey has reached a terminus. Perhaps one of Edgar's motives in assuming his Poor Tom disguise was to provide a solid bottom for Lear's descent. Below or behind him is the chaos-world portended by the storm: the world of the furies and fiends that Edgar is keeping Lear protected from, just as he protects Gloucester later from the self-destructive "fiend" that wants to hurl him over a cliff.

The word "nothing" we remember from Richard II, where it was connected with the conception of the king's two bodies. In both plays "nothing" seems to have the meaning of being deprived of one's social function, and so of one's identity. A king who dies is still a something, namely a dead king; a king deprived of his kingship is "nothing," even if, or especially if, he still goes on living. That is one thing that the issue of the train of knights is about. They represent, for Lear, his continuing identity as king, even though he has abdicated his powers and responsibilities: he wants both to have and not have his royalty. His daughters do not, at least not at first, want to kill him: they want him to go on living without power, once he has renounced it. Regan says, and may well mean it at this point:

> For his particular, I'll receive him gladly,
> But not one follower. (II.iv.293–94)

Such treatment of him is, at least symbolically (and symbolism is immensely important here), what Lear says in another connection is "worse than murder." To kill him would be murder; to let him survive without his identity is a kind of annihilation. Similarly Edgar says, when assuming his Poor Tom disguise: "Edgar I nothing am." He's still alive, but his identity as Edgar is gone, or at least in abeyance.

There is another context, easier to understand, in which the conception of nothing is of great significance. What is the cause of love, friendship, good faith, loyalty or any of the essential human virtues? Nothing. There's no "why" about them: they just are. In putting on his love-test act, Lear is obsessed by the formula of something for something. I'll love you if you love me, and if you love me you'll get a great big slice of England. When Cordelia says that she loves him according to her "bond," she of course doesn't mean anything like Shylock's bond: the word for her has more the modern sense of "bond-ing." Love and loyalty don't have motives or expectations or causes, nor can they be quantified, as in Lear's "Which of you shall we say doth love us most?" Much later in the play, when Cordelia awakens Lear and he finally realizes he is still in the same world, he says:

> I know you do not love me; for your sisters
> Have, as I do remember, done me wrong:
> You have some cause, they have not. (IV.vii.73–75)

Cordelia's answer, "No cause, no cause," is one of the supreme moments of all drama. And yet when Cordelia says that, she is saying precisely what she said at the beginning of the play: she will have nothing to do with these silly conditional games. It is characteristic of such relationships that sooner or later they come to focus on some anxiety symbol, which for Lear is the issue of the hundred knights. Pursuing this anxiety drives Lear toward the madness he so much fears, and forces him into those dreadful bargaining scenes that we can hardly bear to reread:

> Thy fifty yet doth double five and twenty,
> And thou art twice her love. (II.iv.261–62)

As for "fool," we have first of all Lear's version of the common phrase, used several times by Shakespeare, "all the world's a stage":

> When we are born, we cry that we are come
> To this great stage of fools. (IV.vi.184–85)

The word "fool" is in course of time applied to practically every decent char-acter in the play. Those who are not fools are people like Goneril and Regan and Edmund, who live according to the conditions of the lower or savage nature they do so well in. But Albany is called a "moral fool" by Goneril because he is unwilling to accept such a world; Kent is called a fool for tak-ing the part of an outcast king. As for the Fool himself, he is a "natural," a word that again evokes the sense of two levels of nature. As a "natural" in this world, he is deficient enough, mentally, to be put in a licensed position to say what he likes. In his kind of "natural" quality there is a reminiscence of a still coherent and divinely designed order of nature, a world in which no one can help telling the truth. In our world, there is the proverb "children and fools tell the truth," and the Fool's privilege makes him a wit because in our world nothing is funnier than a sudden outspoken declaration of the truth.

There is another sense of the word "fool" that seems to be peculiar to Shakespeare, and that is the "fool" as victim, the kind of person to whom disasters happen. Everyone on the wrong side of the wheel of fortune is a fool in this sense, and it is in this sense that Lear speaks of himself as "the natural fool of fortune," just as Romeo earlier had called himself "fortune's fool." Speaking of Romeo, we raised the question of why he talks so much about the stars as causal elements in his tragedy when we have a simple and human cause ready to hand, namely the feud. And when in *King Lear* Gloucester says:

> As flies to wanton boys are we to th' gods,
> They kill us for their sport. (IV.i.36–37)

he certainly hasn't forgotten that his own plight is the quite understandable result of his own folly, Edmund's treachery and Cornwall's brutality; it doesn't need any gods to explain it. Some nineteenth-century commentators felt that this remark displayed an atheistic pessimism which Shakespeare himself believed in (because they did) and was keeping up his sleeve. I don't know what Shakespeare believed, but he knew what his audience would buy, and he knew they wouldn't buy that. Gloucester is no atheist: he postulates gods, divine personalities, and if he replaced them with a mechanism of fate or destiny he couldn't ascribe *malice* to it. What he feels is that there is some mystery in the horror of what's happened to him that goes beyond the tangible human causes.

Edgar and Albany, on the other hand, are moralists: they look for human causes and assume that there are powers above who are reacting to events as they should. Albany is a decent man, and Goneril a vicious woman, and yet in Goneril's world Albany looks weak and ineffectual. He produces his great melodramatic coup, the letter proving Goneril's intrigue with Edmund, which should overwhelm her with shame and confusion. But Goneril isn't listening: in her world, of course anyone of her social rank who despised her husband would take a lover. It's true that she kills herself when Edmund is fatally wounded, but that too is part of the Goneril ethic. Albany's demonstrations of the workings of Providence also get undercut pretty badly. When he hears of the death of Cornwall he says it shows that "justicers" are above, passing over the fate of Gloucester himself and of Cornwall's servant. He sees a "judgement of the heavens" in the deaths of Goneril and Regan: at once Kent enters, inquires for the king, and Albany says, "Great thing of us forgot!" It looks almost as though the memory of the "heavens" had slipped up along with Albany's. Finally, he tries to set up a scene of poetic justice in which:

> All friends shall taste
> The wages of their virtue, and all foes
> The cup of their deservings. (V.iii.302–304)

What follows this is Lear's terrible lament over the dead body of Cordelia, and in the nuclear-bomb desolation of that speech, words like "wages" and "deserving" fade into nothingness. It may be, as some say, that Lear thinks Cordelia is alive again at the end of the speech, but we know that if so he is being mocked with another illusion.

Edgar too, for all his prodigies of valour and fidelity, gets some curiously limp things to say. At the end of the heath scene he makes a chorus comment (which is not in the Folio):

> When we our betters see bearing our woes,
> We scarcely think our miseries our foes. (III.vi.105–106)

and so on for another dozen sickening lines. After he strikes down Edmund in the final duel, he remarks that the gods are just, and that Gloucester's blindness was the inevitable result of going into a whorehouse to beget Edmund. (I feel very sorry for Edmund's mother, who seems to me to get a quite undeservedly bad press.) Even though Edmund agrees with the statement, it doesn't make much of a point, as we're explicitly told that Goneril and Regan were "got 'tween lawful sheets." In fact, the whole relation between Gloucester and the Lear tragedies seems to have something of a contrast between an explicable and an inexplicable disaster. The Gloucester tragedy perhaps can—just—be explained in moral terms; the Lear tragedy cannot.

There is a lot more to be said about both Albany and Edgar, and I shall be saying some of it myself in a moment. They are not in the least ridiculous characters, but, like all the virtuous people, they are fools in the sense that a fool is a victim: they utter the cries of bewildered men who can't see what's tormenting them, and their explanations, even if they are reassuring for the moment, are random guesses. In this dark, meaningless, horrible world, every-one is as spiritually blind as Gloucester is physically: you might be interested in looking at the number of references to blindness in the play apart from those connected with Gloucester. The moral for us, as students of the play, is clear enough: we have to take a much broader view of the action than either a fatalistic or a moral one, and try, not to "explain" it, but to see something of its dimensions and its scope.

Many critics of Shakespeare have noticed that there often seem to be two time clocks in the action of his plays, the events in the foreground

summarizing slower and bigger events in the background that by themselves would take longer to work out. It's a little like looking at the scenery
from the window of a car or train, with the weeds at the side of the road
rushing by and the horizon turning slowly. In the foreground action the
scene on the heath seems to take place in the same night that begins with
Regan and Cornwall shutting Lear out. In the background we pick up hints
that Albany and Cornwall are at loggerheads, but are forced to compose
their differences and unite against a threatened invasion from France, partly
encouraged by Cordelia, although in the foreground action nothing has yet
happened to Lear that would justify such an invasion. At the end of Act II
we still don't feel that Gloucester's statement "his daughters seek his death"
is quite true yet, though they certainly don't care if he does die. But within
an hour or two Gloucester's concern for Lear becomes strictly forbidden,
and his action in helping the king to get to Dover is, from Cornwall's point
of view, the basest treachery. It's not difficult to get all this from the indica-
tions we're given. I think there's also a third rhythm of time, if it really is
time, in a still larger background.

We remember the phrase that Shakespeare uses twice in the history
plays, in the garden scene of *Richard II* and early in *Henry V*: "a second fall
of cursèd man." Before the play begins, we are in roughly the upper world
of human nature; not a paradisal state, of course, but a world where there is
authority, social discipline, orders of distinction, and loyalty: the conditions
regarded as the central ones in the Tudor world. Then the dreaded image of
the map appears, with a proposal to carve up the country: the same image
we met at the beginning of *Henry IV*. By the end of the scene we have the
feeling of sliding into a different world, and when Edmund steps forth with
his "Thou, Nature, art my goddess," we feel that he's the first person to have
recognized this new world for what it is. He's Gloucester's "natural" son, and
on this level of nature he's the kind of person who will take command. When
the storm begins in Act III it's described in a way that makes it clear that it's
more than just a storm. It's an image of nature dissolving into its primordial
elements, losing its distinctions of hierarchies in chaos, a kind of crossing of
the Red Sea in reverse.

One of the central images of this descent is that of the antagonism of
a younger and older generation. "The younger rises when the old doth fall,"
says Edmund, and Goneril, speaking of Lear, issues a blanket denunciation of
old people generally: "The best and soundest of his time hath been but rash."
On the other side, Lear appeals to the gods, "If you do love old men," and
Gloucester, with a still more futile irony, appeals for help, during the blinding
scene, to any "who will think to live till he be old." The principle that made
hereditary succession so important in the history plays seems to be extended

here, in a world where the honouring of one's parents is the most emphasized of all virtues. Albany regards Goneril's treatment of her father as the key to everything else she does that's wrong:

> She that herself will sliver and disbranch
> From her material sap, perforce must wither
> And come to deadly use. (IV.ii.34–36)

The connection between honouring one's parents and long life is, of course, already present in the fifth commandment, though the characters in King Lear are not supposed to know that. In any case the principle doesn't work in the post-storm world: Cornwall's servant feels that so wicked a woman as Regan can't possibly live out her full life, and Regan does get poisoned, but then Cordelia is hanged, so that again doesn't prove or explain anything. Wherever we turn, we're up against the ambiguity in all tragedy: that death is both the punishment of the evil and the reward of the virtuous, besides being the same end for everybody. Our moralists, Edgar and Albany, the survivors of the play, actually speak as though the length of human life had been shortened as a result of the play's action. The last four lines, spoken by Edgar in the Folio and by Albany in the Quarto, are:

> The weight of this sad time we must obey,
> Speak what we feel, not what we ought to say:
> The oldest hath borne most: we that are young
> Shall never see so much, nor live so long. (V.iii.323–26)

The second line, incidentally, seems very curious. If it's a vindication of the conduct of Cordelia and Kent in the opening scene, it's a bit late in the day; and as a general principle it covers too much ground. When Edmund says, "Legitimate Edgar, I must have your land," he is saying what he feels, and certainly not what he ought to say. Nonetheless, I think it's a very central comment: it points to the fact that language is just about the only thing that fights for genuine humanity in this blinded world.

Let's go back to the conception of the king's two bodies. Lear gives up his second body when he surrenders himself to the power of Goneril and Regan, and consequently, as we said, he no longer has any identity as a king. His loss of identity troubles him, and he says to Oswald: "Who am I?" The question is rhetorical, but Oswald's answer, "My lady's father," has the unusual quality of being both the exact truth and a calculated insult. The next time he asks the question it is the Fool who answers: "Lear's shadow." There follows the expulsion and the storm on the heath, and before long things begin to change in

Lear. We notice the point at which he is suddenly conscious of the misery of the Fool, and an even more significant moment when he says: "I'll pray, and then I'll sleep." The prayer is a strange prayer, not addressed to any deity, but to the "poor naked wretches" of his own kingdom. What is happening is that he has lost his identity as a king in the body peculiar to a king, but is beginning to recover his royal nature in his other body, his individual and physical one; not just the body that is cold and wet, but the mind that realizes how many others are cold and wet, starting with the Fool and Poor Tom. To use religious terms, his relation to his kingdom was transcendent at the beginning of the play; now it is immanent. Whatever his actual size, Lear is a giant figure, but his gigantic dimensions are now not those of a king or hero; they are those of a human being who suffers but understands his affinity with others who suffer.

In the mad scenes (which would have to be very carefully staged in Shakespeare's day because there was a tendency to think mad people funny), we get a negative aspect of Lear's new sense of identity with his subjects. He speaks of the endless hypocrisies in the administering of justice, of the sexual pleasure with which beadles lash whores, of the prurience lurking under the prude, of the shame of living in a society where "a dog's obeyed in office." These things are not exactly news to us, but they are new sensations to him. All Poor Tom's fiends of lust and theft and lying weep through him, but they are not in possession of him: he is, like Prince Hal, though in an infinitely subtler way, absorbing the good and bad of the human nature in his kingdom. He is at the opposite pole from the deposed king who had half expected the storm to take his part:

> Tremble, thou wretch,
> That hast within thee undivulged crimes,
> Unwhipp'd of justice; hide thee, thou bloody hand . . . (III.
> ii.51–53)

We can summarize all this by saying that Lear has entered a world in which the most genuine language is prophetic language: that is, language inspired by a vision of life springing from the higher level of nature. Albany's providence and Edgar's divine justice make sense as a part of such a vision, though as prophecy in the sense of predicting what is going to happen it may fail. Kent, again, is often prophetic; his fury against Oswald is really a prophetic vision of the kind of thing that such people as Oswald do in the world:

> Such smiling rogues as these,
> Like rats, oft bite the holy cords a-twain . . . (II.ii.74–75)

The "holy cords" may be parental or matrimonial: in either case he's dead right about Oswald, as the rest of the play shows. Again, he is someone possessed by a need to have a "master" who represents genuine "authority," as he says to Lear. At the end of the play, when he comes in to "bid my king and master aye goodnight," he of course means Lear; when he repeats this a few lines later, a second or two after Lear's death, he may have some intuition about a bigger master who nonetheless includes Lear:

> I have a journey, sir, shortly to go;
> My master calls me, I must not say no. (V.iii.321–22)

I don't mean that he is moving toward a specific religious belief, Christian or other; I mean only that his vision of the source of authority and mastery is expanding from its exclusive focus on King Lear.

The audience is apparently expected to recognize a number of Biblical allusions that the characters who make them do not know to be Biblical. Cordelia speaks of going about her father's business, echoing a phrase of Jesus in the Gospel of Luke: had she known of the resemblance she would hardly have made the remark in quite those words. A gentleman says of Lear:

> Thou hast one daughter,
> Who redeems nature from the general curse
> Which twain have brought her to. (IV.vi.206–208)

He could, theoretically, mean Goneril and Regan, or he could mean Adam and Eve. I'd say that he means Goneril and Regan and has probably never heard of Adam and Eve. At the same time it would be true to say that Adam and Eve brought a general curse on nature, and a bit overblown to say it of Goneril and Regan, except insofar as they are participating in a "second fall of cursèd man." The statement is unconsciously prophetic, and the audience picks up more than the speaker is aware of.

Lear on the heath, again, is attended by two bedraggled prophets, the Fool and Poor Tom. The Fool is introduced in the somewhat ambiguous role of keeping Lear amused by repeating incessantly, "You are nothing, nothing, nothing." However unhelpful, it is prophetic enough: it tells Lear the outcome of his journey to Regan and what the next stage of his life will be. Goneril, no devotee of either humour or truth, believes that he is "more knave than fool," because the Fool is a "natural" allied to a level of nature that she does not know exists. On the heath the Fool's role is largely taken over by Poor Tom, although the idiot doggerel that he recites (in the Folio text only) at the end of Act III, Scene ii is still called a "prophecy." As for Poor Tom, a ballad on "Tom o' Bedlam" was collected in the eighteenth century, and may well go back to something very similar extant in Shakespeare's time. The last stanza of the ballad goes:

> With an host of furious fancies
> Whereof I am commander,
> With a burning spear, and a horse of air,
> To the wilderness I wander.
> By a knight of ghosts and shadows
> I summoned am to tourney
> Ten leagues beyond the wide world's end,
> Methinks it is no journey.

This kind of imagery reminds us of certain primitive poets and magicians, like the "shamans" of central Asia, who go through long initiations that involve journeys to upper and lower worlds. We are now in a world where all knowledge of anything "spiritual" or otherworldly has been degraded to Poor Tom's fiends, his nightmare with her ninefold, his dark tower of Childe Roland, and other phantasms linked to the night and the storm.

Edgar says explicitly that he is trying to "cure" Gloucester's despair, and to lead him to feel that "ripeness is all," that man does not own his life, and must wait until it concludes of itself. Lear has told Gloucester the same thing earlier, and the fact that the mad Lear is in a position to do so says a good deal about the essential sanity of Lear's madness. What Edgar expects to do for Lear by producing his Tom o' Bedlam act is more difficult to say. He seems to be acting as a kind of lightning rod, focussing and objectifying the chaos that is in both Lear's mind and in nature. He's holding a mirror up to Lear's growing madness, somewhat as, to refer to a very different play, Petruchio tries to cure Katharina's shrewishness by showing her in his own behaviour what it looks like.

The action of the play seems to be proceeding to a conclusion that, however sombre and exhausting, nonetheless has some serenity in it. But just as we seem about to reach this conclusion, there comes the agonizing wrench of the hanging of Cordelia and the death speeches of Lear. Naturally the stage refused to act this down to the nineteenth century: producers settled for another version that married Cordelia off to Edgar. We act the play now as Shakespeare wrote it, but it's still pretty tough even for this grisly century. I said that in the course of the play the characters settled into a clear division of good and bad people, like the white and black pieces of a chess game. The last of the black pieces, Goneril, Regan and Edmund, have been removed from the board, and then comes the death of Cordelia. Part of this is just the principle that the evil men do lives after them, Edmund's repentance being too late to rescind his own order. But there seems to be a black king still on the board, and one wonders if there is any clue to who or what or where he is.

I said that *Hamlet* was the central Shakespeare play for the nineteenth century; in the twentieth century feelings of alienation and absurdity have arisen that tend to shift the focus to *King Lear*. All virtuous or evil actions, all acceptances or rejections of religious or political ideology, seem equally absurd in a world that is set up mainly for the benefit of the Gonerils and the Cornwalls. A generation ago this statement would have stimulated arguments about ways and means of changing such a world, but such arguments are not only irrelevant to Shakespeare's play, but avoid one of its central issues.

I suggested in speaking of *A Midsummer Night's Dream* that Bottom got closer than any other character to the central experience of the play, even if he didn't altogether know it. The implication is that it takes a fool or clown to see into the heart of comedy. Perhaps it takes a madman to see into the heart of tragedy, the dark tower of Lear's fury and tenderness, rage and sympathy, scorn and courtesy, and finally his broken heart. I've often come back to the titanic size of Lear, which is not a size of body or ultimately even of social rank, but of language. This seems to put him at an immense distance from us, except that he is also utterly human and recognizable. Perhaps Lear's madness is what our sanity would be if it weren't under such heavy sedation all the time, if our senses or nerves or whatever didn't keep filtering out experiences or emotions that would threaten our stability. It's a dangerous business to enter the world of titans and heroes and gods, but safer if we have as a guide a poet who speaks their language.

To speak of a black king, however metaphorically, is to make an assumption, and to ask what or who it is makes secondary assumptions. Another step takes us into the blind-men-and-elephant routine, where we "identify" the source of tragedy as the consequence of human acts or divine malice or fatality or cosmic absurdity. I also spoke of three important words in the play, "nature," "fool" and "nothing": perhaps I could have mentioned a fourth, "fortune." Fortune in Shakespeare's day, we saw, was symbolized by a wheel, and there are several powerful images of wheels in this play. In some rural areas at certain times of the year a wheel was made of straw, rolled to the top of a hill, then set on fire and let roll down: the Fool seems to be using this image about Lear's fall from one level of nature to another. Lear himself, waking out of sleep and seeing Cordelia, speaks of himself as bound on a wheel of fire, a spirit tormented in hell, though he soon discovers he isn't. Edmund accepts Edgar's view of him as the nemesis of Gloucester's folly in the phrase "The wheel has come full circle," after which he suddenly changes character. The image is inexact in one essential respect: wheels turn, but they remain wheels.

Whatever is turning in *King Lear* also keeps turning *into* other things. The language of definition is helpless to deal with this: the language of prophecy can come closer, because it's more nearly related to the language of madness. At the beginning of the play Lear is technically sane, but everything he says and does is absurd. In his mad scenes his associations are often hard to follow, but his general meaning is blindly clear. The language is a counter absurdity: that is what the play leaves for us, a sense of what we could release if we could speak what we feel.

I keep using the word "prophetic" because it seems to me the least misleading metaphor for the primary power of vision in human consciousness, before it gets congealed into religious or political beliefs or institutions. In the final scenes particularly, we see both what's in front of us, where "all's cheerless, dark and deadly," and the power of language that will not stop expanding, even when it starts to press into the mystery that's blocked off from us by death. We don't know the answers; we don't know that there are no answers. Tragedy forces on us a response of acceptance: we have to say, "Yes, this kind of thing is human life too." But by making that response we've accepted something much deeper: that what is defined or made finite by words becomes infinite through the power of words.

ARTHUR KIRSCH

The Emotional Landscape of King Lear

The tragedy of *King Lear* raises large religious, as well as political and social, questions, and there is a disposition in recent scholarship to treat the play as if it were an argument that gives unorthodox, if not revolutionary, answers to them. Prominent critics have contended that *Lear* is locked in combat with Elizabethan conceptions of Providence and order,[1] and one influential Marxist critic has maintained that the play constitutes both a specific criticism of Elizabethan ideology and a denial of what he calls "essentialist humanism," the belief that, with respect to tragedy, assumes "a human essence which by its own nature as well as its relation to the universal order of things, must inevitably suffer."[2]

The current popularity of such views makes it urgent, I think, to reassert the less fashionable position that though Shakespeare is "the soul of [his] age," as Ben Jonson wrote, he is also "not of an age, but for all time," and that, as Dr. Johnson argued, his plays have "pleased many, and pleased long," because they are "just representations of general nature," "faithful mirror[s] of manners and of life." Shakespeare's tragedies are, above all else, plays of passions and suffering that we eventually recognize as our own, whatever their social, political, or religious contingencies may have been in the Renaissance. However we may interpret the particular ideological questions *King Lear* seems to pose, it is the universal human anguish that gives rise to them upon

From *Shakespeare Quarterly* 39, no. 2 (Summer 1988): 154–70. Copyright © 1986 by the Folger Shakespeare Library.

31

which Shakespeare primarily focuses and to which audiences have responded
for nearly four hundred years.

The experience of feeling—physical as well as emotional feeling—is at
the core of *King Lear*, as the enlargement of our own capacity to feel is at
the core of any persuasive explanation of why we can take pleasure in such a
tragedy. The word "heart" resonates in the play, describing the extremes of the
play's characterizations, from the "honest-hearted" Kent (I.iv.19) to the "marble-hearted" ingratitude and "hard-hearts" of Goneril and Regan (I.iv.237;
III.vi.36).[3] "Heart" is the metonym for Lear himself in the storm—"poor old
heart, he holp the heavens to rain" (III.vii.60)—and it is the primary register
of Lear's experience. He rejects Cordelia because she cannot heave her "heart"
into her "mouth" (I.i.92), and he pronounces her banishment as the divorce of
her heart from his own: "So be my grave my peace as here I give / Her father's
heart from her" (I.i.125–26), an uncanny line that predicates his eventual
reunion with her in death. The heart is physically palpable to Lear. He says he
is "struck . . . upon the very heart" by Goneril's "tongue" (II.ii.333–34), and the
same tactile sense of the heart emerges in the synapse between physical and
emotional pain that prompts the first movement of fellow-feeling in him:

> My wits begin to turn.
> (*To Fool*) Come on, my boy. How dost, my boy? Art cold?
> I am cold myself. . . .
> Poor fool and knave, I have one part in my heart
> That's sorry yet for thee.
>   (III.ii.67–69, 72–73)

As Lear moves toward madness, he recognizes that his rage against Cordelia
drew from his "heart all love" and "wrenched" his "frame of nature / From
the fixed place" (I.iv.247–48); he then repeatedly identifies his incipient
madness with his heart: "O, how this mother swells up toward my heart!
/ *Histerica passio* down, thou climbing sorrow" (II.ii.231–32); "O me, my
heart! My rising heart! But down" (II.ii.292); "But this heart shall break into
a hundred thousand flaws / Or ere I'll weep" (II.ii.458–59).

The breaking of the heart "into a hundred thousand flaws" defines the
point towards which most references to the heart in *King Lear* eventually
move, and suggests the extremity of pain and suffering that is the play's peculiar concern. In his most famous soliloquy Hamlet speaks of the "heartache"
of human existence. In *King Lear* we hear of and then see hearts "cracked"
(II.i.89) and "split" (V.iii.168). Edgar tells us that his father, Gloucester, died
when his "flawed heart . . . / 'Twixt two extremes of passion, joy and grief, /

Burst smilingly" (V.iii.188, 190–91), and at the moment of Lear's death, Kent says, "Break, heart, I prithee break" (V.iii.288), a line that corroborates the truth of what we have just witnessed, whether it refers to Lear's heart or to Kent's own.

The dramatization of the metaphor of a breaking heart and its association with the extremity of dying are central to *King Lear*, for though, again like *Hamlet*, *King Lear* is essentially concerned with the anguish of living in the face of death, it does not look beyond the grave. It focuses instead, and relentlessly, upon the shattering of the heart and upon actual human deterioration—the physical "eyes' anguish" (IV.v.6) of Gloucester's maiming, the emotional "eye of anguish" (IV.iii.15) of Lear's madness. Nor does the Fifth Act of the play bring relief, as it does in *Hamlet*. There is no recovery from sorrow and grief at the end of *Lear*, and there is no suggestion of the "special providence" that Hamlet, in his luminous reference to Matthew, sees in the fall of a sparrow. The agonized question that Lear asks over Cordelia's lifeless body, "Why should a dog, a horse, a rat have life, / And thou no breath at all?" (V.iii.282–83) is not answered in the play, certainly not by his own few succeeding words; and among those words the ones that are most unequivocal and that we most remember are: "Thou'lt come no more. / Never, never, never, never, never!" (V.iii.283–84). These lines express the immediate, "essential," feeling of all of us in the presence of the death and dying of those we love, but they have an acute and governing power in *King Lear*.[4] They occur at the very end, they occur after protracted suffering, they violate the hopes that appear to be raised by the reunion of Lear and Cordelia, and they occur over the dead body of a character who has seemed to symbolize the heart's undying resources of love in the play. There is no scene in Shakespeare that represents the wrench of death more absolutely or more painfully; and the scene is not merely the conclusion of the action of the play, it is its recapitulation, the moment in which the whole of it is crystallized.

In this regard, as in others, *King Lear* is very reminiscent of Ecclesiastes. The depiction of suffering in *King Lear* has often been compared to the Book of Job,[5] which, of course, focuses upon the suffering of an individual; and the protraction of Job's suffering as well as his protests against it do indeed suggest the magnitude of Lear's heroic characterization. But there is no Satan at the beginning of *King Lear*, nor a whirlwind from which God speaks at the end to make the play's extraordinary sense of heartfelt pain even intellectually explicable. In its overall conception as well as in much of its ironic texture, *King Lear* is closer to Ecclesiastes, the book of the Old Testament that is most nearly pagan in its outlook and that treats human life almost exclusively in terms of the immanence of its ending.

The Preacher in Ecclesiastes speaks over and over again of the heart, occasionally of the "heart of the wise" or "of fooles" (7:6),[6] but most often of his own: "And I haue giuen mine heart to search & finde out wisdome" (1:13); "I thought in mine heart" (1:16); "And I gaue mine heart" (1:17); "I said in mine heart" (2:1); "I soght in mine heart" (2:3). The Preacher's experience of the heart suggests many of the major motifs as well as the specific language of *King Lear*. His announced theme is "vanity," a word whose principal connotation (and whose translation in the New English Bible) is "emptiness," and he speaks of man's identity in this life as "a shadow" (7:2) and his achievements as "nothing" (5:14; 7:16). He likens men to beasts:

> For the condition of the children of men, and the condition of beastes *are* even *as* one condition vnto them. As the one dyeth, so dyeth the other: for they haue all one breath, and there is no excellencie of man aboue the beast: for all *is* vanitie.
> (3:19)

He describes man's nakedness: "As he came forthe of his mothers belly, he shal returne naked to go as he came, & shal beare away nothing of his labour, which he hathe caused to passe by his hand" (5:14). He talks repeatedly of the paradoxes of wisdom and folly and madness:

> And I gaue mine heart to knowe wisdome & knowledge, madnes & foolishnes: I knewe also that this is a vexacion of the spirit.
> For in the multitude of wisdome *is* muche grief: & he that encreaseth knowledge, encreaseth sorowe.
> (1:17–18)

He relates such paradoxes to kingship: "Better is a poore and wise childe, then an olde and foolish King, which wil no more be admonished" (4:13), and he relates them as well to eyesight: "For the wise mans eyes *are* in his head, but the foole walketh in darkenes: yet I knowe also that the same condition falleth to them all" (2:14). He also associates "The sight of the eye" with "lustes" (6:9), and he speaks of how men are killed like fishes in a net and birds in a snare (9:12). And he is preoccupied with the paradoxes of justice and injustice:

> I have sene all things in the daies of my vanitie: there is a iuste man that perisheth in his iustice, and there is a wicked man that continueth long in his malice.
> (7:17)

There is a vanitie, which is done vpon the earth, that there be
righteous men to whome it cometh according to the worke of the
wicked: and there be wicked men to whome it cometh according to
the worke of the iuste: I thoght also that this is vanitie.
　(8:14)

The premise as well as the conclusion of all these experiences is that

All things *come* alike to all: and the same condition *is* to the iuste
and to the wicked, to the good and to the pure, & to the polluted,
& to him that sacrificeth, & to him that sacrificeth not: as *is* the
good, so *is* the sinner, he that sweareth, as he that feareth an othe.
　(9:2)

The "olde and foolish King" is perhaps the most inescapable of the
resemblances between these verses and *King Lear*, but many others are equally
suggestive: the painful paradoxes of folly and wisdom that are the subject of
the Fool's speeches and songs; the realization of the metaphors of sight in
Gloucester's building; the nakedness of birth and death and of man's whole
condition that is lamented by Lear and acted out by both Lear and Edgar;
the random wantonness of death of which Gloucester complains; the com-
parisons of men and beasts that suffuse the language of the play and that are
especially prominent in Lear's speeches, including his last; the vision of the
confluence of the just and the wicked that consumes Lear on the heath and
that leads him to conclude, not unlike the Preacher, that "None does offend,
none, I say none" (IV.v.164).

Ecclesiastes, of course, is not the only source from which Shakespeare
could have inherited such preoccupations. Most of them are prominent in
Montaigne's "Apologie of *Raymond Sebond*," a work that clearly lies behind
the play,[7] and they are present as well in other parts of the Bible itself, especially its depictions of the end of the world.[8] The vision of the Apocalypse in
Mark 13, for example, virtually describes the central action of *King Lear*:

For nacion shal rise against nacion, and kingdome against
kingdome, and there shalbe earthquakes ... the brother shal
deliuer the brother to death, and the father the sonne, and the
children shal rise against their parents, and shal cause them to dye.
　(13:8, 12)

But if the Apocalypse suggests that general social and political outline of
Lear, the large number of evocations of Ecclesiastes (and many more could

be cited) give that outline its emotional definition. The Preacher's lament that "he that encreaseth knowledge, encreaseth sorowe" is a line that the Fool could sing: it evokes the cadence as well as the substance of his characterization and its relationship with Lear's. The Preacher's repeated references to the anguish of his own heart suggest the pain of protest as well as of resignation, a combination of feelings that *King Lear* eventually also elicits—in us, if not also, at the last, in Lear himself. And perhaps most important, if most obvious, *vanitas*, the theme that echoes endlessly in Ecclesiastes and that *King Lear* catches up in its preoccupation with the word "nothing," leads not just to the idea of emptiness, but to its paradoxically full feeling, the feeling to which Edgar refers at the end when he says that we should "Speak what we feel, not what we ought to say" (V.iii.300). This feeling has a far greater amplitude and richness in the play than in Ecclesiastes, but its roots are the same.

Subsuming all of these motifs is the focus upon death as the universal event in human existence that not only ends life but calls its whole meaning into question. The Preacher in Ecclesiastes at one point asks, "Who is as the wise man? and who knoweth the interpretacion of a thing?" (8:1), and the burden of the question is that given the transience and mutability of human life, who *can* know? As in *King Lear*, which also poses this question insistently, there is no satisfying answer, and certainly no consoling one. But again like *Lear*, Ecclesiastes does offer a characteristic perception of human existence in the face of death, if not an interpretation of it. For the Preacher's anguished sense of the dissolution of all things in time almost necessarily impels him to think of those things in terms of polarities—the polarities of beginnings and endings especially, but also of their cognates in creativeness and destructiveness—and to think of life itself as a composition of extremes that have individual moral definition, but that are not necessarily morally intelligible as a whole. He suggests this understanding in the passage already quoted in which he says that "All things *come* alike to all," to the just and the wicked, the good and the pure, and that "as *is* the good, so *is* the sinner," and he does so strikingly in the passage for which Ecclesiastes is now best known and which is regularly cited in liturgies for the dead, the passage that speaks of a time to be born and a time to die, a time to slay and a time to heal, to weep and to laugh, to seek and to lose, to keep and to cast away, to be silent and to speak, to love and to hate (3:1–8).

This polarized landscape suggests the most profound of the affinities between Ecclesiastes and *King Lear*, for the kingdom of *Lear* too is defined by the antinomy of "coming hither" and "going hence" (V.ii.10) and by corresponding oppositions of human states of feeling and being. The association of such oppositions with the experience of death is adumbrated earlier in

Shakespeare's career in *Richard II*, a play that is also concerned with an abdication that is a prefiguration of death:

> What must the King do now? Must he submit?
> The King shall do it. Must he be deposed?
> The King shall be contented. Must he lose
> The name of King? A God's name, let it go.
> I'll give my jewels for a set of beads,
> My gorgeous palace for a hermitage,
> My gay apparel for an almsman's gown,
> My figured goblets for a dish of wood,
> My sceptre for a palmer's walking staff,
> My subjects for a pair of carvèd saints,
> And my large kingdom for a little grave,
> A little, little grave, an obscure grave. . . .
>   (*Richard II*, III.iii.142–53)[9]

Richard's itemization of these oppositions is melodramatic, but the contrasts nonetheless do characterize his sensibility, because once his mind is focused on death there is no middle ground in which he can live. In *King Lear* these meditative antitheses are not only acted out by Lear himself but also inform every part of the play's action. For like Ecclesiastes, *King Lear* is composed of oppositions, oppositions between weeping and laughing, seeking and losing, being silent and speaking, loving and hating. The characters embody such contrasts: Cordelia is schematically opposed to Goneril and Regan, Edgar to Edmund, Kent to Oswald, Albany to Cornwall.

Some of these oppositions are combined in single characterizations, especially those of the Fool and Cordelia, but also those of Gloucester and Lear. The Fool's embodiment of the paradoxes of wisdom and folly that run through Ecclesiastes is of course obvious. He incarnates these paradoxes in his traditional role, in his dress, and in his speech; and he does so with the bias toward the broken heart that is characteristic both of Ecclesiastes and of the play. Enid Welsford remarks that "the Fool sees that when the match between the good and the evil is played by the intellect alone it must end in stalemate, but when the heart joins in the game then the decision is immediate and final. 'I will tarry, the Fool will stay—And let the wise man fly.'" She adds that this "is the unambiguous wisdom of the madman who sees the truth," and that it "is decisive" because it reflects the way that normal human beings see the world feelingly.[10] I think that though this is perhaps true, the Fool's "whirling ambiguities" carry a burden that is further reminiscent of Ecclesiastes and less comforting. The Fool tells Lear that when Lear made his daughters his mothers,

> Then they for sudden joy did weep,
>   And I for sorrow sung,
> That such a king should play bo-peep
>   And go the fools among.
>   (I.iv.156–59)

Besides providing the keynote of his own characterization, this particular condensation of emotions is also eventually associated with the moment of death itself in the play. The paradoxical fusion of the extremities of joy and sorrow was often noted in Renaissance commentaries on the passions,[11] but its identification with death is peculiar to *Lear*. The correspondence between the two is suggested in the old ballad that the Fool seems to be adapting:

> Some men for sodayne ioye do wepe,
>   And some in sorrow syng:
> When that they lie in daunger depe,
>   To put away mournyng.[12]

It is that shadow of mourning in the Fool, the association of the Fool with Death that is always incipient in his traditional role as the teller of the truths of human vanity and mortality, that makes particularly appropriate Lear's conflation of him with Cordelia at the end of the play, when he says, "And my poor fool is hanged" (V.iii.281).

The combination of opposites is especially profound in Cordelia's characterization, but the play's most manifest combinations of the extremes that are traced in Ecclesiastes occur in the actions as well as characterizations of Lear and Gloucester, the two aged and dying protagonists who participate in the being of all of their children, the loving and the hateful, the legitimate and the illegitimate. Indeed a large part of the action of the play consists of Lear's and Gloucester's oscillation between extremes that are never ameliorated, that tear at them, and that ultimately break their hearts.

Gloucester's initial arrogance in his talk of Edmund's bastardy yields very quickly to the demoralizing thought that his legitimate son seeks his death; and the "good sport" (I.i.22) of the scene of Edmund's conception is eventually contrasted with the malignant horror of the scene in which Gloucester is blinded. Edgar, who makes the latter contrast explicit, also tries to treat it homiletically: "The dark and vicious place where thee he got / Cost him his eyes" (V.iii.163–64); but the symmetry of Edgar's formulation does not dispel our own sense of the gross disparity between the two scenes. And the same is true of Gloucester's states of mind on the heath, after his blinding. Edgar's sententious efforts to preserve his father from despair finally only intensify our sense of the alternations between despair and patience that punctuate Gloucester's feelings, alternations that continue to the point of his death, and that actually constitute it. Near the end Gloucester, in his anguish, says to Edgar that "A man may rot even here" (V.ii.8). Edgar's famous response, "Men must endure / Their going hence even as their coming hither. / Ripeness is all" (V.ii.9–11), might well be a verse in Ecclesiastes. (The exhausted tone of Ecclesiastes is generally apposite to the Gloucester plot.) "Ripeness" is a metaphor not for the fullness of life, but for the need to be resigned to the arbitrariness of its ending. As the context itself suggests, Edgar is evoking a traditional image of ripe fruit dropping from a tree and then rotting.[13] "Ripeness is all" is Gloucester's epitaph.

Similar stark contrasts of feeling, on a far more massive scale, inform Lear's movement toward death, and in his case there is not even the patina of moral commentary. The Fool's comments, which are the analogues of Edgar's, are almost always morally equivocal, and they are entirely absorbed with the paradoxical oppositions that compose Lear's condition. In the second childhood of age, Lear is at the same time "every inch a king" (IV.v.107); and though he sometimes enacts these roles simultaneously, he cannot mediate between them: they remain in opposition until the play's end. His sense of humility grows, but it alternates with his wrath, never replaces it. He rages in his last appearance in the play, as he did in his first. His increasing apprehension, early in the play, of the wrong he did Cordelia is balanced by his excoriations of his other daughters and by the fury of his madness, just as later in the play the joy of his recovery of Cordelia is balanced by the desolation of his loss of her. In a wonderful speech, he imagines kneeling and humbling himself as a child before Cordelia:

> Come let's away to prison.
> We two alone will sing like birds i'th' cage.
> When thou dost ask me blessing, I'll kneel down
> And ask of thee forgiveness; so we'll live,
> And pray, and sing, and tell old tales, and laugh
> At gilded butterflies....
> (V.iii.8–13)

But the childlike humility of this speech is a function of its childlike presumption, for Lear also tells Cordelia that they will "take upon" themselves "the mystery of things / As if we were God's spies" (V.i.16–17).[14] And the yoking of such disparities continues until his death, and in the very moment of it. His very last words express the hope—or delusion—that Cordelia is alive. They join with, they do not transform, the knowledge that she will never return.

It is tempting to see in Lear's movement towards death an image of the homiletic journeys of the protagonists of the earlier morality plays, particularly because those plays seem similarly composed of radically contrasting states of feeling and being—virtue and vice, despair and hope, good and evil, angels and devils. But the resemblances only highlight the profound difference. In the moralities, the summons of death is not ultimately an end but a beginning that retrospectively gives meaning to the large contrasts of human existence. In *King Lear*, as in Ecclesiastes, the summons is to an absolute ending whose retrospect of existence is not morally comprehensible. Edgar tries to make it so for his father's death, and there is perhaps a moral, if barbaric, decorum in Gloucester's destruction by his bastard son. But the Gloucester plot is not the primary plot of *King Lear*. That plot is Lear's, and even Edgar cannot moralize Lear's story. He says of the spectacle of Lear's meeting with Gloucester on the heath, "I would not take this from report; it is, / And my heart breaks at it" (IV.v.137–38). The verb *is* in Edgar's comment suggests that Lear's suffering presents us with the world of unmediated existential extremes we find in Ecclesiastes, where "as *is* the good, so *is* the sinner." The growth in Lear's understanding itself suggests this world. Lear does change on the heath. His own suffering allows him to feel, almost literally to touch, the pain of poor Tom and of the Fool and of poor naked wretches everywhere. This compassion is important and deeply moving. The sympathetic experience of pain establishes a human community in a play that otherwise seems to represent its apocalyptic dissolution, and it informs our sense of Lear's heroic stature. But his compassion should also not be misconstrued in a Romantic fashion, for the knowledge of human frailty that his suffering brings him increases his sorrow to the point of madness. Critics sometimes talk of the "privilege" of Lear's madness, but if we examine our own experience of mentally infirm human beings, we will, like Edgar, know better. It is a horror, and an anticipation of "the promised end . . . Or image of that horror" (V.iii.238–39) that we witness in Cordelia's death.[15]

Cordelia's death is, typically, preceded by her reunion with Lear after he awakens from his madness, a scene that has often been treated as if it were the climax of the action and that has frequently been compared with the reunion of Pericles and Marina. The two scenes have many elements in common: both show old and exhausted fathers, discomposed by suffering, reunited with daughters from whom they have long been separated and who seem to bring them back to life. In both, the recognitions are luminous; and both have verse of extraordinary lyric intensity. But the two scenes are also profoundly different in their immediate and eventual effects as well as in their generic contexts. Pericles's recovery of Marina is at once a recovery of his identity and an acknowledgement of its definition in the stream of time. For though, "wild in [his] beholding" (V.i.221),[16] he draws Marina to himself and embraces her, he also immediately dreams of his eventual reunion with his wife and anticipates giving Marina away in marriage. In addition, he hears the music of the spheres, a music that helps give Marina's nurture of him the cosmic sense of the intelligibility, if not miracle, of rebirth: "O, come hither," he tells her, "Thou that beget'st him that did thee beget" (V.i.194–95). The scene invokes the combination of joy and pain that is habitual in *King Lear*, but with a diametrically different accent. As Pericles recognizes Marina, he says:

> O Helicanus, strike me, honour'd sir!
> Give me a gash, put me to present pain,
> Lest this great sea of joys rushing upon me
> O'erbear the shores of my mortality,
> And drown me with their sweetness.
>   (V.i.190–94)

Pericles's mixture of joy and pain is a guarantee of renewed life rather than an expression of its ending; and he later discriminates the pattern of the fortunate fall in all his suffering, suffering that is the prelude to joy and that heightens it: "You gods, your present kindness / Makes my past miseries sports" (V.iii.40–41).

The pattern, as well as the texture, of Lear's experience is the reverse. Lear tells Kent at the outset of the play that he had "thought to set [his] rest / On [Cordelia's] kind nursery" (I.i.123–24), and it is the peculiar nursing, rather than rebirth, of Lear that we witness in the scene in which he is reunited with Cordelia. For Cordelia ministers not only to an aged father but also to a man transformed by age into a child again. The metaphor of age as second childhood pervades the sources of *King Lear*, and as G. Wilson Knight suggested long ago,[17] Shakespeare himself tends to give it a harsh, if not grotesque, inflection in the play. The Fool speaks of the king putting down his breeches and making his daughters his mothers (I.iv.153–55), a metaphor that is painfully acted out as Lear kneels to Cordelia and says,

>   Pray do not mock.
> I am a very foolish, fond old man,
> Fourscore and upward,
> Not an hour more nor less; and to deal plainly,
> I fear I am not in my perfect mind.
>   (IV.vi.52–56)

That Lear should have to kneel and confess the infirmity of age to his evil daughters is "terrible," but that he should do so to Cordelia as well "has also something of the terrible in it...."[18] The Fool repeatedly rebukes Lear for giving away his power and turning his family relationships upside down, and Lear's behavior in the opening scene would seem to justify those rebukes. But there is a sad irony in the Fool's speeches, for as Montaigne suggested,[19] and as the play itself eventually shows, human beings of "fourscore and upward" usually cannot do otherwise. There is often no choice for us but to become the parents of our parents in their old age and to treat them as children, and it is painful because whether our motives verge toward Cordelia's or toward Goneril and Regan's (and they may do both) the nursing of parents is not nurture for future life but the preparation for death. It is directly so for Lear. The music he hears in his reunion with Cordelia suggests no larger life into which he can be incorporated, and his recovery of her is the immediate prelude to his excruciating loss of her as well as to his own death. In the manner of the whole play, it is a joy that heightens sorrow, that makes it heartbreaking.

As is well known, Dr. Johnson found Cordelia's death both bewildering and unendurable, and like many later critics, he wished to deny it. He protested that "Shakespeare has suffered the virtue of Cordelia to perish in a just cause, contrary to the natural ideas of justice, to the hope of the reader, and, what is yet more strange, to the faith of chronicles." He added, "I was many years ago so shocked by Cordelia's death, that I know not whether I ever endured to read again the last scenes of the play till I undertook to revise them as an editor."[20] As Johnson's commentary suggests, there is an inner logic to adaptations of *King Lear*, like Nahum Tate's, that left Cordelia and Lear alive and united at the end of the play. All of Shakespeare's own sources—the old play of *King Leir*, Holinshed, Spenser, and others—end (in the short term, at least) by giving life and victory to Cordelia and Lear.[21] Only Shakespeare does not, and his insistence on Cordelia's death and Lear's final agony, as Northrop Frye remarks, is "too much a part of the play even to be explained as inexplicable."[22] Lear's and Cordelia's union in death is at the heart of Shakespeare's rendition of the Lear story. It is prepared for by every scene in which they appear together, including their earlier reunion, and is the event that not only concludes the tragedy, but wholly informs it. We cannot deny it, however much we wish to and however much the play itself makes us wish to.

A modern understanding of the psychology of dying can help illuminate this phenomenon.[23] Freud's discussion of *King Lear* is especially pertinent. He argues that the choice among the three daughters with which *King Lear* begins is the choice of death. Cordelia, in her muteness, he says, is the representation of death and, as in the depiction of such choices in the myths and fairy tales that *King Lear* resembles, her portrayal as the most beautiful and desirable of the three women expresses the inherent, often unconscious, human wish to deny death. "Lear is not only an old man: he is a dying man," and this reality subsumes both "the extraordinary premise of the division of the inheritance" in the opening scene and the overpowering effect of the final scene:

> Lear carries Cordelia's dead body on to the stage. Cordelia is
> Death. If we reverse the situation it becomes intelligible and
> familiar to us. She is the Death-goddess who, like the Valkyrie
> in German mythology, carries away the dead hero from the
> battlefield. Eternal wisdom, clothed in primaeval myth, bids the
> old man renounce love, choose death and make friends with the
> necessity of dying.[24]

Freud's identification of Cordelia with Lear's death suggests the kind of allegorization that often exasperates literary critics, but in this instance, at least, it seems just. Shakespeare's characterization of Cordelia is very luminous, but it is also very sharply focused. She is from first to last a function of Lear's character, a part of him to which we know he must return. She is clearly the person who counts most to him, and in the extremely crowded action of the play it is his relation to her that we most attend to and that most organizes our responses. Their relationship is the emotional as well as structural spine of the play. Cordelia is the absolute focus of Lear's attention, and ours, in the opening scene; it is Lear's rejection of her that initiates the tragic action; and during that ensuing, often diffuse, action neither he nor we can ever forget her. The Fool, who is Cordelia's surrogate, does not allow us to, both because he keeps her constantly in Lear's mind and because the combination of love and sorrow that he brings to Lear prepares us for a similar combination in Cordelia's final role. The collocation of her reunion with Lear and his loss of her is of a piece with all the words of the Fool that weep for joy and sing for sorrow, and it constitutes the same paradox of heartbreak and death.

Lear himself momentarily associates Cordelia and death in the opening scene of the play, when he says, "So be my grave my peace as here I give / Her father's heart from her," and the association is apparent in the scene's literal action as well. Freud contends that Cordelia's silence directly connotes death, as muteness often does in dreams.[25] But Cordelia also speaks in the scene, and what she says indicates clearly enough that Lear's rejection of her is precisely his denial of the impending death that he ostensibly acknowledges in the very act of dividing his kingdom and in his explicit announcement that he wishes "To shake all cares and business from our age," and "Unburdened crawl toward death" (I.i.39, 41). Cordelia tells her father that she loves him "According to [her] bond, no more nor less." She goes on to say, in a speech that is akin to Desdemona's defiance of Brabantio:

> Good my lord,
> You have begot me, bred me, loved me.
> I return those duties back as are right fit—
> Obey you, love you, and most honour you.
> Why have my sisters husbands if they say
> They love you all? Haply when I shall wed
> That lord whose hand must take my plight shall carry
> Half my love with him, half my care and duty.
> Sure, I shall never marry like my sisters.
>   (I.i.93, 95–103)

Cordelia exhibits not a little of Lear's own stubbornness in this speech, but though that trait may explain the manner of her speech, it does not account for what, as Kent remarks, she "justly think'st, and hast most rightly said" (I.i.182). What she declares quite clearly in these lines is not only that she must have the freedom to love a husband, but also that it is in the nature of things for parents to be succeeded by children and for her to have a future that Lear cannot absorb or control. Her peculiar gravity in this scene, the austerity of her insistence on the word *bond* as well as her reiteration of the word *nothing*, reflects more than her temperament. It also suggests, even this early in the play, the particular sense of the nature of things that is evoked in Ecclesiastes—the sense of human vanity that comes with the awareness of the ultimate bond with death. At any rate, it is to the natural realities given expression in Cordelia's speech that Lear responds. His rage against her, like his cosmological rage throughout the play, is his refusal to "go gentle into that good night," his unavailing, as well as heroic, attempt to deny death and hold on to life.

Shakespeare's portrayal of this rage and denial is intelligible in Renaissance as well as modern terms. Montaigne's discussion of death and dying in "Of Judging of Others Death," for example, is remarkably apposite to Lear. In an argument that has analogies with Freud's, Montaigne remarks that a dying man "will hardly beleeve he is come to [the] point" of death and that "no wher doth hopes deceit ammuse us more...." "The reason," he says,

> is, that we make too much account of our selves. It seemeth,
> that the generality of things doth in some sort suffer for our

annullation, and takes compassion of our state. Forsomuch as
our sight being altered, represents unto it selfe things alike; and
we imagine, that things faile it, as it doth to them: As they who
travell by Sea, to whom mountaines, fields, townes, heaven and
earth, seeme to goe the same motion, and keepe the same course,
they doe. . . . We deeme our death to be some great matter, and
which passeth not so easily, nor without a solemne consultation
of the Starres; *Tot circa unum caput tumultuantes* Deos. *So many
Gods keeping a stirre about one mans life. . . .* No one of us thinkes it
sufficient, to be but one.[26]

Shakespeare's depiction of Lear is clearly informed by such ideas. His
portrait is more sympathetic than Montaigne's, but similarly ironic. Rage and
cosmological pretension characterize Lear throughout the play. These feelings
reach their apogee during the time when his denial of what Cordelia stands
for is literalized by her absence from the play. Her return in Act IV heralds his
significant recognition that he is "but one"—"They told me I was everything;
'tis a lie, I am not ague-proof" (IV.v.104–5)—and permits him to recover
from his madness when he is physically reunited with her. But his inescapable attachment to her, his bond with her, always remains a prefiguration of
his death. It is often difficult in our experience of *King Lear* to understand
that Lear's denial of death is represented as much in his love for Cordelia as
in his rage against her. It is even more difficult, but crucial, to understand that
Cordelia's own love is itself a function of this denial, that the expression of her
love at the end of the play is as much a signification of Lear's death as is the
muteness of that love at the start. Granville-Barker hints at such a meaning as
well as at Cordelia's general symbolic properties in his comments on her characterization. He observes that she does not change in the play, and that her cry
of "No cause, no cause" to Lear at their reunion is essentially of a piece with
her earlier declaration of "Nothing, my lord." He remarks that though "it is
no effort to her to love her father better than herself, . . . this supremest virtue,
as we count it, is no gain to him," and he asks, "Is there, then, an impotence in
such goodness, lovely as we find it? And is this why Shakespeare lets her slip
out of the play . . . to her death, as if, for all her beauty of spirit, she were not of
so much account?"[27] The questions Granville-Barker asks and the paradox he
discriminates are central to Cordelia's characterization and are at the center
of most of the play's other paradoxes as well. They are best explained, I think,
in terms (which Granville-Barker himself does not use) of the phenomenon
of the denial of death, what Montaigne calls "hopes deceit."[28]

   In all the myths of the choice among three sisters that Freud finds analogous to *Lear*, the woman representing the power of death is transformed

into a woman representing the power of love. Contradictions and contraries of this kind are characteristic of the process of condensation in dreams, but Freud relates such contradictions in *King Lear* primarily to the human disposition to make use of the imagination "to satisfy wishes that reality does not satisfy" and to deny what cannot be tolerated. The profound human wish to deny "the immutable law of death" is represented both in the identification of the most beautiful sister with death and in the presence of choice itself:

> Choice stands in the place of necessity, of destiny. In this way
> man overcomes death, which he has recognized intellectually.
> No greater triumph of wish-fulfilment is conceivable. A choice
> is made where in reality there is obedience to a compulsion, and
> what is chosen is not a figure of terror, but the fairest and most
> desirable of women.[29]

In the old chronicle play of *King Leir*, the king has an explicit political motive that is associated with his testing of his daughters' love as well as with the division of the kingdom, and the two wicked daughters are forewarned of it while the good one is not. All three daughters, moreover, are unmarried, and the issue of their marriages is related to the love test and to politics. Shakespeare almost entirely shears away such surface motives and rationalizations for Lear's action in order to make its underlying motive of denial more stark and more compelling.[30] The whole of the scene echoes with negations and contradictions. Its sense of high order and ceremony is prefaced by Gloucester's casual talk of ungoverned instinct. The ceremony itself is a decoronation, deeply reminiscent of Richard II's undecking of "the pompous body of a king" as well as of Richard's ambivalence: "Ay, no; no, ay; for I must nothing be" (*Richard II*, IV.i.240, 191). The pun is not only on "Ay" for "I," but also "no" for "know." Richard knows no "I" and sees that he is to be no "I."[31] He thus seems to indicate and accept, more clearly than Lear ever does, that the loss of his crown also constitutes the loss of his life, that "nothing" is death. This meaning of the word becomes unmistakably plain in his final speech in prison when he says,

> Thus play I in one person many people,
> . . . . .
>   But whate'er I be,
> Nor I, nor any man that but man is,
> With nothing shall be pleased till he be eased
> With being nothing.
>   (V.v.31, 38–41)

Lear himself does not acknowledge the ambivalence that Richard exhibits in resigning the throne, but he unquestionably acts it out. He invests Cornwall and Albany with his "power, / Pre-eminence, and all the large effects / That troop with majesty," but he wishes at the same time to "retain / The name and all th'addition to a king" (I.i.130–32, 135–36). Richard II also cleaves, unavailingly, to the "king's name," and in his case the implications of that wish are explicitly related to the Renaissance concept of the mystical union between the king's two bodies, between the body natural that is subject to time and death, and the body politic that is divine and immortal.[32] Richard's repeated invocations of his name ("Arm, arm, my name!" [III.ii.82]) signify the imminent severing of this union and his growing consciousness of death. Even though the universe of *King Lear* is not Christian, Lear's wish to "retain / The name and all th'addition to a king" would probably have been understood in the same context of ideas and have suggested the same implicit focus upon mortality. But in any case, his wish, even on its face, contradicts his ostensible desire to resign the "sway," "revenue," and "execution" of the king's power (I.i.136–37), and that contradiction governs his manner, his speech, and his actions throughout the opening scene.

The contradictions that govern Cordelia in the scene are less obvious, but more profound and more moving. What is compelling about her from the outset is that she continuously represents both sides of the process of denial: the heart's sorrow as well as its joy. She represents the vanity of denial but also its animating power, the love of life as well as the inescapability of death, the mother that nurtures us, as Freud suggests, as well as the Mother Earth that finally receives us.[33] She tells Lear the truth of his dying in the opening scene: "Nothing, my lord." She stands in mute rebuke to the folly of his attempt to deny it. And she eventually becomes that truth when she lies lifeless in his arms. But at the same time the very telling of that truth is replete with love—"What shall Cordelia speak? Love and be silent" (I.i.62)—which is what makes Lear's rejection of her seem unnatural on the literal as well as the symbolic level. As the play progresses she comes more and more to represent everything that binds Lear most nobly to life and that makes his protest against death at once heartbreaking and heroic. Freud speaks of the resistance to death as essentially a reflex of the ego's wish to be immortal. But he undervalues human love, for another reason that we do not wish to die and see those close to us die, even the very old, is that we are capable of cherishing and loving others. Cordelia is an incarnation of this capacity.

Shakespeare endows Cordelia's representation of such love in *King Lear* with religious, and specifically Christian, overtones, and perhaps the greatest pain of her death, and of her tragic embodiment of the futility of the denial of death, is that the promise of these overtones also proves empty. Cordelia's counterpart in the chronicle play of *King Leir* is, like the whole of that play, explicitly homiletic and Christian. When she is rejected by her father, she turns to "him which doth protect the iust, / In him will poore *Cordella* put her trust," and later, as she acknowledges her sisters' "blame," she prays for God's forgiveness both of them and of her father:

> Yet God forgiue both him, and you and me,
> Euen as I doe in perfit charity.
> I will to Church, and pray vnto my Sauiour,
> That ere I dye, I may obtayne his fauour.
>   (ll. 331–32, 1090–93)[34]

Cordella's trust in God is fully vindicated at the end of the play when she and Leir are triumphantly reunited and he is restored to love and dignity.

Shakespeare intensifies, at the same time that he transmutes, the old play's association of Cordella with Christianity. There are unmistakable New Testament echoes in *King Lear*, and most of them cluster around Cordelia. They start in the opening scene, when France uses the language of miracle and faith to question Lear's judgment of Cordelia (I.i.220–22) and when he takes her as his wife:

> Fairest Cordelia, that art most rich, being poor;
> Most choice, forsaken; and most loved, despised:
> Thee and thy virtues here I seize upon.
>   (I.i.250–52)

The allusion to 2 Corinthians 6:10 is clear—"as poore, and *yet* [making] manie riche: as hauing nothing, and *yet* possessing all things"—and it resonates with the deepest preoccupations of the whole scene. The allusions and associations intensify at the end of the play. When Cordelia returns from France she says, "O dear father, / It is thy business that I go about" (IV. iii.23–24; cf. Luke 2:49); and shortly afterwards, the Gentleman who is sent to rescue Lear says,

> Thou hast a daughter,
> Who redeems nature from the general curse
> Which twain have brought her to.
>   (IV.v.201–3)

At the very end Cordelia's death is associated with the Last Judgment (V.iii.238–39), and Lear himself wishes for her revival in language that seems to echo the most profound of Christian beliefs:

This feather stirs. She lives. If it be so,
It is a chance which does redeem all sorrows
That ever I have felt.
(V.iii.240–42)

But Cordelia does not live, and Lear, whether he dies thinking she does
or not, is not redeemed by her. For in the pagan world of *King Lear* the New
Testament's conception of death, and life, is the denial; the reality is that of
Ecclesiastes, the pilgrimage of the heart in the Old Testament that insists
above all else that death cannot be denied. Shakespeare, in all the plots of
King Lear, at once summons up and denies the most profound energies of
the comic and romantic impulses of the chronicle play of *Leir*, as well as
of his other sources.[35] We expect and wish, for example, for Gloucester to
recognize his good son Edgar, but he does so only at the very moment of his
death and off-stage, and we wish, as Kent does, that Lear will recognize him
as his faithful servant Caius, and he never does. The most painful of these
denials of our romantic expectations, however, is the treatment of Cordelia.
By associating her role with the Christian hope of redemption (an association
that is strengthened by the play's simultaneous evocation and frustration of
the generic expectations of the morality play as well as of romance[36]), Shakespeare deliberately violates, as Dr. Johnson perceived, not only "the faith of
the chronicles" but also the profoundest "hope of the reader." We ourselves are
thus compelled not just to view the process of denial, but to undergo it and
endure it. There is no deeper generic transformation of a source in the canon,
and it is the wellspring of the sense of grotesqueness as well as of desolation
that is so peculiar to this tragedy.[37]

Such an understanding of the Christian evocations in the pagan world
of *King Lear* can help clarify the religious issues that continue to vex criticism of the play, but it should not be interpreted to suggest that *King Lear* is
thus either an argument against Providence or a homily on the inadequacy
of pagan virtue.[38] Nor does it suggest that the play's conception of death is
unique among Shakespeare's tragedies. The tragic sense that death informs as
well as ends human life, and that after it, in Hamlet's last words, "The rest is
silence" (V.ii.310), is as germane to *Hamlet*, *Othello*, and *Macbeth*, which have
manifest Christian settings, as it is to *King Lear*. Christian belief does give
a providential perspective to death in those plays, most strongly in *Hamlet*,
where the intimations of another world of being become a part of the hero's
consciousness; but such a perspective, even in the case of *Hamlet*, cannot
absorb or fully explain the hero's actual suffering. Nor can it finally mitigate
the effect of that suffering on us. We can spend much time gauging the level
of irony in the endings of the tragedies, but when we see or read these great

plays we do not construe the endings, we feel them, and what we feel is a paramount sense of suffering and loss. The distinction of *King Lear* is that the death of Cordelia compounds that feeling and focuses it. All of us are pagan in our immediate response to dying and death. The final scene of *King Lear* is a representation—among the most moving in all drama—of the universality of this experience and of its immeasurable pain.

Notes

1. See, e.g., William Elton, *King Lear and the Gods* (San Marino: Huntington Library Press, 1968), and Stephen Greenblatt, "Shakespeare and the Exorcists," *After Strange Texts*, eds. Gregory F. Jay and David L. Miller (Birmingham: Univ. of Alabama Press, 1985), pp. 101–23.

2. Jonathan Dollimore, *Radical Tragedy: Religion, Ideology and Power in the Drama of Shakespeare and his Contemporaries* (Chicago: Univ. of Chicago Press, 1984), p. 157. His discussion of *Lear* is on pages 189–203. See also Walter Cohen, *Drama of a Nation* (Ithaca: Cornell Univ. Press, 1985).

3. All references to *King Lear* are to the Folio text in *William Shakespeare: The Complete Works*, eds. Stanley Wells and Gary Taylor (Oxford: Clarendon Press, 1986).

4. Significantly, Dollimore's attack on the humanist assumption that in tragedy men must suffer never really comes to terms with the suffering that is produced by death, the one event in human life, besides birth, that is ineluctable and universal.

5. See especially John Holloway, *The Story of the Night* (Lincoln: Univ. of Nebraska Press, 1961), pp. 85–91. For a suggestive survey of biblical echoes in the play, which includes but does not give particular emphasis to Ecclesiastes, see Rosalie L. Colie, "The Energies of Endurance: Biblical Echo in *King Lear*," in *Some Facets of King Lear*, eds. Rosalie Colie and F. T. Flahiff (Toronto: Univ. of Toronto Press, 1974), pp. 117–44.

6. All quotations from the Bible are from *The Geneva Bible, A facsimile of the 1560 edition* (Madison, Milwaukee, and London: Univ. of Wisconsin Press, 1969).

7. See Thomas McFarland, *Tragic Meanings in Shakespeare* (New York: Random House, 1966), pp. 149–71.

8. See Holloway, pp. 75–80; and Joseph Wittreich, *"Image of that Horror": History, Prophecy, and Apocalypse in* King Lear (San Marino: Huntington Library Press, 1984).

9. Allan Bloom comments on this speech in his fine essay on *Richard II* in *Shakespeare as Political Thinker*, eds. John Alvis and Thomas G. West (Durham, N.C.: Carolina Academic Press, 1981), pp. 55–56.

10. *The Fool: His Social and Literary History* (London: Faber and Faber, 1935) p. 267.

11. For thorough discussions of these commentaries, see Elton, King Lear *and the Gods*, pp. 270–72.

12. Cited in the Arden *King Lear*, ed. Kenneth Muir (London: Methuen and Co. Ltd., 1952), p. 45. For a discussion of the ballad, see Hyder Rollins, "'King Lear' and the Ballad of 'John Careless,'" *Modern Language Review*, 15 (1920), 87–89.

13. See J. V. Cunningham, *Tradition and Poetic Structure* (Denver: Alan Swallow, 1960), pp. 135–40.

14. See Elton, pp. 249–53.

15. For the argument that Lear's suffering and madness are purgatorial, see Paul A. Jorgenson, *Lear's Self-Discovery* (Berkeley and Los Angeles: Univ. of California Press, 1967).

16. All references to *Pericles* are to the New Arden edition, ed. F. D. Hoeniger (London: Methuen and Co. Ltd., 1963).

17. "*King Lear* and the Comedy of the Grotesque," *The Wheel of Fire* (London: Methuen and Co. Ltd., 1949), pp. 160–76.

18. Barbara Everett, "The New King Lear," *Critical Quarterly*, 2 (1960), 325–39, esp. pp. 334–35.

19. See especially "Of the Affection of Fathers to Their Children," *Montaigne's Essays*, trans. John Florio, 2 vols. (London: The Nonesuch Press, 1931), Vol. I, 437–59. Montaigne's assumption is that fathers not only often have to give up power to their children, but should do so.

20. *The Yale Edition of the Works of Samuel Johnson: Johnson on Shakespeare*, 15 vols., Vol. VIII, ed. Arthur Sherbo (New Haven and London: Yale Univ. Press, 1968), 704.

21. In the longer term, in the chronicles, Cordelia commits suicide after Lear's own death. Shakespeare's stress, of course, is on Lear's experience of Cordelia's death.

22. *Fools of Time: Studies in Shakespearean Tragedy* (Toronto: Univ. of Toronto Press, 1967), p. 115.

23. The ground-breaking study on this subject is Susan Snyder's "*King Lear* and the Psychology of Dying," *Shakespeare Quarterly*, 33 (1982), 449–60. My own analysis places more emphasis upon Freud's insight into the play, but I remain much indebted to her article.

24. "The Theme of the Three Caskets," *Standard Edition of the Complete Psychological Works of Sigmund Freud*, ed. James Strachey, 24 vols. (London: Hogarth Press, 1953–74), Vol. 12, 301.

25. *Works*, Vol. 12, 295.

26. *Montaigne's Essays*, Vol. I, 694–95.

27. *Prefaces to Shakespeare*, 2 vols. (Princeton: Princeton Univ. Press, 1952), Vol. 1, 305.

28. I think this is the phenomenon Stanley Cavell is really touching upon in "The Avoidance of Love," *Must We Mean What We Say?* (Cambridge: Cambridge Univ. Press, 1976), pp. 272–300, for in *King Lear* the avoidance of love (as well as the embrace of it) is fundamentally the avoidance of death.

29. *Works*, Vol. 12, 299.

30. For an interesting, if highly inferential, insistence on the political motives of the opening scene of *Lear*, see Harry V. Jaffa, "The Limits of Politics," in *Shakespeare's Politics*, eds. Allan Bloom and Harry Jaffa (New York: Basic Books, 1964), pp. 113–38.

31. See Molly Mahood, *Shakespeare's Wordplay* (London: Methuen and Co. Ltd., 1957), p. 87.

32. See Ernst Kantorowicz, *The King's Two Bodies* (Princeton: Princeton Univ. Press, 1957), pp. 24–91.

33. *Works*, Vol. 12, 301.

34. *The History of King Leir 1605*, gen. ed. W. W. Greg (Oxford: The Malone Society Reprints, 1907).

35. For a discussion of the generic expectations of romance in *King Lear,* see Leo Salingar, "Romance in *King Lear*," *English,* 27 (1978), 5–22.

36. See Edgar Schell, *Strangers and Pilgrims: from The Castle of Perseverance to King Lear* (Chicago: Univ. of Chicago Press, 1983).

37. See G. Wilson Knight, "*King Lear* and the Grotesque"; and Susan Snyder, *The Comic Matrix of Shakespeare's Tragedies* (Princeton: Princeton Univ. Press, 1979), pp. 137–79.

38. Cf. Thomas P. Roche, Jr., "'Nothing Almost Sees Miracles': Tragic Knowledge in *King Lear,*" in *On King Lear,* ed. Lawrence Danson (Princeton: Princeton Univ. Press, 1981), pp. 136–62.

DAVID BEVINGTON

"Is This the Promised End?"
Death and Dying in King Lear

Shakespeare's last plays share a common concern about last things. The late romances, *Pericles*, *Cymbeline*, *The Winter's Tale*, and *The Tempest*, have long been regarded as a kind of summation and recapitulation of Shakespeare's artistic career and an extended dramatic statement about the coming of death. The protagonists of these plays, as they grow older, must confront the reality of marrying their daughters off to younger men. The interplay of aging father and marriageable daughter brings with it a kind of renewal as well, but it is a renewal suffused with the melancholy perception of a life no longer recoverable. Pericles, in sackcloth, observing a strict silence on board his own ship, seems in mourning for his life until his daughter, Marina, brings him back to acceptance of life and makes subsequently possible the reunion of aging husband and his aging wife, long given up for dead. The play is marked by threatening portraitures of those who, like Antiochus, refuse to give up their daughters and who are thereupon consumed by the angry heavens for their incest and impiety. Leontes, in *The Winter's Tale*, tortured in the play's earlier scenes by recollections of his own lost innocence, reconciles himself to aging and to the approach of death through the reunion with his now marriageable daughter and his long-lost wife, still beautiful but wrinkled with the years. Posthumus Leonatus in *Cymbeline*, though he is not reunited with a daughter, is called back from his active

From *Proceedings of the American Philosophical Society* 133, no. 3 (September 1989): 404–15. Copyright © 1989 by The American Philosophical Society.

53

longing for a penitential death by a forgiving wife whom he thought he had killed for her imagined infidelity. Prospero, in *The Tempest*, provides a young husband for his only daughter as he simultaneously resolves to lay aside his art and return to Milan, "where / Every third thought shall be my grave" (5.1.314–5). Repeatedly we see an association between the acceptance of aging and the necessity of laying aside burdens, pleasure, and achievements. Finally we must lay aside life itself.

King Lear, written ca. 1605 more or less on the threshold of the late romances, is no less obsessed with last things. It too juxtaposes the difficulty of aging, and especially of confronting the marriage of a favorite daughter, with the harsh necessity of preparing for death. And *King Lear* brings particularly into focus the eschatological dimensions of such a confrontation with death. What judgment will we face? What will be left of us once we are dead? The late romances partially mask these hard questions by providing romance-like solutions: the daughter is successfully married, the wife thought to be dead is recovered, life will renew itself in love and forgiveness and a second chance.

Moreover, the gods preside over these renewals and offer assurance that the heavens will indeed ultimately succor those whom the gods love. Gower in *Pericles* proceeds to show us those in trouble's reign, "Losing a mite, a mountain gain" (2. Chorus 7–8) and ultimately shows us a spectacle of "Virtue preserved from fell destruction's blast, / Led on by heaven, and crowned with joy at last" (5.3.91–2). Jupiter assures us in *Cymbeline* that he deliberately crosses those he loves, but only "to make my gift, / The more delayed, delighted" (5.4.101–2), thus demonstrating once again that "Fortune brings in some boats that are not steered" (4.3.46). Leontes's suffering in *The Winter's Tale* is at last seen not as merely tragic but as a meaningful penance preparing him for a receiving into grace symbolized by the coming of Hermione's statue to life. Juno herself, or rather an illusion of Juno created by Prospero's art, attends the wedding of Ferdinand and Miranda, while a spirit impersonating Ceres promises the couple "Earth's increase, foison plenty, / Barns and garners never empty" (4.1.110–11).

These reassurances of divine caring seem to me unambiguous, even if Juno and Ceres are creations of Prospero's magic. There have been attempts recently to deconstruct meaning in the late romances,[1] but in fact nowhere in Shakespeare are we presented with oracular pronouncements as plain as that in *The Winter's Tale*, taken almost word for word from Shakespeare's source: "Hermione is chaste, Polixenes blameless, Camillo a true subject, Leontes a jealous tyrant, his innocent babe truly begotten, and the King shall live without an heir if that which is lost be not found" (3.2.132–6). Dark uncertainties and tragic potentials abound in the human capacity for self-destruction as manifested in Leontes and Posthumus Leonatus, but the answer of the caring gods is no less audible.

The promise of an afterlife is more problematic. Posthumus Leonatus is visited in *Cymbeline* by the "apparition" of his father in warlike attire, his mother as "an ancient matron," and his brothers "with wounds as they died in the wars" (5.4.29 S.D.), pleading to Jupiter to give justice to the only mortal survivor of their family. Ghosts of the dead have appeared in earlier plays, of course, in both a Christian and a pagan context: Richard III's victims on the eve of Bosworth Field, Julius Caesar just before Philippi, Hamlet's father, Banquo, and others. Only Hamlet's father, among these ghosts, provides us with a description of his current place of residence, and it is far from reassuring. Clarence, in *Richard III*, tells his dream, "lengthened after life" into "the kingdom of perpetual" night, where he visits the souls of those being punished for perjury, but he speaks as a mortal only glimpsing in his imagination that underworld "which poets write of" (1.4.45 ff.). Antony dreams of an afterlife in the Elysian Fields with Cleopatra in which they will make Dido and Aeneas envious by their fame as lovers (4.14.51–4), and Cleopatra too proclaims that she must hurry to join her "curlèd Antony" in their shared afterlife lest Iras get there first and "spend that kiss / Which is my heaven to have" (5.2.301–3), but these pagan visions are presented from the mortal perspective and may tell more about the artist's vision of greatness than about reassurances of an afterlife. Earlier, Antony joshes Lepidus about transmigration as something best applied to the crocodile (2.7.46). Shakespeare's hints in the direction of immortality are gnomic and sparse. In the late plays especially, what we see instead are visions of human reconciliation in which the idea of reincarnation or resurrection is transformed into a human and mundane context; Hermione's coming again to life is like a resurrection, but it is more suitably an emblem of recovered hope and acceptance than a promise of anything after death. Immortality in Shakespeare is more likely to be the fame bestowed on humanity by the poet's art than any kind of life existing beyond death.

Most of Shakespeare's ghosts appear onstage as a means of interpreting the present rather than of offering assurance of life after death. The little princes who return in *Richard III* are a token of judgment for Richard rather than dwellers in an eternal reward; Julius Caesar's return is proof that "the spirit of Caesar" will not leave Brutus until the story is finished; Banquo is the image of Macbeth's guilt, perhaps even a figment of his tortured imagination; and even Posthumus Leonatus's family are more a part of his dream than a promise of what will follow death. The enduring vision is the artist's work, for it is he after all who has created Ceres and Juno, and it is he, typified by Prospero, whose "potent art" and "rough magic" can command the graves to wake their sleepers and bid them come forth (5.1.50). The afterlife in Shakespeare is a consciousness of the past, to which the artist has special access; it is the memory of our achievements, immortalized, if we are lucky enough, in art. Meanwhile, as we unavoidably age and approach death, the reassurance offered by the late plays is a consistent one, and it has little to do with the promise of an afterlife: it is that we accept. "Be content," says Jupiter, simply enough, to Posthumus's family (5.4.102). Be content.

I hope the context of the late plays will clarify Lear's struggle to understand himself in relation to approaching death and what may follow. Even if *King Lear* is devastatingly unlike the plays I have been discussing in its unwillingness to provide assurance, it goes about the painful work of disillusionment by creating and then mocking the very expectations upon which the late romances depend for their sense of artistic closure.[2] Lear is, like Pericles, Cymbeline, and Leontes, reunited with a daughter he thinks he has alienated and lost. That event, and the prospect of her marriage, coincide with Lear's retirement, as with Prospero. Lear lays aside his burdens of office as Prospero lays aside the heavy burden of his magic, ponders the importance of his family in his declining years, and understands intellectually at least that he must prepare for the end: "'tis our fast intent / To shake all cares and business from our age, / Conferring them on younger strengths while we / Unburdened crawl toward death" (1.1.38–41). *King Lear* is not simply a tragedy in which many deaths occur, as usual in Shakespearean tragedy: it is differentiated from *Hamlet, Othello,* and *Macbeth* in its focus on aging and preparation for death.

We have heard a good deal in recent years about the stages of dying: the disbelief or incredulity at the first news that we are about to die, the inevitable question, "Why me?," the impotent anger, the rebelliousness against the seeming arbitrariness and injustice of it all, the refusal to accept (as though one had a choice), the slow coming to terms with the reality of death, and at last the acceptance. Elisabeth Kübler-Ross's five-part scheme for this process moves from denial and isolation to anger, bargaining, depression, and acceptance.[3] E. Mansell Pattison's more recent tripartite scheme of acute, chronic, and terminal phases distinguishes first the severe crisis of learning the bad news, the immobilization, the overwhelming feeling of inadequacy, the bewilderment, confusion, anxiety, and fear, the defensive mechanisms for postponing or disguising what cannot at first be faced (akin to Kübler-Ross's bargaining phase); then, a chronic living-dying phase characterized by fear of the unknown, fear of sorrow, fear of loss of family and friends, fear of loss of body and self-control, fear of suffering and pain, and fear of loss of identity, along with a more positive attempt to start putting our life in perspective and deal with the defense mechanisms we have used to deny reality; finally, in the terminal phase, the full realization that we will not get better and the acceptance of what must be final, accompanied by an increasing blocking out of the external world, what Pattison calls an "acceptable regression," and the exchanging of an unrealistic "expectational hope" for a more appropriate "desirability hope."[4]

These ways of analyzing the process of dying can also be applied, as Kübler-Ross realizes, to other traumatic experiences like bereavement, and so it is not surprising perhaps that we can look at *King Lear* in these terms. Lear does not know that he is dying, in fact is not terminal in the medical sense in which we usually analyze the problem today, and yet *King Lear* portrays an old man whose stages of reaction and suffering are as though a sentence of death has been pronounced. From the very start of the play, what Lear seems to be in need of learning is how to die, if possible with dignity and wisdom. This is a role for which he is, alas, spectacularly unfitted.

To describe Lear's story as the story of the death of a human being, even from the start of the play, is to examine the difficulty we all face in giving up this world, in learning to renounce, just as Prospero learns to renounce. Lear is in this regard a kind of everyman figure, like the protagonist of a morality play: he is King of the World, Rex Humanitas, or, to use the name of a fragmentary early morality play, he is Pride of Life or the King of Life.[5] Most of us are not kings, and we hope we are not as domineering or magisterial as Lear, but, as we approach old age, we do cling to our sense of privilege, to the rights we think we have earned to be treated with veneration. We expect, not without anxiety, to be looked after by our children, if only as a return on what we have done for them. "I gave you all," Lear says in rebuke to Regan and Goneril, only to be answered by Regan, "And in good time you gave it" (2.4.252). Goneril is no one to be speaking here, but the point is not lost on us: a sense of entitlement to happiness is the surest way imaginable to disillusionment and bitterness. We set ourselves up for failure and rejection when we expect or ask too much, and, in *King Lear*, to expect or ask anything is to expect too much.

Lear is not ready for this bitter medicine. However much he may have asserted his readiness in the opening scene to crawl "unburdened" toward death, he has done everything in his considerable power to ensure that he will not in fact be unburdened with those things that Everyman must learn to leave behind—friends, kindred, pleasure, riches. He leaves himself vulnerable not simply by delivering power into the hands of Goneril and Regan while banishing Cordelia, but by insisting on his right to the material comforts of this world. He is to reside by monthly courses with his two daughters, to be followed by a hundred knights, to enjoy "The name and all th' addition of a king" (1.1.136). He deals in the currency of wealth and power, attempting to bribe even Cordelia with "A third more opulent than your sisters'" (l. 86). The unselfknowing blindness of this mighty king, pointed out with brutal irony by his ungrateful daughters ("'Tis the infirmity of his age. Yet he hath ever but slenderly known himself," ll. 296–7), is his fatuous assumption that he can hold on to royal authority and perquisites while yielding the substance of power to others. This paradox is true in the specific political context of scene 1, and indeed is often made to give up a pragmatic and worldly meaning: if Lear wanted to be comfortable and safe, he should not have surrendered authority without sufficient guarantees of his welfare. My reading is quite the opposite: in the context of the approach of death, one cannot retire without also renouncing desire for worldly greatness. One cannot be disappointed in one's hopes if one no longer entertains hopes of this sort.

Thus the Fool becomes indispensable for pointing out to Lear, and to us, the folly of believing that one can give up power, or give up life itself, and still remain immune from any real loss. Lear's denial, his defense mechanisms for refusing to face the reality of his material decline, take the form of supposing, for example, that even when he has been rejected by Goneril, his other daughter will use him "kindly." Any fool can tell that "she's as like this as a crab's like an apple" (1.5.14–15). Lear attempts to explain away the insolence of his not being ceremoniously greeted in Gloucestershire by Regan and Cornwall with the speculation that the Duke "is not well," since "Infirmity doth still neglect all office / Whereto our health is bound; we are not ourselves / When nature, being oppressed, commands the mind / To suffer with the body" (2.4.103–7). The Fool is needed to mock Lear with his own self-deceiving strategies since no one else will be heard by him, and, more centrally, because the essence of Lear's folly is his unwillingness to come to terms with the reality of old age and declining fatherhood.

Anger, as in the second stage of Kübler-Ross's progression, is brought on by a growing awareness of impotence in the face of dissolution. Lear's inability to imagine himself dead takes the form of a fantasy in which he is godlike, immortal, and as wrathful as Jove toward those who dare threaten his invincibility. "Hear, Nature, hear! Dear goddess, hear!" he exclaims, in response to Goneril's refusal to let him have his way unchecked with his hundred knights in her castle. "Suspend thy purpose if thou didst intend / To make this creature fruitful!" (1.4.274–6). The god-father who has created life now claims the power to undo life, though in fact he is impotent to do so. These implorings of the gods, usually looked at as part of the question, do the gods exist and do they listen, are no less useful as a way of seeing how Lear thinks of himself; he supposes that he is, like the gods, beyond mortal vicissitude, able to strike others in the name of justice and above all to ensure his immortality. In this stage of his fury, Lear identifies again and again with the gods, imploring them to take his part and to make his cause their own, for they like him are old. Beneath this grandiloquence is of course the deep fear that he is not god-like, or that the gods are not listening, or that they are not there—all these propositions amounting pretty much to the same thing, that Lear is mortal and vulnerable.

And so Lear playacts at sparing his victims. "I do not bid the thunder-bearer shoot," he replies to Goneril's unyielding demands, "Nor tell tales of thee to high-judging Jove. / Mend when thou canst; be better at thy leisure. / I can be patient" (2.4.228–31). Lear imagines himself able to practice forbearance and mercy as well as vengeance, since the gods also conduct themselves in this way, but Lear is only masking the hard reality that he cannot hurt Goneril. When he dares look at this powerlessness in himself, the response is not only anger but shame. "I am ashamed / That thou hast power to shake my manhood thus, / That these hot tears, which break from me perforce, / Should make thee worth them" (1.4.295–8). The threat of dissolution is a threat to Lear's very manhood, and is exacerbated by the fact that Lear is emasculated by a woman, by his own daughter. Paradoxically, we see that Lear's impotent and furious response to this woman is childlike, babyish: seeing himself denied the absolute control that he has enjoyed as a king, and that an infant too believes it has the right to expect from its maternal source of being, Lear can only assert his sense of wounded potency through outbursts of petulant rage. As the Fool points out, Lear has succeeded in making his daughters his mothers, for he has given them the rod and has put down his own breeches (1.4.169–71). Lear needs to confront the painful and humiliating coming together in his life of old age and infancy, of "second childishness and mere oblivion," as Jaques terms it (*As You Like It*, 2.7.164). At first Lear can do little but scream and rant.

Lear bargains with all three of his daughters, first for their public declarations of affection, then with Goneril and Regan for a hundred knights, for fifty, twenty-five. "Hear me, my lord," Goneril concludes the bargaining, "What need you five-and-twenty, ten, or five, / To follow in a house where twice so many / Have a command to tend you?" to which Regan adds, "What need one?" (2.4.262–5). The bargaining is not with death as such, but it is so closely associated through the link (as in other late Shakespearean plays) between marrying off one's daughters and preparing for the end of life itself that we can see Lear's futile negotiations as a desperate struggle to put off the inevitable. His very identity, his life itself, seems to him to depend on his authoritarian role as father, as king, as god, as giver of life. Lear suffers from that quintessential and incredibly tenacious weakness of Mankind or Pride of Life in the morality play: he is covetous. Not in the sense of miserliness with wealth, but as the middle ages and Renaissance understood covetousness in its broadest sense: a clinging to this world. Coveteise in *The Castle of Perseverance*, that most spectacular of all morality plays, is associated throughout with Mundus, the world itself; to be covetous is to refuse to give up this world.

Lear cannot let go. He sees no justice in the proposition that his reign as King of the World must cease. He enlists the gods as his allies in protesting the injustice of what is, for him, a deposition, and, when the gods fail to respond to his call, he begins to fear some metaphysical conspiracy against his divine and royal might. "If it be you that stirs these daughters' hearts / Against their father," he apostrophizes the gods, "fool me not so much / To bear it tamely" (2.4.276–8). Lear equates his own dethroning, as we all do, and as infants do, with cosmic injustice. The gods must not care if they let us die, or, worse still, may not be there at all. It is the necessity and seeming injustice of death that for Lear, as for all of us, raises philosophical challenges to any meaningful explanation of human existence.

As long as Lear remains sane, his response to the challenge of dissolution is one of denial, outrage, protest, self pity, and evasion. Only in his madness can Lear begin to confront the reality of death. This paradox, as has been so often pointed out, is integral with the play's many inversions of wisdom and folly, seeing and blindness, legitimacy and bastardy, love and hatred, veneration of parents and parricide, justice and injustice, loyalty and disloyalty, true service and flattery. It is also, in this present context, a poignant reminder of how nearly impossible it is, until we are forced against our wills, to confront life's most unavoidable and final reality. Madness provides for Lear a detachment from his former seemingly rational and conscious self (a detachment previously provided by the Fool) in which something like dreamwork can begin to cope with the enormity of death. In his madness Lear can caricature the image his courtiers have thrown up to him of his own invulnerability:

> They flattered me like a dog and told me I had white hairs in
> my beard ere the black ones were there. To say ay and no to
> everything that I said ay and no to was no good divinity. When
> the rain came to wet me once and the wind to make me chatter,
> when the thunder would not peace at my bidding, there I found
> 'em, there I smelt 'em out. Go to, they are not men o their words.
> They told me I was everything. 'Tis a lie; I am not ague-proof.
> (4.6.96–105)

Lear here distances himself from his own earlier claims of invulnerability, of being a god, the King of Life; if he seeks to blame others for leading him into the delusion he has suffered, he at least "sees" it (in his madness) as a delusion.

Lear also ravingly imagines a world of utopian social justice, one in which royal pomp will "Take physic" and exposes itself "to feel what wretches feel," shaking "the superflux" to those wretches in order to "show the heavens more just" (3.4.33–6). This hope, so commendable in any hopeful vision of the world, is plainly delusory in this play about death. Not only Lear but every other well-disposed character who begins to dream of a better world finds that hope crushed. Gloucester's longing for a radical redistribution of wealth in which "distribution should undo excess / And each man have enough" (4.1.69–70), so akin to Lear's mad utopian dream, is spoken as a prelude to his intended suicide and as a form of expiation for his wronging of his loyal son. Edgar, meditating in the depths of his ruined fortune on the truism that things cannot get worse, that "The lamentable change is from the best" whereas "The worst returns to laughter" (4.1.5–6), is immediately assaulted with the spectacle of his blinded father. "O gods! Who is 't can say, 'I am at the worst'? / I am worse than e'er I was." Such a realization leads Edgar immediately to the conclusion that we must not hope for anything. "And worse I may be yet. The worst is not / So long as we can say, 'This is the worst'" (ll. 25–8). So long as we are able to draw breath, the one thing we can count on is that things can in fact get worse; the law of averages, the old cliches about a long road that knows no turning, need not apply in individual cases. Life and old age are unbearable, Edgar knows, without a philosophical awareness of how we must learn to despise the world and its ways. "World, world, O world! / But that thy strange mutations make us hate thee, / Life would not yield to age" (ll. 10–12).

The unstated juxtapositions of *King Lear*'s double plotting make clear for us that what Edgar here "applies" to his father's unhappy story is also relevant to Lear's confrontation with death. Even to the very end of the play, the longing to hope for amelioration in human society leads only to self-deception and a cruel undercutting of that hope. Albany's assurance that "All friends shall taste / The wages of their virtue, and all foes / The cup of their deservings" (5.3.307–9) is at once invalidated by the image of Lear, fleetingly aware that Cordelia is dead and never to return, while the hopeless pronouncement of "Never, never, never, never, never" (l. 314) is a sentence on his life as well. We are not sure that Lear has ever learned what it was he had to learn, or that he is at all reconciled to death, but the pathway to that kind of wisdom is at least clear in outline. Gloucester is close to it when he prays, "You ever-gentle gods, take my breath from me; / Let not my worser spirit tempt me again / To die before your please!" (4.6.219–20). In the words of the Duke in *Measure for Measure*, speaking as a friar: "Do not satisfy your resolution with hopes that are fallible." "Be absolute for death" (3.1.5, 170–1).

Lear does fitfully grasp at the wisdom of acceptance in the last scenes of the play. So does Gloucester, in his resolution to "bear / Affliction till it do cry out itself / 'Enough, enough,' and die" (4.6.75–7). Edgar's word of wisdom to his father, often quoted, is that "Men must endure / Their going hence, even as their coming hither; / Ripeness is all" (5.2.9–11). The play's concluding action is replete with commonplaces on the art of holy dying, as it was practiced in the early seventeenth century by the contemplation of a skull (as in *Hamlet*) or, in John Donne's case, by lying in one's shroud. The difficulty for Lear himself is that he is brought back to sanity not by his perception of the corruption of human nature—"There's hell, there's darkness, there is the sulfurous pit, burning, scalding, stench, consumption. Fie, fie, fie!" (4.6.128–9)—but by the charitable ministrations of a daughter who loves him after all and can begin to inculcate in him some sense of being forgivable. Lear is revived by an image of grace, in other words, and indeed Cordelia looks to Lear like "a soul in bliss" (4.7.47). When Lear is reunited with his loving daughter and then captured in the shifting fortunes of battle, his worldly failure seems unimportant to him; no longer king, no longer even free, doubtless under sentence of death, he rejoices in being what he now is at last, a true father, and he conjures up for us the nearest we ever come in this play to a vision of a blissful afterlife.

> Come, let's away to prison.
> We two alone will sing like birds i' the cage.
> When thou dost ask me blessing, I'll kneel down
> And ask of thee forgiveness. So we'll live,
> And pray, and sing, and tell old tales, and laugh
> At gilded butterflies, and hear poor rogues
> Talk of court news; and we'll talk with them too—
> Who loses and who wins; who's in, who's out—
> And take upon 's the mystery of things,
> As if we were God's spies; and we'll wear out,
> In a walled prison, packs and sects of great ones,
> That ebb and flow by the moon. (5.3.8–19)

Lear is, for the only time in the play, truly happy, enjoying a happiness that grows out of the renunciation of so much of what he previously cared about. This is, moreover, the kind of happiness vouchsafed to Lear's counterparts in the late romances, to Pericles, Cymbeline, Leontes, and Prospero. Lear will live content to have only a daughter's love and his own precious identity as father. I agree up to a point with Helen Luke, who, in a moving book entitled *Old Age*, argues that this key speech in *King Lear* beautifully expresses an idea of acceptance in old age. The prison Lear speaks of is not a literal one so much as an image of the fading power of the human body; Lear's response to the approaching end of life is, as it should be for all of us, to pray, to sing, to tell tales, to laugh, to listen, to be God's spies, to be above the battle of life. There is, however, a powerful sense in which Helen Luke is quite wrong to speak of this passage as one in which, through an old man of eighty, Shakespeare has "condensed all the essential wisdom into which we may hope to grow in our closing years."[6] *King Lear* is a play in which *all* hopes are fallible, not just hopes for power, wealth, and justice. Lear cannot have the one thing that now makes life more than bearable. He cannot have Cordelia. His clinging to her is not the achievement of wisdom Helen Luke would like to have us believe in, but one last unbearably painful delusion of hoping after something that too will fail.

When Lear confronts and fails to cope with this last shattering manifestation of the bleakness of old age, we see the entire process of dying compressed into the last minutes of this play and of his life. Lear recapitulates for us the stages of dying that have been represented earlier, as he now responds to the death of Cordelia with denial, rage, evasion, acknowledgment, despair. The images come so swiftly and so confusedly that we cannot be sure if he is finally overwhelmed by the need to deceive himself or not: "Look on her, look, her lips. / Look there, look there!" (5.3.316–7). Lear has no time to work his way through the sequence of stages, despite his previous anticipations of what it is like to prepare for the end. Nothing can prepare him adequately, and he dies in the very heartbreaking moment of attempting to cope with the death of the one person who has kept him alive until now.

The counseling of the Duke in *Measure for Measure*, not to satisfy our resolution with hopes that are fallible, is sufficiently consistent with orthodox Christianity that we must ask whether Lear's loss of Cordelia and his own death can be reconciled with a vision of reward in the afterlife. On a psychological level, one might be tempted to say, cruel as it sounds, that Lear's clinging to Cordelia is incestuous—not in any carnal sense but still betraying the massive reluctance of a father to give up his daughter, as in so many of Shakespeare's late plays; hence the promise of a reunion with Cordelia is a kind of wish fulfillment, perhaps even a regressive one psychologically, that can serve the artistic purposes of romance but that is unsuited to this uncompromisingly stark tragedy. Lear's original error, perhaps, was to covet Cordelia for his own, to assume his right to be ushered out of this world in the loving arms of the daughter he has engendered; such a possessiveness may be an error of covetousness and hubris for which Lear must be humbled. In orthodox terms, perhaps the heavens are only being consistent in their insistence that human happiness must not rely on those things we all covet—no, not even a daughter's love.

Such an orthodox reading fails, however, because the gods do not seem to be there to offer such a promise, or even to tender an explanation. Images of bliss and reward in the final scenes hover about Cordelia while she is alive,

and she is carried onstage by her father in a poignant recollection of the ico-
nography of the pieta, but in death Cordelia reminds onlookers only of the
apocalypse. "Is this the promised end?" asks Kent, meaning the end of the
world itself. "Or image of that horror?" adds Edgar, refusing to see more than
a representation of something too horrible to behold in its actuality. All death
can do for Lear is to spare him from the "wheel of fire" and the "rack of this
tough world" on which he has been stretched out (4.7.48, 5.3.320). We cannot be sure, despite all Lear has been forced to learn in the course of the play,
that he is in the least prepared to die or disabused of illusory self-deceiving.
Every premise of divine intention or of future reward collapses into the self-
evident emptiness of Albany's wishful hope that "All friends shall taste / The
wages of their virtue, and all foes / The cup of their deservings" (ll. 308–10).

Earlier, in Act 4, scene 6, mad Lear has seemed to the blind Gloucester
the perfect emblem of the apocalypse: "O ruined piece of nature! This great
world / Shall so wear out to naught" (4.6.134–5). By equating Lear's death,
and Cordelia's, with the end of the world itself, beyond which it is impossible
to entertain a vision of any kind of afterlife, *King Lear* forces us to consider
what reason there is to continue living at all, as Edgar urges his father to do
rather than commit suicide. Some answers are in fact discoverable. If we must
learn to covet nothing, absolutely nothing, for ourselves, and must above all
disabuse ourselves of the notion that life owes us anything by right, we can
at least serve and assist those we admire with uncorrupted honesty and love.
We can choose, in other words, to be as like Cordelia, Kent, and Edgar as we
are able, and as unlike Goneril, Regan, and Edmund as our strength permits,
not because the gods will punish or reward us accordingly and comfort us
with an afterlife in which our brief sojourn on earth will seem only a vale of
sorrows and a time of trial—they will not do that, not by any evidence that
King Lear brings to bear on the question. We must try to choose to live well
because that choice at least is ours and because we will define who we are by
the choices we make.[7]

Notes

1. See, for example, Howard Felperin, "'Tongue-tied Our Queen?': The
Deconstruction of Presence in *The Winter's Tale*," *Shakespeare and the Question
of Theory*, ed. Patricia Parker and Geoffrey Hartman (London and New York:
Methuen, 1985).

2. Maynard Mack, *"King Lear" in Our Time* (Berkeley: University of California
Press, 1965).

3. Elisabeth Kübler-Ross, *On Death and Dying* (London: Macmillan, 1969)
and several more recent books.

4. E. Mansell Pattison, *The Experience of Dying* (Englewood Cliffs, N.J.: Pren-
tice Hall, 1977), pp. 43–60.

5. Edmund Creeth, *Mankynde in Shakespeare* (Athens, Ga.: University of Georgia Press, 1976), pp. 111–51, presses this idea too far and with distressing imprecision in his idea that *King Lear* is some kind of avatar or reincarnation of *The Pride of Life*; for Creeth, the later play embodies the earlier one with a definable connection and indebtedness. I believe it may be useful to think briefly of these two plays side by side, but without positing any more of a connection than to suppose that Shakespeare absorbed, at a remove, something of the morality play's interest in representative and generic characters who must face the various stages of human existence and death.

6. Helen M. Luke, *Old Age* (New York: Parabola, 1987), pp. 25–33, esp. p. 32.

7. This essay owes a general debt to Susan Snyder, "*King Lear* and the Psychology of Dying," *Shakespeare Quarterly*, 33 (1982): 449–60, and to Arthur Kirsch, "The Emotional Landscape of *King Lear*," *Shakespeare Quarterly*, 39 (1988): 154–70.

PAUL A. CANTOR

King Lear: *The Tragic Disjunction of Wisdom and Power*

What is the price of Experience do men buy it for a song
Or wisdom for a dance in the street? No it is bought with the price
Of all that a man hath his house his wife his children.
                                   —William Blake, *The Four Zoas*

I

Many critics regard *King Lear* as the greatest of Shakespeare's plays and also as his most tragic. Indeed, many would claim that it is the most tragic play ever written. And yet, curiously, in most critical accounts of the play it is difficult to see why we should even regard it as tragic at all, whether we are using an Aristotelian or a Hegelian definition of tragedy. In the view of most critics, Lear is basically a pathetic old man, vain and foolish, rash in his judgment and incapable of controlling his emotions—and he is all these things from the very beginning of the play.[1] This characterization seems to preclude viewing Lear on the Aristotelian model of a tragic hero, as someone raised above the ordinary level of humanity, except in the most conventional sense of his social status. Moreover, in the view of the majority of critics, the play charts the growth of Lear's wisdom, as he learns the emptiness of worldly glory and comes to embrace the love of his daughter Cordelia as the one true value in his life.[2] As consoling as this vision of Lear's education through suffering may be, it leaves us with a sense that the

From *Shakespeare's Political Pageant: Essays in Literature and Politics,* edited by Joseph Alulis and Vickie Sullivan, pp. 189–207. Copyright © 1996 by Rowman and Littlefield.

dramatic issues of the play can in the end be fully resolved. But if that is the case, then Lear cannot be in a tragic situation as Hegel defines it, that is, he is not caught in the clash of two legitimate principles, a situation from which there is no simple escape, no matter how much he learns. In concrete terms, critics generally do not view Lear as caught between genuinely conflicting loyalties, his political and his personal obligations; on the contrary, in their reading of the play, Lear would simply be right to abdicate the throne and retire into private life.

In short, in the view of most critics, at the beginning of the play Lear is simply mistaken in both his attitudes and his actions, and the course of the drama should in effect teach him the error of his ways.[3] This reading of *King Lear* makes it an edifying play, but it drains it of its tragic power by oversimplifying Shakespeare's understanding of the complexities of political life. Ultimately, this kind of reading threatens to reduce *King Lear* to a form of melodrama, a story of the straightforward conflict of clearly identifiable and separable forces of good and evil, in which the outcome is tragic only in the sense of being disastrous for the main characters. Above all, many critics end up undermining the stature of King Lear as a tragic figure by suggesting that with a little more wisdom he could have avoided the catastrophes in his life. Critics may go on speaking of the grandeur of Shakespeare's achievement and of Lear as a character, but if the standard readings of the play were correct, a more honest reaction would resemble that of Groucho Marx, when, in a meeting almost as improbable as Lear's encounter with Tom o' Bedlam, he was attempting to explain the play to T. S. Eliot:

> I said the king was an incredibly foolish old man, which God knows he *was*; and that if he'd been *my* father I would have run away from home at the age of eight—instead of waiting until I was ten.... I pointed out that King Lear's opening speech was the height of idiocy. Imagine (I said) a father asking his three children: Which of you kids loves me the most?[4]

I am sure that most critics would, as Eliot evidently did, reject this characterization of *King Lear*, but the question remains: is there anything in their readings of the play that would allow them to counter this view of its hero? As convinced as critics are of the greatness of *King Lear* as a work of art, they evidently have a hard time giving an account of the play that explains that greatness. In the delightfully insouciant way in which Groucho projects himself into the world of *King Lear*, he unwittingly reveals the problem with many interpretations of the play. In our eagerness to identify with Shakespeare's characters, we run the risk of bringing them down to our own level.

The Lear described in many critical essays sounds less like Shakespeare's monarch than the middle-class recreations of Lear in the nineteenth-century fiction of writers like Balzac and Turgenev.[5]

From this perspective, the turning point in the criticism of *King Lear* was Harry Jaffa's brilliant analysis of the opening scene of the play, in which he shows that Lear has a sophisticated scheme in mind for dividing up his kingdom, one in which he hopes to secure the bulk of his land for Cordelia, together with an alliance with the House of Burgundy.[6] As Jaffa shows, Lear's plan, far from being the product of senility, is, if anything, too clever for his own good. I will not go over the details of Jaffa's subtle analysis; suffice it to say here that he points the way to understanding Lear as a tragic figure. The king is not behaving like a doddering old fool in the opening scene, but attempting a remarkable political feat: to pass on his royal inheritance in a way that will avoid the defects of following the conventional rules of primogeniture. Lear fails in his plan, but in Jaffa's view, he fails nobly and hence tragically. Jaffa's reading is true to the text of the play and also to the impression Lear in fact makes on stage in the opening scene. Far from coming across as a pathetic old man, Lear projects a commanding presence in his first appearance, dominating the action and, for all his errors, towering over the other figures on the stage.

In another essay on *King Lear*, I have tried to extend Jaffa's analysis, analyzing the process of education the king undergoes when he loses power.[7] Like Jaffa, I try to show that Lear's errors are not, so to speak, *vulgar* errors; they do not simply proceed from stupidity or lack of thought. I argue that, in tragic fashion, Lear's failings are bound up inextricably with his greatness. Precisely what makes him powerful as a king incapacitates him for seeing the truth about himself and his kingdom. In part this outcome results from his being surrounded by hypocrites and flatterers, who reinforce his self-image and his confidence in the justice of his rule. But as Shakespeare presents it, the problem runs deeper. Lear's errors are a kind of occupational hazard of his kingship. In order to exercise command, he must project an aura of authority, and this need in turn dictates that he have a high opinion of himself, thus fatally tempting him to overestimate his capabilities in such tasks as disposing of his kingdom.

The powerfully tragic vision of *King Lear* is rooted in Shakespeare's understanding of political life, its limitations and its demands. The play turns on what I will call the disjunction of wisdom and power. When Lear is in command as king, he is tragically cut off from the wisdom he needs to rule justly. He gains access to this wisdom only when he loses power, but that process in turn incapacitates him for further rule. In this essay, I will examine largely the second half of *King Lear*, and trace what happens to Lear when he learns the truths to which his position as king initially blinded him. Acts

4 and 5 are crucial to a full understanding of Lear as a tragic figure, but most critics fail to follow the subtle turns Shakespeare portrays in the king's attitudes, because they do not think through the implications of Lear's radically changed view of the world. In many accounts of the play, Lear's education is presented as an unequivocal good, as if there were nothing problematic about his experience. These accounts in effect present private life as simply superior to public life, suggesting that Lear has everything to gain and nothing to lose when he is thrust out of power. Without questioning Lear's legitimate gains in wisdom in the course of the play—indeed I have discussed them at length elsewhere—I want to explore here the possibility that *King Lear* is tragic precisely because of the complexity of the process Shakespeare is portraying in the king's development. Lear's gains in wisdom come at the expense of his initial grandeur and hence his ability to rule. In the unsettling logic of the world of *Lear*, the characters pay a terrible price for the wisdom they gain, and none more so than Lear himself.

II

Lear's process of education reaches its crisis in act 3, especially with his encounter with Edgar disguised as Tom o' Bedlam, and the insights he gains and even articulates as a result are indeed remarkable. It is tempting but far too simplistic to treat Lear's shattering experience in act 3 as a kind of civics lesson or a seminar at a school of public administration. However much Lear grows in wisdom in act 3, he could not simply translate that wisdom back into a form of rule. For one thing, the wisdom Lear gains in act 3 has a questionable character. In trying to articulate what Lear learns, it is easy to distort the nature of his experience, presenting in an organized and coherent form insights that in fact come to Lear in fits and starts. Lear gains many insights in act 3, but we cannot grasp what he is going through if we do not see how deeply unsettling and disorienting these truths are for him, shattering his self-image and his whole view of humanity. However disturbing it may be to admit, the Lear of act 3 is in no condition to walk back into the court and resume command of his kingdom. What is precisely characteristic of Lear in act 3 is that he cannot hold together the two images of human nature he observes in Edgar as first Tom o' Bedlam and then as the "noble philosopher" (3.4.172), and that is the deepest reason why his experience on the heath at least momentarily unfits him for rule. Lear is agonizingly wrenched back and forth between images of the lowest degradation of the human body and images of the highest development of the human soul. Obsessed with his insights into the extremes of humanity, Lear understandably loses sight of the middle range, but that is precisely the realm where politics ordinarily takes place.[8]

Shakespeare repeats this pattern in Lear's appearances in act 4. The juxtaposition of scenes 6 and 7 shows Lear recapitulating his encounter with the lower and higher sides of human nature, and once again he is unable to integrate his widely diverging images of humanity. Encountering the blind Gloucester in act 4, scene 6, Lear dwells obsessively on the animal side of man and above all woman:

> Behold yond simp'ring dame,
> Whose face between her forks presages snow;
> That minces virtue, and does shake the head
> To hear of pleasure's name—
> The fitchew nor the soiled horse goes to't
> With a more riotous appetite.
> Down from the waist they are Centaurs,
> Though women all above;
> But to the girdle do the gods inherit,
> Beneath is all the fiends'. (4.6.118–27)[9]

This vision is the equivalent of Lear's earlier view of the "bare, fork'd animal" in Tom o' Bedlam (3.4.107–8), as he effaces the distinction between human being and beast. Because Lear is convinced that all human beings are consumed by sexual appetites, he refuses to see anyone punished anymore for violating the conventional rules of sexual conduct:

> I pardon that man's life. What was thy cause?
> Adultery?
> Thou shalt not die. Die for adultery? No,
> The wren goes to't, and the small gilded fly
> Does lecher in my sight. (4.6.109–13)

In Lear's refusal to support conventional marriage contracts, we see what the political consequences would be of the new doctrine of natural justice he learns during the storm on the heath. As ruler he would no longer have any legitimate basis for punishing any of his subjects or enforcing any law. Once Lear views all human beings as alike in their animal urges, for him the difference between legally constituted authorities and criminals dissolves: "see how yond justice rails upon yond simple thief. Hark in thine ear: change places, and handy-dandy, which is the justice, which is the thief?" (4.6.151–54). Though Lear once embodied the majesty of the law in his own person, he loses faith in all authority once he concludes that conventional appearances hide an inner corruption:

Thorough tatter'd clothes small vices do appear;
Robes and furr'd gowns hide all. Plate sin with gold,
And the strong lance of justice hurtless breaks;
Arm it in rags, a pigmy's straw does pierce it.
None does offend, none, I say none. (4.6.164–68)

Speeches such as this continue Lear's impulse in act 3 to reject a conventional view of political reality in the name of what is natural to human beings. In particular he displays the same hostility to clothing because it hides the truth about humanity.[10]

Lear's speeches in act 4, scene 6 are very powerful and express some fundamental truths about politics; Edgar is moved to comment on the king's words: "O, matter and impertinency mix'd, / Reason in madness" (4.6.174–75).[11] But before we are tempted simply to equate Lear's viewpoint here with Shakespeare's, we need to look more critically at what the king says. Shakespeare deliberately builds an error into Lear's reflections in this scene: "Let copulation thrive; for Gloucester's bastard son / Was kinder to his father than my daughters / Got 'tween the lawful sheets" (4.6.114–16). These lines should give us pause; Lear's preference for the natural over the conventional child is clearly as mistaken as his earlier tendency to accept conventional professions of love over his true daughter's natural feelings. Like Lear's two auditors at this moment, Edgar and Gloucester, we know how misguided the king's praise of Edmund is. Modern interpreters seem disposed to follow Lear in his thoroughgoing disillusionment with politics and human nature in this scene,[12] but Shakespeare took pains to prevent us from wholly identifying with Lear's one-sided view of man as beast. Even Lear momentarily recognizes the diseased character of his imagination in this scene (4.6.130–31).

Indeed, Lear's jaundiced view of women as all "centaurs" is immediately contradicted by Cordelia's appearance in the next scene. Lear's reunion and reconciliation with his true daughter is one of the most beautiful and moving scenes Shakespeare ever wrote. Act 4, scene 7 provides the dreamlike answer to Lear's nightmare vision of humanity in act 4, scene 6. From his obsession with human carnality in act 4, scene 6, Lear moves to a vision of human spirituality. He is barely aware of his own body in this scene ("I will not swear these are my hands," [4.7.54]) and in his eyes Cordelia has transcended the physical level: "You are a spirit, I know" (4.7.48). By trying to kneel to Cordelia, Lear is finally willing to reverse their relative positions of power. In act 1, scene 1, Cordelia could not express her true love for her father because his power over her stood in the way, threatening to obliterate the distinction between a sincere profession of devotion and the hypocritical and self-serving flattery of her two sisters. Now that Lear has lost his power and admits to being nothing but "a very foolish fond old man" (4.7.59), Cordelia can no longer be accused of any base motives in her love for her father. In rallying to his cause, she, like Kent and the Fool, has nothing to gain and everything to lose. Free of the conventional political roles that complicated and distorted their relationship earlier, Lear and Cordelia are finally able to be simply father and daughter.

Indeed in view of the reversal of their customary positions in this scene—the fact that Lear is willing to kneel to Cordelia—it is arguable that they are liberated even from the conventional roles of parent and child, and face each other as human being to human being in a condition of equality.[13] Lear and Cordelia move beyond any kind of conventional moral accounting, as she rejects his seemingly justified assumption of guilt for their breach:

> *Lear:* I know you do not love me, for your sisters
> Have (as I do remember) done me wrong:
> You have some cause, they have not.
> *Cordelia:* No cause, no cause. (4.7.72–74)

In act 4, scene 6, Lear rejected conventional morality out of contempt for human nature and on the basis of the lowest possible view of human beings as indistinguishable from beasts. In act 4, scene 7, Lear and Cordelia rise above conventional moral considerations just as they appear to rise above the level of their bodies.

Shakespeare's juxtaposition of act 4, scene 6 and act 4, scene 7 conveys a deeper wisdom than Lear is able to encompass in either scene alone: the two scenes embody alternative and complementary visions of what is natural to humanity. It is a sad commentary on our times that we are all too eager to acknowledge that Lear is talking about what is natural to the human condition in act 4, scene 6. But on reflection, we can appreciate that in some sense of the term the behavior of Lear and Cordelia in act 4, scene 7 is also a paradigm of nature, now thought of in terms of human perfection, rather than some kind of lowest common denominator of humanity. The simplicity of their dialogue in this scene, the fact that they speak in brief, declarative sentences, above all, the fact that they are finally speaking *to* each other, no longer *at* each other, lends what can be called a natural quality to their interaction here. Neither act 4, scene 6 nor act 4, scene 7 tells the whole truth about the human condition, and to accept one at the expense of the other is to risk falling prey to an overly cynical or an overly idealistic understanding of human nature. Shakespeare was guilty of neither.

However contradictory the images of humanity presented in act 4, scene 6 and act 4, scene 7 may be, the two scenes have one thing in common: in both Lear effectively rejects political life. In act 4, scene 6 his cynical view of humanity undermines all claims to legitimate authority by political figures. In act 4, scene 7 his idealistic view of the human condition leaves all ordinary political considerations far below. The juxtaposition of these two scenes thus points to an important truth about politics. In act 4, scene 6 Lear talks about human beings as if they were all body and no spirit; the result of this view of human nature as purely animal is to eliminate every possible justification for political action. In act 4, scene 7 Lear talks about himself and Cordelia as if they were all spirit and no body; the result of this contrary view of human nature as purely spiritual is to eliminate every need for political action; Lear and Cordelia pass beyond the world of good and evil. The conjunction of these two scenes suggests that either of these views is one-sided and hence incomplete. As the bifurcation of vision throughout acts 3 and 4 of *King Lear* suggests, man is a composite being, a perplexing mixture of body and spirit. It is precisely for this reason that human beings require political life: to deal with the problems created by the tension between body and spirit. Neither animals nor angels require politics.

We can now see more fully why Lear's gains in wisdom in acts 4 and 5 come at the expense of his ability to rule. At the beginning of the play Lear is the captive of many illusions about himself and his world, but his very overestimation of his own powers is what gives him the aura of authority he needs to command his subjects. The Lear of act 4, scene 6 has learned a great deal about his own limitations, but the result is that he has developed a universal contempt for political authority. He has lost all faith in the ability of political action to improve the human condition, or even to control its worst excesses of passion. The Lear of act 4, scene 7 is simply indifferent to politics; having achieved a spiritual communion with Cordelia in an intensely private moment, he no longer has any interest in public life. Failing to integrate his antithetical visions of humanity in act 4, scene 6 and act 4, scene 7, Lear is unable to grasp the fundamental truth that the political authority he despises and rejects in act 4, scene 6 would be necessary to protect the fragile spirituality he comes to cherish in act 4, scene 7.

III

Lear's loss of his ability to rule is not simply to be traced to the change in his opinions about politics in acts 3 and 4. Shakespeare also focuses on the matter of Lear's temperament. The Lear of act 1, scene 1 is headstrong and rash; those are not the virtues of a philosopher, but they are the qualities of the kind of man who often succeeds in getting other men to obey his will. When we say that Lear has a kingly temperament, we mean in part that he is a spirited man, capable of what he himself calls "noble anger" (2.4.276). His capacity for indignation is one of the forces that attaches him to political life and fuels his ability to get things done. Lear's tendency to identify his personal cause with justice pure and simple is unphilosophic and leads to many of his errors in judgment. Nevertheless, his pride and titanic overestimation of himself are also what makes an admirable man like Kent say that he can see authority written on Lear's face (1.4.26–30).

Thus the more Lear comes to think of himself as an ordinary man, sharing the weaknesses of his fellows, the less capable he becomes of inspiring their awe and hence their obedience. To be sure, Kent, the Fool, and Cordelia come to love Lear more in his defeat and humiliation, but that is precisely a private reaction on their parts and not the same as political loyalty. The Lear we see in the second half of the play has become temperamentally unfit to rule England. We must realize that Lear's learning in the play is not a purely intellectual process; it is not a matter of Lear picking up a textbook in political science and calmly reading about what went wrong with his administration. Lear's education in self-knowledge is a soul-wrenching experience. It rips asunder the deepest fibers of his being. For Lear's titanic ego to be shaken, he must be painfully humiliated, and that is the terrifying process we witness in acts 1 and 2, as his wolfish daughters strip away every shred of dignity he has left. With all his pride, Lear resists this process:

> You see me here, you gods, a poor old man,
> As full of grief as age, wretched in both.
> If it be you that stirs these daughters' hearts
> Against their father, fool me not so much
> To bear it tamely; touch me with noble anger,
> And let not women's weapons, water-drops,
> Stain my man's cheeks! (2.4.272–78)

Lear realizes that nothing less than his manhood is at stake in this scene, and he futilely wishes that he had the power to act like a manly king and take vengeance on all those who have slighted his dignity. When Lear is confronted by the cruelty of his daughters, he is torn between the contradictory emotions of anger and grief. His anger is rooted in his pride as a king, and makes him ashamed of the grief he feels as an ordinary human being. As Lear himself recognizes, the tension he experiences between wanting to express his grief as a wronged father and the need he feels as a king to suppress any such public display of weakness eventually causes his mind to snap: "O Fool, I shall go mad" (2.4.286).

As much as we are moved by seeing what Lear gains in the process of his education, we should not blind ourselves to what he loses. The Lear of act

4, scene 7 is a broken man, his pride in himself and in his regime shattered. He is a wiser man in this scene, more capable of love, and in many important respects this Lear is preferable to the one we saw in the opening scene of the play. But not in all respects. Unlike the Lear we saw in act 1, scene 1, the Lear of act 4, scene 7 could not walk into any room and just by his regal bearing command the instant respect of any human being in range of his voice. A king who expects to be obeyed cannot go around proclaiming: "I am old and foolish" (4.7.84). We may admire Lear for this frank admission of his weakness, but we must also recognize its consequences for his ability to rule in the future as anything other than a figurehead. The Lear of act 4, scene 7 is completely without anger; as the Doctor says: "the great rage, / You see, is kill'd in him" (4.7.77–78). It may be a relief for us as audience to see this calm descend upon Lear, but we must recognize that with his rage, something else is for the moment killed in Lear: his pride. And, bound up as it is with his spiritedness, Lear's pride was the source of his greatness as well as of his failures as a king. Up to this point in the play, even in his madness, Lear has displayed an acute awareness of everything going on around him. If anything, he has been too ready to see affronts to his dignity in his subjects' actions, but that hypersensitivity has been profoundly linked to Lear's concern for justice. In act 4, scene 7, he ceases to be aware of his surroundings; he even has to be reminded that he is in Britain (4.7.75). With Lear's "great rage" goes his "noble anger," and with that, his ability and even his desire to govern his kingdom.

In short, we must realize that Lear cannot absorb the kind of unnerving truths he learns about himself and remain the same man. The Lear we see in act 4, scene 7 is profoundly changed from what he was in act 1, scene 1. His newfound wisdom and self-awareness are purchased at the price of his original grandeur.[14] We may ultimately judge the result worth the exchange, but we should not deny that Shakespeare is confronting us with a kind of choice. Shakespeare's tragic world is profoundly disturbing to us. We do not like to think about the tragic disjunctions he presents. We would like to think that it is possible to be a powerful ruler and a wise man at the same time. Perhaps it is possible, and in the case of Henry V Shakespeare offers an example of a man who seems to unite wisdom and power (Prospero is another such case).[15] But even if it is possible, the conjunction of wisdom and power is surely not easy to achieve, and in King Lear Shakespeare most fully explores the problems of bringing the two together. When Lear is in power, he is blind to his own limitations, not just out of stupidity, senility, or simple error, but because, as Shakespeare shows, there is something in the very nature of kingship that blinds even and perhaps especially a successful ruler to fundamental truths about his situation. When Lear finally gains access to those truths, it is only through a process that disillusions him about politics in general and shatters the very spirit that made him a commanding figure. That is why *King Lear* is such a tragic play, perhaps the most profound of all tragedies. It offers no easy way out of Lear's dilemma. Shakespeare uncovers a deep and abiding tension between the preconditions of power and the preconditions of wisdom.

IV

The Lear we see in act 5 has recovered his sanity, but he is still a far cry from the regal figure we first saw in act 1. He has become totally absorbed in his private bond with Cordelia:

> Come, let's away to prison:
> We two alone will sing like birds i' th' cage;
> When thou dost ask me blessing, I'll kneel down
> And ask of thee forgiveness. So we'll live,
> And pray, and sing, and tell old tales, and laugh
> At gilded butterflies, and hear poor rogues
> Talk of court news; and we'll talk with them too—
> Who loses and who wins; who's in, who's out—
> And take upon's the mystery of things
> As if we were God's spies; and we'll wear out
> In a wall'd prison, packs and sects of great ones,
> That ebb and flow by th' moon. (5.3.8–19)

This is a beautiful speech, and we want to rejoice in Lear's newfound happiness with his daughter. But Lear here betrays his complete indifference to conventional politics; what once was his greatest concern has been reduced to the level of gossip, a mere matter of "who loses and who wins; who's in, who's out." Lear now looks down upon politics as a realm of merely transitory triumphs. He seems to have achieved a kind of philosophic detachment from life, which allows him to see human affairs as if from a contemplative height. But Lear's indifference to politics extends even to an indifference to his own freedom, and hence he seems happy to endure what formerly would have struck him as the ultimate humiliation: to be imprisoned by his enemies. Lear is now content to live like a bird in a cage; as attractive as this image may seem, there is something demeaning about it as well: the majestic lion of a king has been reduced to a tame house pet.[16] As if to remind us that Lear may be indifferent to politics but cannot escape its power, Shakespeare punctuates the king's lyrical fantasy with Edmund's curt and peremptory order: "Take them away" (5.3.19). We may applaud Lear's rising above his earlier conventional devotion to political life, but the fact is that his indifference to power in this scene is about to lead directly to the death of Cordelia.

If basically decent men like Lear renounce political life, however justified they may be in their contempt for corruption in high places, no one will be left to defend the Cordelias of this world. Thus if Lear comes to understand the supreme worth of Cordelia, he cannot simply abandon political life to men like Edmund, who will ruthlessly stamp out all that Lear legitimately has come to value in the realms that transcend politics.

It is thus characteristic of the complexity of the movement of *King Lear* that Shakespeare has Lear at least partially rediscover the value of political life just before his death. Lear does not go to the grave still believing that there is no difference between a human being and an animal; on the contrary, he powerfully asserts the superiority of Cordelia to other forms of life: "Why should a dog, a horse, a rat, have life, / And thou no breath at all?" (5.3.307–8).[17] Recapturing his sense of human excellence, the man who in act 4 could see no reason to punish any malefactor, returns in act 5 to his role as judge and executes the subordinate sent by Edmund to eliminate Cordelia: "I kill'd the slave that was a-hanging thee" (5.3.275). With his unique grasp of psychology, Shakespeare chooses just this moment for Lear to recapture a bit of his old pride and anger, and at the same time to recall his youth, as he responds to the confirmation of his surprisingly valiant deed: "I have seen the day, with my good biting falchion / I would have made them skip" (5.3.277–78).

This is a fascinating moment, as we finally get the briefest glimpse of the young King Lear. Nearing the end of his life, Lear thinks back presumably to the earliest days of his political career, remembering what he forgot in his plan for dividing the kingdom, that the ability to do justice must ultimately be backed up by the sword. Lear's execution of the man who killed Cordelia tells us as much about the nature of justice as his speeches about the hollowness of authority back in act 4, scene 6. It is not that his final act cancels out the truths he articulated earlier; it is only that his deeds bring out the partiality of his speeches. To get at Shakespeare's understanding of justice, we cannot identify it with any single statement by his characters, but must take into account the pattern of the whole play, both deeds and speeches.

The fact that Lear thinks back to his youth at the conclusion of the play provides a clue to its structure; as Edmund's line "The wheel is come full circle" (5.3.175) suggests, the end of *King Lear* harks back to the beginning. At the start of the play the British regime, like Lear himself, has grown old. At the end of the play, the regime renews itself. Like Lear recalling the powerful sword strokes of his youthful arm, the regime must get back in touch with its foundation in the ultimate guarantor of political right: military force. At the beginning of the play, as a result of Lear's peaceful reign and his unquestioned authority, his regime has lost touch with political reality and he himself thinks that he can maintain control even while turning military power over to his children. Act 5 takes us back to the brute facts of political life and reminds us that in the end the deepest political divisions can be settled if not healed only by war.

This consideration explains why the trial by combat of Edmund and Edgar figures so prominently in act 5. Edgar has an airtight legal case against Edmund and one might imagine that their conflict would be settled in a court of law, where a juridical process could establish Edmund's guilt unequivocally. But Shakespeare shows a more primitive form of justice, trial by combat, because the thrust of act 5 is to keep reminding us that angels may dispense with violence in settling their disputes, but human beings cannot. The point is not that might makes right; we have seen the limitations of that savage principle in the destruction of Cornwall, Regan, Goneril, and now finally Edmund, whose careers in evil all go to prove the self-defeating and self-destroying character of a purely low-minded conception of justice.[18] But what Edgar's resort to the sword shows is that right cannot be entirely divorced from might. It is not that the good cause always triumphs in battle, only that if the good cause is to triumph, it ultimately must be in battle (recall that Lear must resort to force in this scene as well).

Edgar has had to learn how to turn some of the weapons of evil men and women against them in order to protect what he values in life.[19] Starting the play as a naive young man, untutored in the deceptive ways of the world, Edgar has had to don one disguise after another in the course of the play to come to terms with the evil in the world. Though he remains almost comically scrupulous in dealing with his enemies,[20] the Edgar at the end of the play can at least no longer be called naive. When Edgar kills Edmund in combat he establishes his right to rule in the realm, and seems to have absorbed whatever was best in his enemy, much as Prince Hal does when he defeats Hotspur.

The fact that Edgar can stake out a claim to rule only with a sword reminds us of the violence at the basis of politics, and we have more confidence in the capacity of this temperamentally mild man to maintain political order once we have seen that he can answer the savagery of evil antagonists with some brute force of his own. But it would be a mistake to fall into a totally cynical reading of the end of *King Lear*, arguing that the good party has had to become as savage as the evil in order to overcome it. The Edgar at the end of the play is not the same Edgar we saw at the beginning, but he has not become an Edmund. In general, in the end the good characters maintain their distinction from the evil, in part because they have been spared the necessity of descending to the barbaric level of their antagonists by the fact that the evil characters have largely destroyed each other. Edgar and Albany never display the lust for power that is the hallmark of their counterparts Edmund and Cornwall. At most they have learned the need for political action to counter the machinations of their enemies, but that means that they resort to morally dubious actions with a marked reluctance. Unlike Edmund, Edgar never takes pleasure in deceiving others, and he never glories in evil deeds. Hence the end of the play forms a sharp contrast to the beginning:

> *Albany*: Friends of my soul, you twain
> Rule in this realm, and the gor'd state sustain.
>   *Kent*: I have a journey, sir, shortly to go:
> My master calls me, I must not say no.
>   *Edgar*: The weight of this sad time we must obey,
> Speak what we feel, not what we ought to say:
> The oldest hath bourne most; we that are young
> Shall never see so much, nor live so long. (5.3.320–27)

At the beginning of *King Lear* we are in a world where many of the characters, though not all, are hungry for power; at the end we see characters who apparently cannot wait to hand over power to others. The course of the action has evidently been a sobering experience for decent men like Albany, Kent, and Edgar. No one of them is Plato's philosopher-king—Edgar perhaps comes closest—but they have developed some of his reluctance to rule. As Edgar acknowledges in the final lines, even his experience cannot match the journey Lear went through in the course of the play,[21] but the way in which he accepts rule as a duty imposed on him and not something he eagerly sought shows that he has come to share some of Lear's doubts about political life. Because of his consciousness of the limits of power, Edgar will presumably rule more moderately.

After a period of political chaos, we see a regime refounded at the end of *King Lear*. Like all regimes, its foundation may ultimately be traced back to an act of violence, but given the character of its founders, we may reasonably expect that it will not be a violent regime. All signs in fact point to the inevitability of entering a diminished and tamer world. The precondition for refounding the regime has been the elimination of the evil extremes of humanity who threatened all conventional order. But the extremes of good in Britain have been destroyed as well; Lear, Cordelia, and the Fool are dead, and Kent apparently does not have long to live. A political regime tends to compress the range of humanity, trying to force people into conventional molds, to moderate their passions, to move them toward a comfortable center. The world Edgar will rule will be a safer world, but it will be a world without Lear's grandeur or Cordelia's beauty. That is another way of saying that it will no longer be a heroic or a tragic world. The moderation—one might even say the mediocrity—of the characters left standing at the end of the play is the truest measure of the greatness of King Lear and the tragic nature of his story. No ending of a Shakespeare play captures more perfectly the fundamental contrast at work in tragedy between the ordinary human beings who are content to stay within the limits of the conventional world and the heroic souls who try to go beyond them.

Notes

1. In his *Shakespeare Our Contemporary*, trans. Boleslaw Taborski (Garden City, N.Y.: Anchor Books, 1966), 130, Jan Kott makes explicit what many critics assume about Lear: "He does not see or understand anything. . . . Lear is ridiculous, naive and stupid."

2. The classic statement of this view is to be found in A. C. Bradley, *Shakespearean Tragedy* (1904; rept. New York: Meridian Books, 1955), 258–60. See especially Bradley's attempt to state the moral of the play on p. 260: "The good are seen growing better through suffering. . . . The judgment of this world is a lie; its goods, which we covet, corrupt us. . . . Let us renounce the world, hate it, and lose it gladly. The only real thing in it is the soul, with its courage, patience, devotion. And nothing outward can touch that." For a similar view of *King Lear,* see G. Wilson Knight, *The Wheel of Fire* (1930; rept. New York: Meridian Books, 1957), 195–201, and Reuben A. Brower, *Hero and Saint: Shakespeare and the Graeco-Roman Heroic Tradition* (New York: Oxford University Press, 1971), 415. For a more recent statement of this position, see Barbara Everett's essay, "*King Lear*: Loving," in her *Young Hamlet: Essays on Shakespeare's Tragedies* (Oxford: Clarendon Press, 1989), 59–82.

3. See, for example, Knight, who speaks of "the absurdity of the old King's anger" in the first scene, describes him as "cutting a cruelly ridiculous figure" and as "selfish, self-centered," and characterizes him as "a tremendous soul . . . incongruously geared to a puerile intellect" (*Wheel of Fire*, 161–62).

4. Letter to Gummo Marx, June 1964, in Groucho Marx, *The Groucho Letters* (New York: Simon & Schuster, 1967).

5. Knight says that *King Lear* "resembles a Hardy novel" (*Wheel of Fire*, 202). Shades of Groucho, Knight remarks: "It is, indeed, curious that so storm-furious a play as *King Lear* should have so trivial a domestic basis" (161). So curious that one might question whether the basis is really trivial or domestic.

6. Harry V. Jaffa, "The Limits of Politics: *King Lear*, Act 1, Scene 1," in Allan Bloom, *Shakespeare's Politics* (New York: Basic Books, 1964), 113–45. This essay was originally published in *The American Political Science Review* 51 (1957): 405–27. Briefly stated, Jaffa's thesis is that the intent of Lear's original plan was to give Cordelia the bulk of his kingdom (the middle portion), while giving Goneril the extreme northern and Regan the extreme southern portion, regions their husbands already controlled as feudal lords. Lear intends to marry Cordelia to the Duke of Burgundy, a foreign power strong enough to give her support but not strong enough to conquer and absorb Britain (as the King of France might). Jaffa is the only critic of the play to have articulated the strategy of Lear's original plan, but he was not the first to note that Lear enters act 1, scene 1 with a division of the kingdom already worked out (after all, maps have been drawn up and Lear's counselors Gloucester and Kent are evidently already aware of the details when the play opens). See Samuel Taylor Coleridge, *Shakespearean Criticism*, ed., Thomas Middleton Raysor (London:

J. M. Dent, 1960), 49–50, Bradley, *Shakespearean Tragedy*, 202–3, and Kenneth Muir, *Shakespeare: King Lear* (Harmondsworth: Penguin, 1986), 32, 55. For a further elaboration of Jaffa's analysis of Lear's plan, see David Lowenthal, *"King Lear,"* *Interpretation* 21 (1994): 393–96.

7. "Nature and Convention in *King Lear*," to be published in Joseph Knippenberg and Peter Lawler, eds., *Poets, Princes, and Private Citizens: Literary Alternatives to Postmodern Politics* (Lanham, Md.: Rowman & Littlefield, 1996).

8. Compare Apemantus's criticism of Timon of Athens: "The middle of humanity thou never knewest, but the extremity of both ends" (4.3.300–1).

9. All quotations from Shakespeare are taken from G. Blakemore Evans, ed., *The Riverside Shakespeare* (Boston: Houghton Mifflin, 1974).

10. On the significance of clothing in act 3, see Lowenthal, *"King Lear,"* 403.

11. For a similar analysis of Lear's speeches in act 4, scene 6, see Lowenthal, *"King Lear,"* 407–9.

12. See, for example, Knight, who speaks of Lear "penetrating below the surface shows to the heart of human reality" here (*Wheel of Fire*, 192), or Derek Traversi, *An Approach to Shakespeare* (Garden City, N.Y.: Anchor Books, 1969), vol. 2, 164, who sees Lear revealing "the true state of man" in this scene.

13. The idea of breaking with the conventional parent–child relationship and replacing it with something more "natural" is presented earlier in the play in demonic form when Cornwall tells Edmund after he betrays Gloucester: "thou shalt find a dearer father in my love" (3.5.24–25). Here the conventional bond between father and son is replaced by a bond of pure self-interest between villains; in the case of Lear and Cordelia, the conventional bond is replaced by a higher bond of spiritual love.

14. One must be very careful in formulating one's estimation of King Lear. Even as perceptive a critic as Bradley, who has a better feel for what is tragic in *King Lear* than almost anyone else who has written on the play, gets carried away with his own rhetoric: "there is no figure, surely, in the world of poetry at once so grand, so pathetic, and so beautiful as [King Lear]" (*Shakespearean Tragedy*, 228). It is very difficult to be grand and pathetic *at once*. What is precisely characteristic of Shakespeare's portrayal of King Lear is that he shows a grand political man at the beginning of the play, who becomes a figure of great pathos in his reunion with Cordelia. The dramatic movement of *King Lear* is so extraordinary, the contrast between Lear at the beginning and at the end of the play is so great, that we must be wary of making statements that conflate what I might refer to as the public and the private Lears.

15. See my essays "Shakespeare's *The Tempest*: The Wise Man As Hero," *Shakespeare Quarterly* 31 (1980): 64–75 and "Prospero's Republic: The Politics of Shakespeare's *The Tempest*," in John Alvis and Thomas West, eds., *Shakespeare as Political Thinker* (Durham, N.C.: Carolina Academic Press, 1981), 239–55. For a brief but insightful comparison of *King Lear* and *The Tempest*, see Lowenthal, *"King Lear,"* 416.

16. Bradley is aware that a change has occurred in the Lear of act 5; of his utterances toward the end of the play, Bradley writes: "We feel in them the loss of power to sustain his royal dignity" (*Shakespearean Tragedy*, 234). But Bradley blurs the issue by trying to redefine magnanimity in Christian terms: "what remains is 'the thing itself,' the soul in its bare greatness" (234).

17. On this point, see Lowenthal, *"King Lear,"* 413.

18. This outcome fulfills Albany's ominous prediction at 4.2.49–50. For the self-destructive character of evil, see Lowenthal, "*King Lear,*" 409.

19. For a different view of what Edgar learns in the course of the play, see Joseph Alulis, "The Education of the Prince in Shakespeare's *King Lear,*" *Interpretation* 21 (1994): 373–90.

20. Consider, for example, Edgar's hesitation in opening the letter from Goneril to Edmund when it falls into his hands (4.6.259–61).

21. I take "the oldest" in Edgar's speech to refer to Lear; some critics feel the words refer to Kent. This suggestion seems unlikely; usually at the end of a Shakespearean tragedy, the highest-ranking character surviving speaks of the tragic hero of the play. In any event, the closing lines round out the play effectively. The play opens with a discussion of how the difference between two men has been obscured in a political settlement. It closes with lines stressing the way in which one man is distinguished from his fellows; moreover the criterion by which he is distinguished is the depth of his experience, more specifically how much he has been able to "see." Edgar's respect for wisdom is reflected in the fact that he values age (with its greater experience) over youth; at the beginning of the play, Edmund spoke out for youth over age. (On the issue of youth vs. age in the play, see Lowenthal, "*King Lear,*" 399.) Finally, in the first scene of *King Lear* hypocrisy governed the court; at the end Edgar is calling for a new honesty when he enjoins: "Speak what we feel, not what we ought to say." In sum, Edgar's final words manifest a new regard for truth.

RALPH BERRY

Lear's System

"In his sane moments Lear hardly ever makes an intelligent remark."[1]
Trenchant as always, Orwell directs us to the key issue of the play's opening,
and therefore of the play. He cannot, naturally, be taken too literally. Intel-
ligence does not always express itself in manifestly "intelligent" observation.
Still, if Orwell is essentially right, the opening ceremonial is a mere dotage.
And this is a view commanding wide support. "In the first scene of the play,
Lear is a foolish old man . . . who is led in the vanity of dotage to stage a
scene to gratify his craving for affection."[2] Thus Kenneth Muir, in the New
Arden. For Wilson Knight, "A tremendous soul is, as it were, incongruously
geared to a puerile intellect."[3] These are solidifications of Bradley's percep-
tion of the event:

> The rashness of his division of the kingdom troubles us, and we
> cannot but see with concern that its motive is mainly selfish.
> The absurdity of the pretence of making the division depend on
> protestations of love from his daughters, his complete blindness to
> the hypocrisy which is patent to us at a glance, his piteous delight
> in these protestations, the openness of his expressions of preference
> for his youngest daughter—all make us smile, but all pain us.[4]

From *Tragic Instance: The Sequence of Shakespeare's Tragedies*, pp. 137–49, 220–21. Copyright
© 1999 by Associated University Presses.

Bradley had obviously been unlucky with the productions he saw. Accept his perception, and a dimension of the tragedy is already irrecoverable. *King Lear*, on the view cited, shows us an old fool who, tautologously, commits an act of folly, thus confirming the soundness of judgment of those who have written him off as an old fool. To be taken in by Goneril and Regan, whose hypocrisy is patent to us! Not a commentator in the land would be deceived by them. Such a man deserves our pity, not our sympathy. King Lear is already being ushered, gently, toward the geriatric ward. He will not be accorded there the dignity of intelligent choice, of responsibility for his actions. But his energetic ravings will be followed closely, and his death allowed as cathartic.

Now Bradley's position is not, of course, universally accepted. The opening ceremonial has its purpose, like all ceremonials. Elder Olson puts it well: "if Lear is giving up his authority and still wants security and dignity, he can only trust to their love; and his insistence upon their public profession of it is an attempt to have it warranted and witnessed as a formal part of the compact of the delivery of property and power."[5] The public affirmation of love is an exercise that no power in the world disregards. In the same vein, Winifred Nowottny writes that "At the heart of Lear's tragedy there lies the great problem of traditional symbolic forms. These are the only language of love and reverence; they have, however, to be maintained against attack, and the function of authority is to enforce reverence of form on those who repudiate it."[6] That is pertinent and true; but Nowottny goes on to say that "Authority takes the tragic step of asking for a token of love beyond that reverence for the forms of duty it knows itself able to enforce, whilst at the same time abrogating its powers." That, I think, is more questionable. Asking for a token of love, clearly, is neither unreasonable nor wrong. And Lear, with reason, believes himself to be capable of enforcing it. It is the form of Lear's question that irritates ("Which of you shall we say doth love us most"), by pretending that extent and quality of reward can be made immediately commensurate with the love-protestation. That is a logical absurdity; but it is the form which Lear imposes. In any case, the language of formal protestation is often hyperbolic to the point of absurdity. When the Spaniard says "My house is yours," he merely means that one is welcome. The form of words that Lear chooses to cue in the love-protestation is not, in itself, a cause for rebellion or proof of dotage.

The Olson-Nowottny line does narrow the "folly" of Lear's early actions, since it cedes to him the dignity of staging a ceremonial that is valuable and pointed. But such writers defend only the ceremonial itself. They have little or nothing to say concerning the substantive arrangements that Lear has in mind, which are generally thought of as indefensible. I propose here to consider the political hinterland of the opening scene, the dispositions which Lear makes for the security of his realm.

* * *

King Lear is a tragedy of identity, in the sense that the King has created a system that is his own identity. It is precisely a play of old age, for its subject is responsible for arteriosclerotic structures of rule that malfunction through their rigidity. Nevertheless, the failure lies in that rigidity, not in the structures themselves. Lear's system of rule is perfectly logical, and has seen him safely into his eightieth year.

The system is based on competition and rivalry among Lear's dependents. With three children-dependents, that is an easy game to play; but its dynamics are complex. Goneril has presumably married first, but has no children, and her full dowry has yet to be determined at the play's opening ("With my two daughters' dow'rs digest the third," 1.1.128). Regan likewise has married, has borne no children, and awaits her dowry. Cordelia is destined for a Continental alliance, but it has not yet happened, and her child-bearing potential is yet to be tested. Everything is open-ended, undetermined, requiring the King's will to cooperate with events as they occur. And the King wishes it that way. France and Burgundy, "Great *rivals* in our youngest daughter's love," have been frozen in that posture of rivalry: "Long in our court have made their amorous sojourn" (46–47). Their position is figured in the opening scene, for France and Burgundy have to wait offstage for matters to be concluded onstage. The negotiations have, in fact, been stretched out to the limits. Only at the latest moment will the King decide.

Uncertainty in the governed is the secret of government. Lear keeps everyone guessing. The point about the opening lines is not only that the division of the kingdom is fixed, but that Kent and Gloucester (who are better placed than anyone else, elderly and privileged courtiers near to the King) are taken by surprise. *Kent*: "I thought the King had more affected the Duke of Albany than Cornwall." *Gloucester*: "It did always seem so to us." Only in his opening speech does Lear "express our darker purpose." And even then, the small print is worth looking at.

Lear's opening move is maliciously unsettling: "Our son of Cornwall, / And you our no less loving son of Albany" (41–42) is a reverse bid, for the later precedence (Goneril, Regan) would seem to call for Albany, then Cornwall. (Cornwall must think, for a moment, have I got it? Albany, have I lost it? The thoughts of their ladies must run interestingly parallel, but not geometrically so.) And then, the dowries. "To thine and Albany's issue" (66) is at once ambivalent, skeptical, reserved. If one reads it "To [thine and Albany's] issue," there's no problem. If there's a fractional pause after "thine," it comes out as "To [thine] [and Albany's] issue." The old man is saying: "If you can't bear Albany a child, he may have to look elsewhere. If Albany can't give you a child, you may have to look elsewhere. If you want future trouble, try to arrange the succession for someone who isn't 'thine and Albany's issue.'" Without taking the banal pro-Goneril position, one does see her point of view.

Regan gets terms that are similar, if not identical: "To thee and thine hereditary ever" (79). This is clear enough, surely? Not to me. To begin with, there's no mention of Cornwall, so Regan has theoretically more room for maneuver than Goneril (whose issue is coupled with Albany's). Then, much depends on the Folio's comma after "thee." All modern editors abandon that comma, and most of them leave the line open to inflection and parsing. Two consequences flow. If we retain the comma, it means that the territory is bequeathed to Regan, and thereafter to her heirs. "Hereditary" thus becomes a noun, for which there is indeed no instance cited by the *OED*, but that of course is no conclusive argument against Shakespeare's creating a noun for the occasion. If we abandon F's comma, we understand, if we do not insert, a comma after "To thee and thine." That makes "hereditary" an adjective, as it is in the seven other instances in Shakespeare. But it leaves "thine" open (thine and Cornwall's, or thine alone?). The salient point is that "hereditary" is not "issues": heirs are not the same as children. There is no need to look beyond the *OED*'s first sense of *hereditary*: "*Law and Hist.* Descending by inheritance from generation to generation; that has or may be transmitted according to definite rules of descent; legally vesting, upon the death of the holder, in the person designated by the law as his heir." One can effortlessly imagine the lawyers having good sport, as Gloucester would put it, over the terms of Lear's will. What it means for the moment is that Regan has secured a better deal than Goneril. She has much wider terms in which to dispose of her inheritance; she has greater freedom from her husband; her power to dispose is power to propose, simply power. And she has earned it.

Regan has earned her reward by surpassing Goneril. Her prize-winning speech is quite different in quality from her sister's. Peter Brook recounts a telling anecdote, of how he asked an audience member at a lecture (to whom the play was unfamiliar) to read Goneril's first speech. She did so,

> and the speech itself emerged full of eloquence and charm. I then
> explained that it was supposed to be the speech of a wicked woman,
> and suggested her reading every word for hypocrisy. She tried to
> do so, and the audience saw what a hard unnatural wrestling with
> the simple music of the words was involved when she sought to
> act to a definition ... [Goneril's] words are those of a lady of style

and breeding accustomed to expressing herself in public, someone with ease and social aplomb. As for clues to her character, only the façade is presented and this, we see, is elegant and attractive."[7]

In other words, Goneril is trying—successfully—to reconcile the needs of a public occasion with her own sense of identity. Regan is evidently another matter. Her speech is indefensibly glutinous and false in tone. But this merely ministers to Lear's requirement, and he demonstrates that the winning competitor receives the rewards of competition: which include not only the territory (fixed, in advance) but the terms on which the dowry is made over (open, until Lear speaks). It must be dispiriting to be asked by Lear to bat first. The other side always has a target, and should score more heavily.

Goneril and Regan are rivals, not close allies. Obviously, the course of the play bears this out. I need to stress the point here, because Shakespeare artfully contrives a different impression at the close of the first scene. The intimate, prose-after-verse dialogue, political in tone and context, leads to an easy misjudgment. It conduces to a perception of legend: here are the two Ugly Sisters, ganging up on poor Cinderella as they always have. I point out that the dialogue can as easily be read the other way. Goneril and Regan are *not* close; the opening address, "Sister," is cool and functional, and no first-name terms are exchanged, nor is the "thou" form. Anyone who has ever quoted "Let us hit together" will know that one addresses the remark, not to friends, but to (temporary) political allies of whom one needs to be wary. Why should Goneril say it now, if she and Regan have been practicing the injunction already? Cordelia, so far from being Cinderella, is her father's favorite daughter, set to receive her father's greatest gift: Prince Charming, and the best third of the kingdom. Let us examine the elements of Lear's gift.

* * *

It is an error of interpretation to go all the way down the Stonehenge route. *King Lear*'s primitivism is not in doubt, yet at least two distinguished productions of recent years (Trevor Nunn's, for the RSC, 1976, and Robin Phillips', for Stratford, Ontario, 1979–80) have set the play successfully in the nineteenth and early twentieth centuries.[8] We perceive in the play civilization and its discontents, not merely a falling-out of Druids. Similarly, the play's locations and titles are far from lost in the swirling mists of prehistory. There are five British place-names in *King Lear*: Albany, Cornwall, Gloucester, Kent, Dover. They are hieroglyphs of value, from which a complete system can be reconstructed. The map that Lear calls for is real.

"Albany" signifies Scotland, or the northern region of the Island. The Variorum quotes Holinshed:

> The first and last part of the Island he allotted unto Albanacte hys youngest sonne … This later parcel at the first, toke the name of Albanactus, who called it Albania. But now a small portion onely of the Region (being under the regiment of a Duke) reteyneth the sayd denomination, the reast beyng called Scotlande, of certayne Scottes that came over from Ireland to inhabite in those quarters. It is devided from Loegres also by the Humber, so that Albania as Brute left it, conteyned all the north part of the Island that is to be found beyond the aforesayd streame, unto the point of Cathenesse.[9]

"Cornwall" is the western region, together with a portion of the heartland. The title is literal. The present Duke of Cornwall, who is also Prince of Wales, owns extensive estates in Cornwall and elsewhere. Alvin Kernan notes that James I's sons had the same ducal titles.[10] "Gloucester" fits easily into the system, for the Earl of Gloucester is the Duke of Cornwall's vassal: this approximates to our sense of Gloucestershire as being, rather tenuously, connected with the West Country. Always one must think of titles as denoting possession of land, and not as empty honorifics. There is no name for Cordelia's portion, but it must be the South-East jut of the Island, together with its share of the heartland. That, indeed, would bear out Lear's statement that Cordelia is to "draw / A third, more opulent than your sisters'" (85–86). Kent's regard for Cordelia is more than a purely personal sympathy. She would have been his regional overlord. Dover is the regional port.

Through Dover, the Continental alliance is activated. Which alliance is it to be? Bradley puzzled over this: "Why Burgundy rather than France should have first choice of Cordelia's hand is a question we cannot help asking, but there is no hint of an answer."[11] In his footnote, he speculates that "Burgundy is to be her husband, and that is why, when Lear has cast her off, he offers her to Burgundy first." I doubt this. At the point when Lear offers Cordelia to Burgundy, all bets are off; the explosion has already occurred. If we read any significance into the order of asking, my earlier point applies: to speak first, in Lear's system, is to accept the position of disadvantage. But the French alliance is manifestly preferable. The Duchy of Burgundy was always landlocked (save, apparently, for a brief spell in the tenth century when there was a claimed opening to the Mediterranean). No easy, maritime communications could exist between Burgundy and England. France offers an inexpungable base, with the eternal assurance of support for or intervention in British affairs, just as in the subsequent play. It would always have been France, in the competition for Cordelia's hand. Burgundy was there to make it an auction.

But should not Lear have preserved the Unity of the Kingdom? That is the sort of second-rate maxim that a first-rate fact rebuts. If the kingdom is to be united, it must be under Albany. Albany, a man who spends most of the play backing off from his responsibilities, and in the final page offers, incredibly, to abdicate twice! (Once to Lear, once to Edgar and Kent.) To abdicate in favor of an abdicator is scarcely the pinnacle of political wisdom. And Albany has no children. Since Britain was not actually united under a Scots king until 1603, one wonders at those who reproach Lear for not arranging this coup, one thousand years ahead of its time. We need not be concerned with the questions an appointments committee might raise concerning the moral standing of Cornwall. It is sufficient to note that he has married the second daughter, has no children, and operates from a base in the South-West, from which at no time in history has the Island ever been governed. The political problem is not which of these unappealing satraps to hand over power to. It is to set up a system which will survive Lear, while permitting him a guiding hand in late old age.

That system will not be a unitary state. Rather, it will illustrate, and indeed dramatize, Lear's propensity to divide and rule. The post-abdication outcome will be a dynamic tripartition, which is the political extension and reflection of Lear's relations with his daughters (and sons-in-law). Put differently: in what sense is the Britain of the play's opening a unitary state? It is already divided, as it must be, into regional suzerainty, with a quantum of bad feeling thrown in ("future strife," predicated on the understandable attitudes of the three daughters to each other).[12] What maintains unitary rule, of a sort, is precisely the policy of sectional division which Lear has successfully pursued.

This division is not really arbitrary. Since the great dukes already possess their regional structures, Lear's planned settlement merely formalizes the present state of affairs with the addition of heartland areas. It also maintains the present jealousies and rivalries of the inheritors, which are neatly contained within a triadic system. The map of Britain that Lear unfolds is a working diagram of a settlement that corresponds reasonably well to the current situation and its realities. The future will have to depend on the fertility of the three daughters, anyway—or their husbands.

We now have the essence of Lear's gift to Cordelia. She is to receive the most desirable portion of Britain, the South-East, together with a Continental alliance, probably France. To call these dispositions "favouritism,"[13] as though the term were self-refuting, is to miss the point. ("Favouritism," said Admiral Fisher, "is the secret of efficiency.") Cordelia holds all the cards.

By continuing Lear's balancing act, she can dominate Goneril/Albany and Regan/Cornwall, playing off one against the other. Even if they combine against her (inherently unlikely, on personal grounds), an established kingdom of the South-East, with Continental backing, should easily hold its own. If Cordelia should bear a child, that opens up the prospect of a future reunification of the Island under her issue. Over these agreeable political maneuvers the elder statesman will preside, happy to continue the great political game while monopolizing ("We two *alone*") his favorite daughter. I see no folly in this scheme. On the contrary, it appears to me that Lear has planned his retirement rather well.

In all this, the geography of *King Lear* is a primitive algebra. The place-names are not mere banners, colorful fictions designed to settle a vague Englishness on the events of the play. The mist swirls around the name-counters, but the values they stand for are real. Albany and Cornwall denote wealth, power, and land in specific regions. They are grand theatrical translations of what all dowries and wills are about. Gloucester and Kent denote vassalage and fealty, as well as certain parts of the land. The rage that Lear, Cornwall, and even the mild Albany show in turn is the rage of authority defied by vassals. Dover is the line of communication, the great link with the landmass that from time immemorial has threatened the identity of the island itself. It is Dover that causes the Duke of Cornwall to turn round and bite, tigerishly, at the threat to identity. Ultimately, the land is the identity of Lear. Britain and its king are metonymy. When Lear says, "Give me the map there" (1.1.37) we should look at it, hard.

* * *

All Cordelia has to do is to accept the gift gracefully. "At a moment where terrible issues join, Fate makes on her the one demand which she is unable to meet," says Bradley. "Cordelia cannot, because she is Cordelia."[14] Most people, I suppose, go through life under the impression that Fate is imposing a series of unfair demands on them, which by sheer ill-chance they are unable to meet, because they are themselves. To have this impression sanctioned by Bradley goes some way toward accounting for Cordelia's popularity—and perhaps Bradley's. It is unnecessary here to sift the range of emotions and motives which Cordelia may be supposed to experience. (Though I would add to the traditional range Cordelia's sense of being placed in a false position, that the combination of suitor-choice and dowry-division ought not to be synchronized with a declaration of filial love.) She mutinies, anyway. Lear, predictably and with justice, is wounded and shocked. Has he not done everything a King and father can to ensure the stability of the realm, and the security and happiness of his favorite daughter? Does he not merely ask to be given a vote of thanks, for the record?

More, has not Cordelia committed the grossest of solecisms? The opening scene is a great public spectacle, the division of the realm. It is the theatre of monarchy. On such occasions the roles are determined, the individual compressed within his part. For the individual to assert himself against the programming is, in this context, intolerable. It is like using an award-giving ceremony to make a radical speech, an action widely despised. The general understanding is plain: if you don't like the ceremony, stay away; if you come, you enter into a compact to abide by the rules of the occasion. There are decencies which in aggregate conduce to the decorum of existence. Cordelia, in making her demonstration, flouts them all.

Are these reflections on the event available during the performance of scene one? Not at all. Shakespeare stills such thoughts as subversive to his immediate dramatic purpose. He does so with the simplest of technical tricks, the aside. When the actress swivels round, eyes the audience directly, and asks "What shall Cordelia speak? Love, and be silent," there is no question of an option. We have been got at. The audience is bidden, not invited, to take Cordelia's side. It is tampering with the jury, but no one ever said that drama should be fair. Nothing in this explains the tragedy. It merely explains our immediate responses. Thinking comes later. With it, we can recognize that the aside is a form of ingratiation that no other character in this scene is permitted to practice. Lear, above all, has no aside. This is a case that Shakespeare has no intention of permitting his immediate client to lose.

Suppose those two devastating appeals to the jury were struck out, what then? It has been done. Peter Brook, in his RSC production of 1962, was widely and erroneously criticized for cutting the post-blinding Servants' dialogue,[15] but he retained Cordelia's asides. He also cast the glamorous and appealing Diana Rigg as Cordelia, allowing her as the traditional focus of audience sympathy. But when Brook made his ensuing film of *King Lear* (1969), his thought had moved to an even bleaker statement of the play. The film Cordelia was an abbreviated part, by no means attractive or engaging, and her asides were cut. The film audience was given no reason to side with Cordelia, or indeed with Lear. On the contrary, the case for Goneril—the outrageous behavior of the knights, Lear's impossible entourage—was fully rehearsed. Neither early nor late was there an easy resting point for the audience. (Kozintsev's film, also of 1969, offered a traditional, radiant Cordelia, complete with aside.) Brook's later version of *King Lear* may appear as a branch line in theater history. It remains a powerful questioning of the natural flow of the play, a text as we receive it that is determined to support Cordelia. Cordelia/audience becomes a special relationship, which the more impressionable of commentators take over, eventually translating their esteem for Cordelia into the honorific "Christ figure."

Bradley's transports over Cordelia ("She is a thing enskyed and sainted"[16]) are well known, but still astonish. Dover Wilson temperately describes her as "conceived as a Christ-like figure."[17] As Jonson remarked of Donne's "Anniversary," "if it had been written of the Virgin Mary, it had been something." But this is no place to indulge in a critical brawl over whether Christ-figures ought so readily to precipitate tragedies in Act I through suppressing their Christ-like qualities of humility. I shall confine my remarks to the technical. Cordelia's part is defined by its brevity, both in length and in style. She is indeed laconic, even if her reputation for saying little is grounded upon talking out of turn to the audience. The part is easy, verging upon the actress-proof. And it is a part that does not show signs of extensive re-writing between Q and F. Shakespeare had no important second thoughts about Cordelia. He did not need to.[18] Cordelia is to be retained within an intense, narrow band of effects: any expansion would create ambivalence, additional possibilities, a shade of reservation. Her role is to ambush Lear in Act I, be reconciled with him in Act IV, and make a final appearance symbolically and actually carried by Lear. To continue the metaphor, I conceive of Shakespeare as counsel directing his client: "*And don't say another word.*" Excellent advice, and it continues to dominate *Lear* criticism.

The catastrophe occurs because everyone is fixed in a role which is rigidly maintained by the programming of State. The daughters' functions are prescribed. Cordelia, in rebelling, brings upon herself the unappeasable wrath of the State's main agent. Kent, "'Tis my occupation to be plain" (2.2.93), is blunt when any second-rate supple courtier could and should avert the crisis by calling for an adjournment. By confronting Lear, by losing his temper ("Be Kent unmannerly / When Lear is mad. What wouldst thou do, old man?" [145–46]), Kent offers his master no escape, and compels him to *be* King. Everyone else keeps clear, beyond staying Lear's hand from homicide. Lear himself sees the reimposition of monarchic rule as the only response to the provocation:

> Hear me, recreant, on thine allegiance, hear me!
> That thou has sought to make us break our vows,
> Which we durst never yet, and with strain'd pride
> To come betwixt our sentence and our power,
> Which nor our nature nor our place can bear . . .
>   (168–72)

In the theatre of State, all works perfectly so long as everyone hews to the role. A single rebellion and the system is fractured; no one knows how to repair it. In the scene as written, it takes only three hotheads and a crowd of innocent bystanders to make a catastrophe.

* * *

The impressions we receive, and are meant to receive, of the catastrophe are subtly at odds with the judgments we arrive at later. Lear commits an irreparable folly in banishing Cordelia, but his appraisal of forces, up to that point, is highly defensible. Goneril and Regan have a case, whatever their later conduct. Kent's loss of temper, like Cordelia's, is unpardonable: they have a duty to handle an elderly and splenetic monarch, a duty which can hardly come as a surprise to them. The Continentals look different, too. France has evidently not seen *1 Henry VI*: if he had, he would remember that the much-derided Henry married for love, not State, a decision seen and demonstrated as disastrous. Burgundy, so apparently pusillanimous in his scene, has done well in staying clear of the British entanglement, and of Cordelia's advanced sense of duty. The realm of Burgundy, at least, will be spared the ministrations of a Christ-figure in Act V. No one will remember Burgundy anyway: even the actor has to get changed into one of the minor military functionaries, and may end up being ordered to execute Cordelia. The play, in fact, tries to put the opening scene out of mind. But this it cannot altogether succeed in doing. In the theatre we are all naive spectators; but we retain the faculty of memory; our backward glance does not confirm in all respects the impressions of the opening.

What the play has done is to evoke, in a distorted and nightmarish way, some premonitions of the opening and of Lear's mind. The French alliance becomes the French invasion. Regan's freedom to bequeath becomes the claimed right to make Edmund Earl of Gloucester, and her agent "In my rights / By me invested" (5.3.70–71). Lear's curse on Goneril's fertility (1.4.272–78) foreshadows the state of all three daughters. If there is one moment in the later stages that is a cracked echo of the earlier, it is Lear's glimpse of a future in which "We two alone will sing like birds i' th' cage" (5.3.9). It is not so far from the opening, and his confession in the aftermath of shock—it is conceivable that he never told Cordelia—"I loved her most, and thought to set my rest / On her kind nursery" (1.1.123–24). Of the tragedy of *King Lear* there will be as many formulations as spectators. Not least, I think, of the tragedies is that the final stages mock Act I, and Lear's not despicable, not unintelligent vision of order.

NOTES

1. George Orwell, "Lear, Tolstoy, and the Fool," in *Selected Essays* (Harmondsworth: Penguin Books, 1957), p. 116.

2. Kenneth Muir, New Arden edition of *King Lear* (London: Methuen, 1964), p. liii.

3. G. Wilson Knight, *The Wheel of Fire* (London: Methuen, 1930), p. 162.

4. A. C. Bradley, *Shakespearean Tragedy* (London: Macmillan and Co., 1904), p. 232.

5. Elder Olson, *Tragedy and the Theory of Drama* (Detroit: Wayne State Univ. Press, 1961), p. 201.

6. Winifred Nowottny, "Some Aspects of the Style of *King Lear*," *Shakespeare Survey*, 13 (1960), 53.

7. Peter Brook, *The Empty Space* (London: MacGibbon and Kee 1968), p. 14.

8. See Richard David's *Shakespeare in the Theatre* (Cambridge: Cambridge Univ. Press, 1978), pp. 95–105; and my reviews of the Stratford, Ontario seasons, "Stratford Festival Canada," in *Shakespeare Quarterly*, 31 (1980), 167–75, and 32 (1981), 176–80.

9. *King Lear: A New Variorum Edition*, ed. H. H. Furness (New York, 1880).

10. Alvin Kernan, *Shakespeare, the King's Playwright: Theater in the Stuart Court 1603–1613* (New Haven and London: Yale University Press, 1995), 96.

11. Bradley, p. 211.

12. "Behind the façade of unanimity, all dictatorships are to a large extent centrifugal: the rule of a court conceals a political anarchy in which jealous feudatories, with private armies and reservations of public resources, are secretly bargaining, and may openly fight, for the reversion or preservation of power." Hugh Trevor-Roper, *The Last Days of Hitler* (New York: Macmillan, 1947), p. 233.

13. E.A.J. Honigmann, *Shakespeare: Seven Tragedies: The Dramatist's Manipulation of Response* (London: Macmillan, 1978), p. 103.

14. Bradley, p. 265.

15. Most notably in Maynard Mack, *"King Lear" in Our Time* (Berkeley and Los Angeles: University of California Press, 1965). But the later scholarly view of the Folio as a fully revised text makes Mack's strictures look much less telling. If Shakespeare could cut the post-blinding dialogue in his revision, why not Brook?

16. Bradley, *Shakespearean Tragedy*, p. 264.

17. John Dover Wilson, *King Lear*, New Cambridge edition (Cambridge: Cambridge Univ. Press 1960), p. xx.

18. It is worth noting, though, that 4.3, with the Gentleman's description of Cordelia, disappears in what we are now to think of as the Folio revision. Those who wish to make much of Cordelia's "holy water" and "heavenly eyes" must reconcile themselves to the willed departure of those pointers.

FRANK KERMODE

King Lear

The relationships between the extant versions of *King Lear* are, at present, the subject of intense research and dispute, but I think it is agreed on all sides that any of the versions of the play we are accustomed to reading in the standard editions[1] cannot be very like any text performed in Shakespeare's time, or indeed long after that.

The question of the texts, briefly summarized in the footnote, is of great interest in itself, but it is only marginally relevant to the purposes of this book. Wherever it seems necessary or helpful I will mention Quarto-Folio differences, usually accepting the Folio version, though I am partial to the argument that F might actually represent an earlier form of the text than Q.[2]

It is curious that this play, which it is surely impossible for anybody who cares about poetry to write on without some expression of awe, should offer few of the local excitements to be found, say, in the narrower context of *Measure for Measure*. The explanation must be that the subjects of *King Lear* reflect a much more general, indeed a universal tragedy. In *King Lear* we are no longer concerned with an ethical problem that, however agonising, can be reduced to an issue of law or equity and discussed forensically. For *King Lear* is about suffering represented as a condition of the world as we inherit it or make it for ourselves. Suffering is the consequence of a human tendency to evil, as inflicted on the good by the bad; it can reduce humanity

From *Shakespeare's Language*, pp. 183–200. Copyright © 2000 by Frank Kermode.

to a bestial condition, under an apparently indifferent heaven. It falls, insistently and without apparent regard for the justice they so often ask for, so often say they believe in, on the innocent; but nobody escapes. At the end the punishment or relief of death is indiscriminate. The few survivors, chastened by this knowledge, face a desolate future. The play demands that we think of its events in relation to the last judgement, the promised end itself, calling the conclusion an image of that horror (V.iii.264–65).

Apocalypse is the image of human dealings in their extremity, an image of the state to which humanity can reduce itself. We are asked to imagine the Last Days, when, under the influence of some Antichrist, human beings will behave not as a rickety civility requires but naturally; that is, they will prey upon themselves like animals, having lost the protection of social restraint, now shown to be fragile. The holy cords, however "intrinse," can be loosened by rats. Gloucester may be credulous and venal, but his murmurings about the state of the world, which do not move Edmund, reflect the mood of the play: "in cities, mutinies; in countries, discord; in palaces, treason; and the bond crack'd 'twixt son and father ... We have seen the best of our time" (I.ii.107–12). The voices of the good are distorted by pain, those of the bad by the coarse excess of their wickedness.

The rhetoric of the play is accordingly more explicit, less ambiguous, except—and it is admittedly a large exception—in the apparent unreason of the Fool and Poor Tom and the ravings of the mad King, where the imaginations of folly flood into the language and give it violent local colour. These wild linguistic excursions come later; the opening scene is in cool, even bantering prose, but as always in Shakespeare, it achieves much more than mere exposition. Coleridge understood its depth; the opening conversation between Gloucester and Kent makes it plain that Lear has already arranged the "division of the kingdom" before the ceremony in which he formally announces it, which was therefore intended to be less the declaration of a secret intention ("our darker purpose" [I.i.36]) than a self-gratifying charade. Lear can already be seen as imperious and selfish; we discover that even giving his kingdom away is a selfish act. And immediately we are offered a critical view of the other main sufferer, Gloucester, and his relations with his natural son, Edmund. Gloucester treats Edmund's birth as an occasion for bawdy joking and does not explain why, unlike his legitimate brother, Edgar, he should have been so long absent or why "away he shall again" (32–33). All this has much to do not only with their characters but with the nature of the ensuing action in so far as it depends on the folly of Gloucester and the ingenious unregenerate wickedness of Edmund.[3]

Such economical writing is perhaps no more than should be expected of a dramatist in his prime. The ceremonial love competition that follows of course requires verse. The verse of the daughters Goneril and Regan has to be formal, manifestly insincere. Goneril is using what rhetoricians called "the topic of inexpressibility," standard fare in the eulogy of kings and emperors— "I love you more than words can wield the matter, / Dearer than eyesight . . . A love that makes breath poor, and speech unable . . ." (55–60). Regan follows with the well-established topical formula that Ernst Curtius calls "outdoing," or the "*cedat*-formula"—"let her yield": her sister has expressed Regan's sentiments quite well, "Only she comes too short" (72). Cordelia, coming third in order of praising, would have a hard task, but shuns this competition, meaning nevertheless to outdo her sisters by exposing their rhetorical falsity. She would prefer to be silent, but the only way to announce that intention is to speak about it, which she does.[4] She does not come out of the archaic and artificial contest well, defeated by the genuineness of her love, as France recognises; but she is far from passively yielding.

> LEAR. . . . what can you say to draw
> A third more opulent than your sisters'? Speak.
> COR. Nothing, my lord.
> LEAR. Nothing?
> COR. Nothing.
> LEAR. Nothing will come of nothing, speak again.
> (85–90)

She does speak again, but virtually only to say nothing.[5] Here rhetorical formulae are used for a dramatic purpose. The rage of the King confirms that he cannot be temperate in the absence of ceremony; the love he seeks is the sort that can be offered in formal and subservient expressions, and he therefore rejects the love of Cordelia and of Kent. The rest of the scene is equally well contrived. The style of personal pronouns is worth attention: Lear is almost always, regally, "we," until he loses his temper with his daughter, when he uses "I." Kent is truly "unmannerly," freely addressing the King as "thou": "What wouldest thou do, old man? . . . Reserve thy state, / And in thy best consideration check / This hideous rashness" (146–51).

Lear has already given away everything except an imaginary possession: "Only we shall retain / The name, and all th' addition to a king" (135–36). The word "addition" seems to have interested Shakespeare. It can refer to "honours, prerogatives, titles"—as when, in *Othello*, Cassio, after his disgrace, reacts to Iago's calling him "lieutenant" by saying he is "The worser that you give me the addition / Whose want even kills me" (IV.i.104–5). In *Lear* there is a way of looking at people as if they were simply basic human beings, naturally naked, wretches whose standing as more than that depends on their additions, without which they might be indistinguishable from Poor Tom: "unaccommodated man is no more but such a poor, bare, fork'd animal . . ." (III.iv.106–8). Not only honours but clothes are "additions": splendid in the case of Goneril and Regan, though meant for ostentation of rank rather than warmth; deemed unnecessary by Lear, who tries to take his off in the storm and at the moment of death; fraudulent in the case of corrupt judges, as we see in Lear's extraordinary tirade: "Robes and furr'd gowns hide all" (IV. vi.164). Clothes are emblems of "addition"—what is added, out of pride or wickedness, to the natural man.

Enid Welsford, in her valuable book on the Fool, found in the action of this tragedy "the great reversal of the Saturnalia." The Saturnalia was classical Rome's winter festival, remembered in the Christian Twelfth Night, when masters and servants changed places and a mock-king or boy-bishop ruled for a day over an upside-down world. Here Lear, stripped of additions and in his dotage, "discovers . . . what the evil have known from their cradles, that *in this world there is no poetic justice*."[6] The Renaissance, like St. Paul, found much value in folly, and Erasmus, who wrote a famous book about it, also recorded the adage "Kings and fools are born, not made," which Shakespeare may have recalled when he has Lear ask, "Dost thou call me fool, boy?" and receives the reply "All thy other titles thou hast given away, that thou wast born with" (I.iv.148–50, Q only).[7]

Some understanding of the history and privileges of the Fool is essential to understanding *King Lear*; he is a perpetual reminder of Carnival, of the commentary on grandees allowed by custom to the humble. The Fool is both loyal and bitter; his master has reduced himself absurdly to a fool's role, and the Fool is now the source of wisdom, fantastically delineating a world turned upside down. The proper additions of the Fool include a coxcomb, and the Fool offers his to the King to take the place of a crown.

Among the additions Lear vainly wants to keep are his hundred knights, but they are reduced to none by the savage calculations of Goneril and Regan. In the opening scene he has amused himself with calculations: how much love is due from her, how much from her, what exactly their rewards will be. He bargains with Burgundy: as a result of new calculations "her [Cordelia's] price is fallen" (I.i.197). In his turn he hears the Dutch auction conducted by his daughters: what need has he of a hundred knights, indeed of fifty, even of five-and-twenty, even, finally, of one? Lear joins pathetically in the bargaining: "fifty yet doth double five and twenty, / And thou art twice her love" (II.iv.258–59). "O, reason not the need!" (264) he cries; to reduce a man to no more than what he needs, he remarks prophetically, is to make his life as "cheap as beast's" (267). For this is the moment when the storm is first heard; Lear is to find himself totally unprovided for, with shelter fit only for an animal. Now, more and more, the text begins to be full of animals—the bear, the lion, the wolf; and the King's life, without additions, is truly as cheap as a beast's.

The Gloucester plot is introduced immediately after the departure of Cordelia. First Edmund invokes nature as his goddess, a goddess who despises such human, social contrivances as primogeniture. His argument contests the legitimacy of legitimacy in a purely natural world. But there is more at stake than the ambition of the bastard. At the very outset of his scheming he and Gloucester have a perfectly motivated exchange on the subject of nothing:

> Glou. What paper were you reading?
> Edm. Nothing, my lord.
> Glou. No? What needed then that terrible dispatch of it into
> your pocket? The duality of nothing hath not such need to hide
> itself. Let's see. Come, if it be nothing, I shall not need spectacles.
> (I.ii.30–35)

Much of the poetry in the play depends on these echoes or repetitions; here nothing" is associated with seeing, sight, and the loss of it, which Gloucester is soon to suffer. Edmund plays his trick on the foolish old man and on his brother, whose fault is "foolish honesty" (I.ii.181). The scene is followed at once by another in which we see Goneril's contempt for her father ("Old fools are babes again" [I.iii.19]) and another displaying the loyalty or foolish honesty of Kent, who is at once stripped of his additions and reduced to the status of a servant.

There are so many significant juxtapositions and encounters in the play that one might overlook the importance of Kent's assault on another servant, Goneril's steward Oswald, who has been told to insult the King. Their relationship is brief and violent. Kent comes across Oswald again in II.ii and provokes him to fight. Prevented by Cornwall, he characterises his opponent in words that apply to all the evil persons in the play and to many in anybody's acquaintance:

> Such smiling rogues as these,
> Like rats, oft bite the holy cords a-twain
> Which are t' intrinse t' unloose . . .
> (73–75)

The figure is of rats biting through the complicated knots that bind together families, friends, societies; they cannot be untied and are destroyed by the evil gnawing of vermin. Shakespeare nowhere else used "intrinse," but it is a mistake to emend the word to "intrench," as some editors have done; that reading loses the idea of bonds that are visible and owe their integrity to their complexity. The lines are applied immediately to Oswald, the sycophantic evildoer, but they apply with equal force to the wicked daughters and Edmund. The basic idea lingered in Shakespeare's mind: Cleopatra asks the asp "With thy sharp teeth this knot intrinsicate / Of life at once untie" (*Antony and Cleopatra*, V.ii.304–5). Both words seem to be of Shakespeare's invention. But in the lines from Lear the knot intrinse or intrinsicate (perhaps, as has been suggested, a blend of "intrinsic" and "intricate") is made up of holy cords (the word "holy" is missing from Q1, but I guess it was present in a lost original; it carries so much of the sense of the simile).

Immediately after the scene in which Kent first accosts Oswald, another loyal dependant of the King, the Fool, makes his first entrance (I.iv.94). This is something of a crisis, for from now on the play develops a dialect of folly and madness, to be heard in counterpoint with the language of an evil that remains horribly sane. The Fool's significant first gesture is to offer his coxcomb to the King; then he sings, and the King tells him the song is "nothing"; and the pair have a dialogue on the nature of nothing (128–33). The King has divided his wit in two, like an egg cut in half, and given both sides away, leaving nothing in the middle. He is a "sheal'd peascod" (200). The Fool is insistent: "Thou hadst little wit in thy bald crown when thou gav'st thy golden one away" (162–63; note his privileged singulars, "thou" and "thy"). When Goneril insults him, Lear asks, "Does any here know me? This is not Lear. . . . Where are his eyes? . . . Who is it that can tell me who I am?" (226–230). (Here one notes a strain, only later perceptible, on the use of the word "eyes"; Lear's question is nothing one could expect: "Who am I? Where are my eyes?" is surely, on reflection, strange.) "Lear's shadow," replies the Fool: shadow, being the opposite of substance (an antithesis I have noted earlier as a favourite theme of Shakespeare's), is therefore a form of nothing.[8] One could compare Donne's calling a shadow "an ordinary nothing" in the "Nocturnal upon St. Lucy's Day." Lear is already thus drastically reduced.

The languages of excess and folly allow the intrusion of images and ideas that do not seem immediately relevant but are essential to the fabric of the play. After his frantic curse on Goneril, dismissed by her as "dotage" (293), Lear threatens to pluck out his eyes (301–2), and the mild Albany wonders how far his wife's "eyes may pierce" (345). The Fool asks Lear a riddle: "why one's nose stands i' th' middle on 's face?," the answer to which is "to keep one's eyes on either side's nose, that what a man cannot smell out, he may spy into" (I.v.19–23).

Now, in Act II, comes the disastrous gathering at Gloucester's house of the daughters and their husbands, with Kent and Lear arriving later. The plot of Edmund ("Loyal and natural boy" [i.84])[9] against Edgar is afoot. Regan's wicked opening question to Gloucester was much admired by Coleridge: "What, did my father's godson seek your life?" (91). Here the supposed crime of Edgar is, as it were, by association exclusively attributed to Lear, his god-father. This periphrastic trick of identifying guilt by tracing kinship relations reminds one of *Hamlet*: "your husband's brother's wife" (III.iv.15) is an incriminating way of specifying the Queen his mother. Here the language of Regan, as always, characterises her as without mercy, cold and cunning. That of Lear, in reply to the Fool's tauntings, introduces his first thought and fear of madness (II.iv.56).

From this moment on, the language of *King Lear* has such force and variety that to give a convincing account of it seems close to impossible. Lear rages, and his rage is rant:

> And thou, all-shaking thunder,
> Strike flat the thick rotundity o' th' world!
> Crack nature's moulds, all germains spill at once
> That makes ingrateful man!
> (III.ii.6–9)

Nature is again to take his part against his "unnatural" daughters; again the plea is for sterility, anything rather than the kind of vitality they display. The next appeal is to justice, which it was once his prerogative to dispense; now it will come, if at all, from elsewhere. It is at the disposal of the criminal, the perjured, the incestuous; the elements have become the "servile ministers" of his daughters, and the punishments fall on him, even though he is "More sinn'd against than sinning" (60). The sheer noise of Lear's speeches is a necessary prelude to his sudden turning in compassion to the Fool, and later to Poor Tom. The shouting of the King and the barbed chatter of the Fool accompany this recognition of what it is to be cold and poor, to be at the bottom level of nature. The tone changes in the lines beginning "Poor naked wretches, whereso'er you are, / That bide the pelting of this pitiless storm" (III.iv.28–29); and Lear sends the Fool before him into the hovel. There they find Poor Tom. It is superbly apt that Lear imagines Tom's troubles to have come from the ingratitude of his daughters, a punishment for his having begotten them.

Once more the theme is justice. Edgar-Tom provides a vision of unjust luxury; he has been a fine courtier,[10] but now, without shoes and clothes and perfume, his is an image of destitution: "here's three on 's are sophisticated. Thou art the thing itself: unaccommodated man is no more but such a poor, bare, fork'd animal as thou art" (105–8). And Lear begins to tear off his own clothes: "Off, off, you lendings! Come, unbutton here" (108–9).

This scene is in prose and yet it is poetry of the highest quality. Shakespeare had mastered the device of allowing a pattern of language to irrupt into violent dramatic action. This shedding of "additions" or "lendings" is an instance. Another, equally extraordinary, is the tearing out of Gloucester's eyes, for which all the references to eyes and to sight and to "nothing" might have prepared us, save that the sheer violence of the act, and of all anger displayed—Cornwall's cold and Regan's sadistically excited—makes us, even four centuries later, turn our heads away from the sight.

The crazy chatter of Tom is now heard together with the lament of the newly arrived Gloucester:

> GLOU. Our flesh and blood, my lord, is grown so vild
> That it doth hate what gets it.
> EDG. Poor Tom's a-cold.
> (144–46)

The themes intertwine as it were musically; the cruelty of children, the unsheltered life of unaccommodated man. Gloucester himself says his wits are crazed. Lear believes that Edgar has shown himself to be a philosopher, a student of thunder, one who is so close to being the thing itself that he will understand other elemental phenomena.

The play now maintains a double movement: the craziness on the heath and the treachery of Edmund, with the cruel calculations of Cornwall, indoors. The next scene on the heath (III.vi) presents an image of mad justice in the fantasy trial of Goneril and Regan. (This is only in the Folio, but it is hard to believe this amazing scene, so much of the very substance of the work, was an afterthought.) The "justicers" are a Fool (dealing with equity rather than unmitigated justice) and a Bedlam maniac ("Thou robed man of justice" [35]). "Let us deal justly," says Tom (40). Lear, now quite mad, still in his babblings, does not stray far from the obsessive language of the play: "Is there any cause in nature that make these hard hearts? [It is a philosophical question, like inquiring into the cause of thunder] . . . You, sir . . . I do not like the fashion of your garments" (77–80). As Lear sinks into sleep, the Fool makes his last quip and disappears from the play.

The action proceeds with another trial, this time the interrogation and punishment of Gloucester. In the midst of this obscene horror the words "justice" and of course "eyes" and "seeing" are repeated again and again, even with an echo of the Fool's earlier joke about the use of the nose to separate the eyes. The vile jellies are trampled on, and Gloucester, now an "eyeless villain," must "smell / His way to Dover" (III.vii.93–94). In the end, there are compassionate servants to bring him "flax and whites of eggs" (106) for his bleeding face;

but only in Q. Whether or not this passage existed only in the Quarto, or in a lost archetype, it would seem that some hand, not willing to forgo absolute cruelty, removed it. In Peter Brook's unforgettable 1962 production, it was omitted, not on textual grounds, but because "a note of sympathy" was not wanted in this "Theatre of Cruelty."

The suitability of this play for such a theatre is well suggested in IV.i, when Edgar congratulates himself on having fallen so deep into misery that he can fall no further, at which point his eyeless father enters and Edgar understands that as long as we are capable of saying we are "at the worst" we have not yet reached that point: "the worst is not / So long as we can say, 'This is the worst'" (27–28). This might be the motto of the play, an unrelenting study in protraction; patience, which is continually recommended, is defeated by fortune, by nature, by the indifference of heaven to justice. Gloucester's famous observation "As flies to wanton boys are we to th' gods, / They kill us for their sport" (IV.i.36–37) is often contradicted by other characters, including Albany, Cordelia, and eventually Gloucester himself; but in the context it carries conviction. When father and son have met, the old countryman brings to the naked Tom "the best 'parel that I have" (49). He provides him with additions. There is something rather terrifying about the way in which, having created this nightmarish scenario, Shakespeare continues his clinical insistence on a linguistic subplot: "'Tis the time's plague, when madmen lead the blind"..."the best 'parel"..."naked fellow" ..."Poor Tom's a-cold"..."Bless thy sweet eyes, they bleed" (46–54). Much of the effect of *King Lear* seems to me to arise from its own unsparing cruelty, which can sometimes seem to be an almost sadistic attitude to the spectator, an attitude enhanced by the coolness with which we are manipulated, forced to deal with a pain that does not hinder the poet from playing his terrible games.

The strongest hints that goodness can survive these trials come from Kent and, more strikingly, Albany; easily put down by his wife, Goneril, in the early scenes, Albany can now tell her she is "not worth the dust which the rude wind / Blows in [her] face" (IV.ii.30–31). This fine speech reminds us of another Shakespearian style, the one in which an initial idea makes itself more complex in its expression:

> That nature which contemns its origin
> Cannot be bordered certain in itself.
> She that herself will sliver and disbranch
> From her material sap, perforce must wither,
> And come to deadly use.
> (32–36)

The sentiment is fairly clear in the first two lines; this is another excursion into the semantics of "nature"; and the second line carries the implication that Goneril's contempt for her progenitor must be a kind of self-contempt which she will be unable to control. The remaining lines move silently to the image of the family as a tree; in destroying her father she must destroy herself, here represented as vegetation ruining itself; the "deadly use" may be the equivalent of being burned.[11] Goneril finds this "foolish," and Albany follows her contemptuous remark with the famous speech that ends:

> If that the heavens do not their visible spirits
> Send quickly down to tame these vild offenses,
> It will come,
> Humanity trust perforce prey on itself,
> Like monsters of the deep.
>   (46–60)

These lines are missing from the Folio and the cut is attributed by some to "authorial revision."[12] The cut again diminishes any confidence that evil will be overthrown, and it certainly makes a difference to the character of Albany, but he is voicing a sentiment and a mood that are found throughout the play. A little later Lear takes Cordelia to be a visible "spirit" (IV.vii.48), another bleak, insane error. Albany is soon to say that the fate of Cornwall demonstrates that there are "justicers" above (IV.ii.79), another remark that is stronger in the Folio, where the earlier pessimistic utterance is cut; but the concurrent lamentation for Gloucester's eyes (72 twice, 81, 88, 96) restores the mood of despair and horror. There is something appalling about the thought of an author who will submit his characters and his audiences to such a test.

   IV.iii is the scene, already mentioned, that was cut from the Folio text. In IV.iv we see something of the Cordelia that is lost when the scene is excised. The lines "O dear father, / It is thy business that I go about" (23–24) inevitably recall Luke 2:49: "I must be about my Father's business." The echo is very bold, but probably without the allegorical significance sometimes attributed to it, for Lear is not God, and Cordelia could not save him, even if, absurdly, he would in that case have needed to be saved. Once again the effect is of a sort of authorial savagery; irony is too civilised a word for it.

   Regan and Oswald are again at their horrible worst in IV.v ("It was great ignorance, Gloucester's eyes being out, / To let him live" [9–101]). IV.vi is probably the cruellest and paradoxically the most beautiful scene in Shakespeare. Nowadays a comparison with Samuel Beckett seems inevitable. First there is the wild moment when Edgar leads his father to the edge of an imaginary cliff top and vividly describes to the blind man the nonexistent drop beneath him. Here the energy of the verse goes into imagining the scene: the birds are below them, and "Half way down / Hangs one that gathers sampire, dreadful trade!" (14–15). Once more one feels that this trick, using great poetic resource, is cruel; the scene must look either absurd or deeply shocking. One notices that Edgar insists on the "eyes' anguish" (6), on the act of casting down one's eyes, on "the deficient sight" (23), even as he is demonstrating what it is to see. He also contrives to mention his change of "garments" (10). The obsession with additions and with vision is not peculiar to Edgar; he is serving the play as a whole. When he takes on his second role as the man who comes to the aid of Gloucester on the beach, he again stresses the vastness of the cliff face: "Do but look up. / Alack, I have no eyes" (59–60). Edgar tells his father that he has been preserved from a devil by "the clearest gods" (73), a lie in the service of filial piety, followed by a plea for patience in circumstances that will make patience less and less useful or possible.

The hopelessness of patience is at once demonstrated when Gloucester encounters the mad King. The thread of sense in Lear's ravings is his memory of kingship ("they cannot touch me for coining" [83]) and forfeited power, along with the ingratitude of his daughters. The King, accustomed to being the agent of justice, now finds he is human, and since man's life is now known to be as cheap as beast's, he concludes that crimes such as lechery should not be punished. But the great speech turns into a disgusted rejection of sexuality, stronger even than Iago's. There follows an amazing passage in which the topics of the King's mortal body, the authority of kings, justice, nature, clothes (additions), lust, eyesight, nothingness, and apocalypse are all introduced.

> GLOU. O, let me kiss that hand!
> LEAR. Let me wipe it first, it smells of mortality.
> GLOU. O ruin'd piece of nature! This great world
> Shall so wear out to nought. Dost thou know me?
> LEAR. I remember thine eyes well enough. Dost thou squiny at me? No, do thy worst, blind Cupid, I'll not love. Read thou this challenge; mark but the penning of it.
> GLOU. Were all thy letters suns, I could not see.
> . . .
> LEAR. Read.
> GLOU. What, with the case of eyes?
> LEAR. O ho, are you there with me? No eyes in your head, nor money in your purse? Your eyes are in a heavy case, your purse in a light, yet you see how this world goes.
> GLOU. I see it feelingly.

LEAR. What, art mad? A man may see how this world goes with
no eyes. Look with thine ears ...
   (IV.vi.132–51)

Lear speaks prose and Gloucester verse. The prose is appropriate in the
same way as Poor Tom's; this is "matter and impertinency mix'd, / Reason in
madness!" (174–75), which also resembles in some ways the Fool's, for Lear
is now, with the privilege of madness, playing a fool's role, being "The natural
fool of fortune" (191). The dreadful emphasis on blindness is the prime mark
of Lear's madness and the play's cruelty, but nothing could be more sanely
calculated than this dialogue. At one point Lear takes over the talk, curses
authority in disgusted verse, and advises Gloucester, "Get thee glass eyes, /
And like a scurvy politician, seem / To see the things thou dost not" (170–
72)—after which he tries to remove his boots, and does remove his "natural"
crown of wildflowers and weeds; they have helped to cover the naked wretch.
Offering Gloucester his eyes, Lear counsels him to be patient, for the world is
so designed that endurance of sorrow is required from the moment of birth.

Gloucester, now acquainted with apparently inescapable demands
for patience, is willing to call the gods "ever-gentle" (217), a view of them
inconsistent with the arrival of Oswald, in search of Gloucester's "eyeless
head" (227). Edgar dispatches this "post unsanctified / Of murtherous lech-
ers" (274–75), and Gloucester ends the scene wishing he could be as mad
as the King:

   Better I were distract,
So should my thoughts be sever'd from my griefs,
And woes by wrong imaginations lose
The knowledge of themselves.
   (281–84)

This coiled sequence is characteristic of Shakespeare in this period: If I were
mad, I should be unaware of my huge sorrows—that is the simple sense,
but the idea grows complicated: thoughts and griefs are severed, as if one
could experience griefs as griefs without being aware of them. That idea is
then rephrased: "wrong imaginations" are crazy fantasies, which disable the
holder of them from knowing about his woes.

When we think of Shakespeare's imagination at its most incandescent,
as perhaps we do in the foregoing dialogue between Gloucester and Lear, it
is well to remember that the more normal business of playwriting can also
be intellectually challenging; indeed, it habitually is so in Shakespeare, from
Hamlet on. Cruelty is always a matter of a poet's calculation, like Cornwall's

or Regan's. Dr. Johnson said he could hardly bear to read *Lear* to its conclusion, and Keats spoke of having to *burn* through the "fierce dispute / Betwixt damnation and impassioned clay." Somewhere in our heads we have, as Johnson quite expressly had, a desire that some justice will prevail, that Cordelia should not be allowed "to perish in a just cause, contrary to the natural ideas of justice, to the hope of the reader, and, what is yet more strange, to the faith of the chronicles." For although several versions of Cordelia survive in chronicles and other poems, including the old *King Leir*, on which Shakespeare drew, no Cordelia except his is murdered. Johnson seems to be expressing dismay at a cruelty inflicted on him personally, and I think he is not alone in feeling like that. There is a cruelty in the writing that echoes the cruelty of the story, a terrible calculatedness that puts one in mind of Cornwall's and Regan's. Suffering has to be protracted and intensified, as it were, without end.

The Book of Job, which was so obviously in the playwright's mind, ends with Job's patience rewarded and his goods restored; Lear has no such restoration. It is in the imagery of torment proper to representations of the Last Judgement that we might find parallels;[13] they envisage an endlessness of torture and are often beautiful. It is the play itself that is an "image of that horror" (V.iii.264).

The King is captured and in friendly hands; the "kind gods" (IV.vii.13) appear to have relented; he sleeps and has been clothed in "fresh garments" (21). Music plays (but only in the Quarto), and in Shakespeare music is often a signal of peace and reconciliation, as in *The Merchant of Venice* and *Pericles*. Here it is meant to be restorative, and is followed by the blissful recognition scene of Lear and Cordelia. It has extraordinary beauty, resembling the recognition scene in *Pericles*, which is an exercise in that mode of a virtuosity that betokens long research. There is forgiveness and mutual benediction, and no real reason to think they are not final; but of course they are not.

In the midst of the happenings that are to bring disaster there occurs a brief scene[14] that is a miniature of the play's intentions. Edgar brings his father to a shelter and goes off to fight: "If ever I return to you again, / I'll bring you comfort" (V.ii.3–4). Nothing is heard except the sound of battle. Gloucester is alone and silent on the stage, using his ears as eyes, as Lear had told him to. Then Edmund returns, but with no comfort: "King Lear hath lost, he and his daughter ta'en" (6). He offers a hand, tries to drag his father away; but Gloucester has had enough: "No further, sir, a man may rot even here" (8). Edmund then speaks the famous lines "What, in ill thoughts again? Men must endure / Their going hence even as their coming hither, / Ripeness is all. Come on"—to which Gloucester replies, "And that's true too" (9–11).

Edmund uses the obvious point that his father must leave his refuge just as he arrived at it, to make a more general stoical point about death. "Ripeness is all," though much quoted, is not an unambiguous piece of wisdom; is the ripeness of time referred to, or the preparedness of the sufferer? Edmund wants to hurry away; his "Come on" may strike a note of impatience at the old man's "ill thoughts." And Gloucester, trailing off, seems to treat the observation as a mere platitude. What is certain is that he waited in the shadow of his tree for good, conclusive news and comfort and got neither. That is the way *Lear* works.

The King himself, a prisoner with his daughter (V.iii), now vainly imagines a happy ending, while Cordelia imagines they have reached the worst (4), not having heard Edgar's lesson in IV.i. Lear is given the kind of fantastic poetry Shakespeare had long known the trick of: Lear's thoughts are on the court he has lost; he cannot hope to have another, but he remembers, in a gently satirical way, the customary talk of courtiers: "Who loses and who wins; who's in, who's out"—only with this addition: he and his daughter will

> take upon 's the mystery of things
> As if we were God's spies; and we'll wear out,
> In a wall'd prison, packs and sects of great ones,
> That ebb and flow by th' moon.
>   (15–19)

Here the simplicity of the beginning ("We two alone will sing like birds in a cage") gives way to more compacted language, with its hints of a wider frame of discourse. And Lear continues with even more intellectual force and originality:

> He that parts us shall bring a brand from heaven,
> And fire us hence like foxes. Wipe thine eyes;
> The good-years shall devour them, flesh and fell
> Ere they shall make us weep!
>   (22–25)

The biblical image of foxes attacked or flushed out by fire (Judges 15:4–5) is combined with the obscure "the good-years" ("the good" in Q), never properly explained but seemingly a disease; the relations between these items are no longer those of demented association; the King is not fully sane, but no longer raving.

The rest of the story concerns Edmund's fatal move to kill Cordelia and the King, the love lives of Regan, Goneril, and Edmund, and the fuller emergence of Albany as the man in charge. Edmund dies at his brother's hand, Edgar tells his father's story, Goneril and Regan die, and with all this going on, everybody forgets about Lear and Cordelia until it is too late. The King enters with his daughter in his arms, thinking she is dead, wondering if she still breathes. Amidst the pathos of this ending the King complains of his eyes (V.iii.280), asks for a button to be undone so that he can once more shed an addition. Within these intensities the words "see" and "look" resound, the latter four times in Lear's last ten words.

This is the craftiest as well as the most tremendous of Shakespeare's tragedies. One can imagine awestruck colleagues wondering what the author, with three great and wholly distinct tragic achievements behind him, could possibly do next. There is a finality about *Lear*, it even instructs us to think that. But another great tragedy followed, and it was in its turn very different, though possessing, like its predecessors, its own dialect.

NOTES

1. The *King Lear* familiar to most of us is an amalgam of the first Quarto, Q1 (1608), and the Folio, F (1623), with some hints from the second Quarto, Q2 (1619, falsely dated 1608). Q1 is a poor text, careless, contaminated, and generally prone to error; F, partly dependent on Q1 and Q2, is also faulty. At present there is a tide of opinion in favour of the view that F, based on a theatrical document, perhaps a prompt-book, incorporates revisions from Shakespeare's hand. Q contains about 288 lines or part-lines not in F, including the whole of IV.iii; F includes 133 lines or part-lines not in Q1. These editorial problems occasionally have an effect on the responses of general readers; for example, the omission of IV.iii, the Gentleman's description of her struggle with emotion, her tears "as pearls from diamonds dropp'd" (IV.iii.22Q), can surely change our view of Cordelia. Some changes and omissions were apparently made with the object of muffling the idea that Cordelia headed a French invasion of Britain. Others have a quite marked effect on our response to other characters (Lear, Albany, the Fool, and Goneril). The grim closing lines of the play are spoken by Albany in Q and by Edgar in F.

Modern editors, whether or not they favour the theory that there are two distinct versions of the play, tend to choose the Folio as copy-text. Evans, in *The Riverside Shakespeare*, bases his text on F without subscribing to the theory. Halio (Cambridge, 1992) chooses F because he believes in it. The Oxford editors, confident that there are two distinct states, print Q1 and F separately. Anybody interested in scrutinising the differences between the two may consult the parallel texts in Michael Warren, ed., *The Complete Lear; 1608–1623* (1989), or *The Parallel King Lear, 1608, 1623* (1989), or, more accessibly, more cheaply, and by and large more persuasively, in René Weis, *King Lear: A Parallel Text Edition* (1993).

2. I proposed this view, with far less documentation and far more cursory arguments, in "Disintegration Once More," British Academy Shakespeare Lecture, *Proceedings of the British Academy* (1994), pp. 84, 93–111. The authority of the Oxford editors is opposed to the idea of a common archetype for Q1 and F. But see Weis on this point.

3. See also, on this scene and on many other points, Stanley Cavell's penetrating essay "The Avoidance of Love," in *Disowning Knowledge* (1987).

4. Ernst Curtius, *European Literature in the Latin Middle Ages* (1953), pp. 162–66.

5. This is the F reading; Q has "Nothing, my lord, / How! Nothing can come of nothing; speak again." We have either a revision in F or an omission in Q. The word "nothing" is to become a motif in the play, and so it is given heavy emphasis here and again at line 245: "Nothing. I have sworn . . ." In a rather similar way, the words "dearer than eyesight" are given in Regan's oration as an early warning of another powerful motif. It is very soon repeated in the exchange between Lear and Kent ("Out of my sight! / See better, Lear, and let me still remain / The true blank of thine eye" [157–59]). I have often noted the tendency of the mature Shakespeare to allow a word or set of words to occur almost obsessively: in this play there is an awful deliberation about the practice, though the full effect cannot of course be felt in the early scenes. A fine full-length study of repeated figures, "families of words and their functioning," in *King Lear* is R. B. Heilman, *This Great Stage* (1948, 1963). Heilman is particularly good on the imagery of eyes and sight.

6. Enid Welsford, *The Fool: His Social and Literary History* (1935, 1968), p. 265.

7. The connection with Erasmus is revealed in a lecture by Dominic Baker-Smith, "Counsel and Caprice: Seneca at the Tudor Court" (1999), p. 12.

8. The words "Lear's shadow" are spoken by Lear in Q and by the Fool in F.

9. "Natural" here means, primarily, "dutiful to his father," but the sense of "natural = bastard" is ironically present. The idea of nature is, in *King Lear*, buffeted by ironies: invoked by Edmund as the goddess of natural sons, by Lear as the corrupter of fertility, and as a norm of conduct and temperament he is about to desert. According to Kent, "Nature disclaims" the foppish Oswald (II.ii.54–55); to Cornwall Kent's bluntness shows him to be acting a part not proper to his "nature" (98), which here means something like his servile place. More often the state of nature is what Edgar imitates when he takes "the basest and most poorest shape / That ever penury, in contempt of man, / Brought near to beast" (II.iii.7–9). Another way he expresses this aim is to say, "Edgar I nothing am" (21).

10. I don't know if anybody has noticed the resemblance between Tom's lines—"Let not the creaking of shoes nor the rustling of silks betray thy poor heart to woman" (94–96)—and this couplet from Donne's "Elegy IV": "I taught my silks their whistling to forbear, / Even my opprest shoes dumb and silent were." The furtive lover is given away by his perfume, and perfume is mentioned in Lear's pitying reply. The poem was written earlier than *King Lear*; but I suppose it cannot be thought very likely that Shakespeare had read it in manuscript.

11. René Weis sees a reference to Hebrews 6:8; "But that which beareth thorns and briars is rejected, and is nigh unto cursing, whose end is to be burnt" (p. 224).

12. *King Lear*, ed. Jay L. Halio (New Cambridge edition, 1992), p. 272. Halio does not print the missing lines, even in square brackets, in his main text.

13. English churches often had Doomsday paintings over the chancery arch. There is such a painting in the Guild Chapel at Stratford. For more details about such paintings, their defacement and recovery, see Mary Lascelles, "*King Lear* and Doomsday," in K. Muir and S. Wells, eds., *Aspects of King Lear* (1982), pp. 55–65.

14. See above, p. 11, in my discussion of Shakespeare's silences.

ROBERT LANIER REID

Lear's Three Shamings

The face is the trace of the Other.... [One] cannot say whether this Other
... is another person whom I can look in the face or who can stare at me,
... or my ancestors for whom there is no representation, to so great an
extent does my debt to them constitute my very self, ... or *God*.... or *an
empty place.*

Paul Ricoeur, Oneself as Another

I colde also speake as ye do: (but wolde God your soule were in my soules
stead).... I wolde aswage *your sorowe.*

Job 16.4–5

Despite *King Lear's* impressive enlargement of the Oedipus-Job-every-
man myth of human sufferance,[1] critics as astute as A. C. Bradley and
Emrys Jones find its plot structure lacking. They blame the growing madness and passivity of the king (inadequately causing the action, even retard-
ing it in half-mad reverie) as well as the double plot that further diffuses
Lear's agency.[2] For Susan Snyder and Stephen Booth, the audience's shock
at watching Lear's loss of control and of certitude is compounded by deliberate undoings of plot: Shakespeare's persistent miscues, reversing generic
expectations and denying conventional closure, enforce a moral, teleological
indeterminacy.[3]

From *Shakespeare's Tragic Form: Spirit in the Wheel*, pp. 123–44, 165–69. Copyright © 2000
by Associated University Presses.

Yet each of these unsettling features—the protagonist's growing "passivity" and "madness," the various splittings of character and of plot, and the subversion of expectations—has a paradoxical complexity that subsumes the imputed weaknesses into a larger, stronger vision of what it means to be human. Lear is engaged in what Ernest Becker describes as the definitive human quest, the "*causa sui* project." Through the illusion of self-creation Lear asserts his absolute Godlike being and potency against the ultimate human anxiety, the "terror of death," dissolving his powers into non-being, nothingness.[4]

In this struggle against mortality Lear is far from passive: he never ceases to exhibit tremendously willful self-assertion; and—even more than Oedipus, Job, and Everyman—he displays considerable powers of self-obstruction. Lear is a cynosure of repression and all its subordinate defenses. Surely Elton and Berger are right to note the aggressiveness of Lear's apparent yieldings.[5] Each withdrawal (from kingship, from loving bonds, from facing malice) is actively and proudly self-enforced, not just the feeble reactions of a fading old man to the commands of selfish children.

Equally deceptive is Lear's "madness." As he, even more than Edgar and the other exiles, is stripped of civilization's comforting illusions, exposing him to bodily impotence and communal shame, and as he simultaneously sees the reality of human bonding and the pervasiveness of inequity, he begins to demonstrate the indefinition of reason, its alliance with an insightful mode of madness.

Paradox likewise informs *King Lear*'s division of characters into mirroring and conflicting quests. Tragedy's usual focus on a single protagonist (or a single loving couple) here divides into planes of increasing complexity. Many commentators assume that Lear's executive power is utterly displaced by that of Goneril, Regan, their spouses and henchmen, and eventually Edmund; yet their opportunistic and divisive sway does not seriously challenge Lear's centrality since they do not validate their authority. Never do they command the audience's respect, never do they demonstrate true sovereignty—as is evident in their impulsive indictment and blinding of Gloucester and their final hasty self-destruction. Second, Lear's agon is more seriously displaced, though only intermittently, by the suffering consciousness of Edgar and Gloucester; yet ultimately their drama reinforces that of Lear, both as a mirroring analogue and as an intensely realized drama of Otherness by which Lear can resolve his own crisis of identity and selfhood. The third and subtlest form of character-diversification involves Cordelia, who in her silent goodness, her presence-heightened-through-banishment, truly displaces Lear's moral and spiritual authority as sovereign. Instead of diffusing the dramaturgical focus, however, all three modes of splitting/displacement contribute to the play's main action—its revelation of human nature's liability to dispersal and consequent need of communion. For Lear and the audience each alternate drama clarifies the central mystery of monarchy: *the king's two* (or perhaps three) *bodies*. Since the vicious characters who oppose Lear are hollow and envious, and since the compassionate characters (whose moral goodness and suffering might challenge Lear's moral hegemony) all seek to restore and sustain his authority, all three levels of displacement ultimately affirm Lear's central habitation of the problematic role of sovereign.

Similar paradox shapes the play's dramaturgical form. Its cycles of action subtly contain the anxiety of generic reversals by disclosing a deeper plan, a deeper purpose; for the plot of *King Lear* exhibits the same exacting symmetry that informs all Shakespeare's mature plays, a pattern closely resembling that of *Macbeth*. In both tragedies an evolving crisis of kingship and of psyche occurs in three cycles of action: first, acts 1–2, with 2 reversing the arc of 1; next act 3, an action-reaction within itself; and finally acts 4–5, with 5 reversing the arc of 4.[6] Using the same pattern, these plays show obverse sides of human tragedy: the two monarchic crises, springing from Lear's abdication and Macbeth's usurpation, have contrary effects on their souls.

The complementarity of *King Lear* and *Macbeth* is Shakespeare's culminating meditation on this central theme. In each history tetrad he had depicted the contrary monarchic crises in causal conjunction: in the first series, the childish abdication of Henry VI invites Richard III's ruthless usurpation; in the more complex second series, Richard II, though weak and self-indulgent, matures through deposition, as does the usurper Bolingbroke through assuming the tasks of rule. Abdicator and usurper reach full complexity in King Lear and Macbeth: each fully *causes* the personal/monarchic tragedy; and each, despite madness and repression, is conscience-struck by his mistakes.

In both plays, especially *King Lear*, the assertion of monarchic power is impelled by personal relationship, making Lear seem closer to the family romance of Oedipus than to the God-centered dialogues of Prometheus, Job, and Everyman; yet for Lear, as for Hamlet and Prospero, human relationship becomes a mirror and impetus for the relation with divinity.[7] Thus in *King Lear*, as in *Macbeth*, an epiphanic (or anti-epiphany) human encounter serves as a central axis for each of the three cycles of action. Lear undergoes increasingly illuminative confrontations with the "fiend" Goneril (1.4); with the "spirit" Poor Tom (3.4); and with the "soul in bliss" Cordelia (4.7). Contrarily, in the three powerful scenes involving the "spirit"-possessed Lady Macbeth (1.7), Banquo's ghost (3.4), and Macduff's response to his family's slaughter (4.3), Macbeth increasingly evades epiphany. By having Macbeth command but not join the execution of Macduff's family, and having him assiduously avoid Macduff himself as long as possible, Shakespeare distinctly alters the chronicles (which say that Macbeth led the force to Macduff's castle and only killed the family as an afterthought—in frustration at Macduff's absence).

Each of these encounters has been treated as a crux, especially the three scenes in *King Lear* Gary Taylor explicates the deep significance of Lear's clash with Goneril (1.4) in *To Analyze Delight*.[8] The central import of Lear's meeting with Tom (3.4), axis of the play, is often noted, for example, by Robert Heilman and Maynard Mack.[9] Lear's reunion with Cordelia (4.7) is commonly viewed as Lear's (and the play's) goal, the essential moment of accession to self-knowledge.[10] Though intensely painful, Lear's epiphanies expand into fuller vision; Macbeth's anti-epiphanies contract into evasion.

In each play the three cycles reverse the sequence of metapsychic development (whether we borrow the terminology of Ego Psychology, Object Relations Psychology, or Self Psychology): building on each other, the three sequences enforce a cathartic regression to primal selfhood. These complementary tragedies draw us back to the two "archaic relational" scenes: in *King Lear* the "nurturant scenario," where anticipated loss of a caring other "awakens the infant to its own dependence, helplessness, and impotent rage"; in *Macbeth* the "antagonistic scenario," where "one is either predator or prey, ... master or slave."[11] In these contrary psychic processes the protagonists inversely apprehend the spirit world as a direct outgrowth of the recovery or loss of human kinship. Macbeth increasingly seeks and reifies the phantasmic witches, becoming fiendish himself as he massacres loving innocents; Lear, at first obsessed like Tom with "fiends" he has helped to create, turns from their grotesque reality to Cordelia as a "soul in bliss." Thus Macbeth's three murders systematically deconstruct the three cathexes of human identity; Lear's three self-mortifying experiences reestablish those three basic bondings of human, and sovereign, selfhood. Having traced the 2–1–2 pattern of devolution in *Macbeth*, we shall now observe the same pattern in *King Lear* but with inverse psychogenesis and outcome.

Seeing Goneril: Superego Disabled by False Sublimation

Whereas Macbeth in his initial two-act cycle usurps authority, Lear in acts 1–2 awkwardly relinquishes it. In *King Lear* this cycle opens with the long scene (310 lines) in which Lear asserts godlike power, humiliating and banishing Cordelia and Kent for refusing to confer idolatrous flattery; and it concludes with a closely analogous degenerating ritual of 311 lines (2.4) in which Lear enforces his own humiliation and exile.

Near the end of this two-act sequence Kent and the Fool draw attention to Fortune's ironic cycling. In *Fortune and Elizabethan Tragedy* Frederick Kiefer notes that "in no other of Shakespeare's plays do characters invoke

Fortune so insistently," especially "at pivotal points in the action"[12]—that is, near the end of each completed turning. Kent's Stoic, proto-Christian view—"Smile, . . . turn thy wheel" (2.2.175–76)—allows for wisdom through sufferance: "Nothing almost sees miracles but misery" (165–69). The Fool stresses the more humbling lesson of material needs and humankind's willful role in shaping Fortune's cycle (2.4.70–73).

And Lear does shape it. He is Shakespeare's most complex version of the Abdicating King, whose evasion of rule incurs moral decay, usurpation, and civil butchery. Unlike earlier portraits of the withdrawing monarch (meek Henry VI in the first tetralogy of history plays, diffident Richard II in the second), Lear aggressively directs his abdication-deposition and helps enforce each subsequent cycle of shaming. Elton rightly contrasts Leir's passivity in the source-play with Lear's active role.[13] Lear's aggressive abdication parallels Hamlet's occluded kingship and delayed revenge, and Prospero's initial evasion of rule. All three, though capable of extraordinary agency, incline to skeptical detachment and, like Vincentio in *Measure for Measure*, suggestively mirror the *deus absconditas* of Reformation controversy. Yet of all Shakespearean protagonists, Lear experiences the fullest passion, raises the most disturbing questions, dominates plot and audience with the greatest psychic energy, and most fully exemplifies sovereignty—his mad reveries evoking a lifetime of authority and proud accomplishment. It is thus inaccurate to call him passive. A "repetition compulsion" drives Lear's three acts of self-abasement no less than Macbeth's three murders.[14]

Shakespeare's plot structure highlights the centerpiece:[15] in each of Lear's shamings, Fortune's wheel turns on a central encounter. The axis for the initial two-act cycle is his fiery meeting with Goneril near the end of act 1, a scene looking back to his disowning of Cordelia and forward to his total emasculation by the older daughters. When Goneril rebukes Lear's governance and withdraws half of his hundred knights, he endures his first shameful anagnorisis, an anti-epiphany in which the disclosure of Goneril's consummate evil inverts his mood, self-image, and actions. His explosive reaction, a defensive evasion of the distasteful mirror-image of his own selfish will, shivers the glass of his personal, parental, and sovereign identity; and the recoil draws Lear to the cycle's conclusion, the protracted humiliation at the end of act 2.

The face-off with Goneril closely resembles Macbeth's fiery confrontation with Lady Macbeth at the same central turning point of the two-act cycle that begins that play. Each fierce virago, reflecting the protagonist's pitiless urges, is portrayed as a demonic spirit. Lear calls Goneril a "marble-hearted fend, / More hideous when thou show'st thee in a child / Than the sea monster!" (1.4.257–59).[16] Albany also depicts Goneril as a monstrous fiend, stressing that in turning against her parent she commits herself to a disturbing uncertainty principle, unaware of itself and thus losing true being: "That nature which contemns its origin / Cannot be bordered certain. . . . / Like monsters of the deep. . . . / See thyself, devil!" (4.2.33–34, 51, 60–62). Like Lady Macbeth's fiendish threat of infanticide (1.7.55–59), Goneril's antimaternity draws from Seneca's *Medea*.[17] In both tragedies the abuse of Authority in acts 1–2 is portrayed as an exclusively male dominion: each protagonist suppresses in himself the "female" component of maternal nurture, the "mother" (*King Lear* 2.4.55–57)[18] and "the milk of human kindness" (*Macbeth* 1.5.17); and this self-reduction is enforced through a Medea-figure whom he has helped to create and who mirrors his own willful obduracy.

Though both Lear and Macbeth have partly elicited and sponsored this demonism, their responses are diametrically opposed: Macbeth embraces his spouse's regicidal lust; Lear is repulsed by Goneril's cold, measured lovelessness. The same galling infertility he invokes Goneril ("Into her womb convey sterility; / Dry up in her the organs of" increase," 1.4.277–78) is voluntarily assumed by Lady Macbeth ("Stop up th' access and passage of remorse, / . . . take my milk for gall," 1.5.43–48). The unveiling of Goneril's and of Lady Macbeth's life-denying *weltlust*, mirroring the dark power-hunger of Lear and Macbeth, serves as pivotal experience for the cycle of self-discovery, passional release, and inner change in acts 1–2.

This initial two-act sequence is in each play dominated by the mechanism of *sublimation*, the most refined ego-function in the service of superego. Hans Loewald and Heinz Kohut have explained sublimation's important role in forming superego or conscience (internalized parental authority); and they have also stressed its synthesizing of gender roles into a comprehensive androgynous adulthood, while also learning to resist the lures to false images of what Kohut calls the "grandiose self."[19] The soul's aim in sublimation is self-aggrandizement, seeking through abstraction and spiritualization to achieve the "be-all and end-all"—genuine sovereignty, androgynous wholeness, omnipotence and immortality. The Macbeths' thrilling soliloquies in acts 1–2 voice their aspiration for such "greatness," though without comprehending its nature. Prior to murdering Duncan the Macbeths refer seventeen tunes to the "greatness," promised by the Weird sisters, for which they yearn. The long opening ritual of *King Lear* demonstrates Lear's assumption that he already possesses, in Godlike fullness, such greatness, which the love-test is designed to confirm. In keeping with the mythic content of the love-test,[20] Lear's ritual demands lavish flattery to affirm his sovereign magnanimity (and implicitly, his immortality): "Which of you . . . doth love us most?" The command to praise proves a devastating test for monarchic absolutism as well as for proud superego: it deflates the "great image of authority" (4.6.158), the integrity of state and self-hood, as effectively as Macbeth's murder of Duncan. Paul Ricoeur explains the signal role of hyperbole in efforts to attain "absolute Otherness" through "Elevation" and "Exteriority," producing an utter breakdown in relationship.[21] Those who do evil, says Boethius, "cease not merely to be powerful, but simply to be.... For that is, which keeps its order and preserves its nature":

> Those lofty kings you see seated high on thrones, ...
> Threatening with visage stern ...—
> If a man strip from those proud kings the cloak of their empty splendour,
> At once he will see these lords within bear closely bound chains;
> ... anger whips the mind as a whirlwind.[22]

Lear's anger sweeps hire from all housing and official community, revealing his "mind-forg'd manacles" as well as the hollowness of his love-ritual. Disowning all responsibility for relationship, all truthful mirroring by others, he ceases "not merely to be powerful, but simply to be": "Who is it that can tell me who I am?" (1.4.227). Contrary to Macbeth's violent but furtive claimancy, however, Lear's public shaming exposes him to a painful anger which is cleansing and restorative.

Seeing Poor Tom: Reconstituting Ego by Projection

The superego's cyclic loss of authority in acts 1–2 leads to the ego's cyclic loss of rational control in act 3, a sequence neatly demarcated by a repeated gesture. *King Lear*'s third act is framed on each side by a slamming door: at each juncture an aged father is expelled but with increase in savagery ("Shut up your doors, my lord," 2.4.310; "Go thrust him out at gates," 3.7.95). Similarly, *Macbeth*'s third act is framed on each side by a prayer for holy succor (2.4.41, 3.6.46–51). In each play this gesture helps to close the cycle of acts 1–2 (Lear's loss of authority, Macbeth's grasp of it), and then the cycle of act 3 (Lear's psychic splitting on the heath, Macbeth's at the banquet).

Act 3 is also set apart by Lear's exposure to contrary characters and setting, outcasts on a barren heath.[23] Unlike the courtly affairs of acts 1–2 which build on elaborate rituals of privilege, the more primitive events of act 3 are dominated by a storm, matched by the exiles' mental anguish. Fortune (in its intensest form as "tempest")[24] wheels on a deeper level as Lear's wits "begin to turn" (3.2.67). Again the cycle opens with Lear assuming Godlike power, commanding the storm to destroy sinners, and Gloucester plotting war against the new order; and it ends, like each of the cycles, with both

fathers' deepened impotence: Lear's madness and sleep, Gloucester's blindness and exile.

The axis for this second cycle of psychic divestiture is the meeting with
Tom, combining Lear's neglect and Edgar's embodiment of spiritual poverty.
Edgar's riveting enactment serves as peripety for Lear's change in act 3: preceded by Lear's care for the suffering Fool and "poor naked wretches," Tom's
naked crying "spirit" appears almost magically, as if called forth (or projected)
by Lear's evolving consciousness of need. In this central confrontation the two
plots meet and join, showing how intrinsic is doubleness of plot to the play's
meaning—not only providing complementary analogues of self-abasement
but promoting selfhood through relational awareness: *oneself as another.*

Again Lear's epiphany of human Otherness is shown as a supernatural ontology: Tom, whom the Fool perceives as a vexed "spirit" (3.4.39, 42), is
haunted by "fiends," though unlike Goneril he fears them and tries to "defy"
them (3.4.45, 51, 60, 79, 97, 114, 130, 139, 157; 3.6.8, 17, 29). In act 4, after a
brief reprise of such fantasies on becoming Gloucester's guide (4.1.57), Edgar
disengages from demonism, spatially distancing it on the cliff of pride, and
exaggerating it into farce: "his eyes / Were two full moons; he had a thousand
noses, / Horns whelked and waved like the enridged sea" (4.6.69–72). No viewer,
however, can easily judge the genuineness of Edgar's obsession with demons.

By echoing Harsnett's exposure of fraudulent exorcisms, Edgar's ghoul-
babble seems to parody Gloucester's superstitious credulity; moreover, it
stands in sharp contrast to the staged reality of Macbeth's witches.[25] Yet the
strenuousness of Edgar's performance makes it more than hoax: "Though we
may not believe literally in the devils with outlandish names . . . Flibbertigibbet, Smulkin, Modo and Mahu," still "Poor Tom's rhapsodies bring an inti-
macy with them and with the natural world through which he is driven."[26]
For Edgar, each aspect of otherness (his body, his social connections, his conscience) has become a genuine hellish torment, until Lear's anguish moves
Edgar to abandon his nightmarish role in an aside—"My tears begin to take
his part so much / They mar my counterfeiting" (59–60)—and then to emerge
fully as chorus (102–15). Edgar-as-Tom epitomizes the "poor player" who
recurs at the heart of Shakespeare's vision, where duplicity and authenticity
persistently mingle. Like Hamlet's use of players to test the veracity of the
supernatural, Edgar's survivalist role-playing does not discredit his genuineness, as Lear attests: "Thou art the thing itself." The allusions to Harsnett,
instead of demystifying God, providence, and the spirit world, affirm the
potent immanence of spirit: humankind's genuine capacity to fashion itself as
deluded fiend, its need of charity to become *imago Dei.*

Nor are the fiends mere fancy. As Gulstad notes, Lear's fantasy-trial of
his daughters (3.6) is encoded as witch-trial;[27] and Edgar's persecution fear is

reified, starkly contextualized when, at the cycle's end (3.7), Goneril, Regan, and Cornwall "rash boarish fangs" in Gloucester's flesh. The savage blinding, no less than Iago's treachery and Macbeth's blood lust, suggests cloven feet, demons incarnate. The explicit witchcraft of *Macbeth* generalizes the fiendish behavior in all three plays.

Each protagonist's failure to sublimate or exalt himself as omnipotent parent or superego in acts 1–2 gives way to a more primitive functioning in the central cycle, where *projection* accommodates ego's doublings.[28] Macbeth's bloody assertion of omnipotence in acts 1–2 gives way in act 3 to envious rivalry with peers, evoking the mangled Banquo as his double. Lear's failed fantasy of omnipotence in acts 1–2 gives way in act 3 to a contrary form of splitting, empathetically projecting himself in victims: the shivering Fool, naked wretches, and especially Poor Tom. The same psychic division that makes Macbeth waver between public praise and secret murder of his noble double makes Lear waver between indicting his proud children and exalting his wretched double, Tom. Such projective splitting—crucial to the secondary stage of self-composition in early childhood—serves contrary ends in Macbeth's and Lear's central phase. Macbeth's sadistic projections enforce self-alienation; Lear's empathetic projections begin to restore sovereign selfhood.

Some recent critics question Lear's moral probity in act 3, viewing his identification with Tom as irresponsible self-obsession ("Did'st thou give all to thy daughters, and art thou come to this?" 3.4.46–47). According to Berger, Lear's sympathy for "poor naked wretches" vanishes at the sight of an actual wretch. Leggatt sees Lear "losing touch with literal reality—and losing his selflessness as well"; "his pity for Tom is all too obviously a projection of his pity for himself." With Dollimore they see Lear, until the reunion with Cordelia, driven by lunacy and self-concern, generally ignoring his auditors.[29]

I would offer a more optimistic, at least more ambivalent, reading of this central sequence. First, that Lear's pity springs from self-pity is only natural: there is no shame in "loving one's neighbor as one loves oneself." From Augustine to Kohut, healthy self-love is the key to ethics and psychological well-being.[30] Self-love may sponsor blind exercise of power as in the initial love-test, but also genuine (though confused and deflected) sympathy as in the meeting with Poor Tom, and meek gratitude as in the reunion with Cordelia. As Lear learns, self love may be distorted by excessive privilege and commodities (as also by their absence, wretched poverty). Though act 3 begins with an inner storm of wounded pride and exclusive self-love, these motives form a tension with shame and compassion, beginning with sympathy for the shivering Fool. Lear in his "madness" instinctively extends charity, partly recovering the sovereign nature that originally drew the devoted loyalty of Cordelia, the Fool, Kent, Gloucester, Edgar, and other "gentlemen." Their devotion, especially their pursuit of the king in his madness, seems more than habitual servitude. The "authority" in Lear's countenance which Kent "would fain call master" implies not merely Lear's anointed sovereignty but his effective exercise of that power (1.4.27–30). Berger faults both Lear and his supporters for subverting love;[31] yet plain-speaking Kent and Cordelia do not simply antagonize Lear but express admiration for his lifetime of fatherly/kingly guidance (1.1.95–98, 139–42), and the suffering caused by Lear's shame and compassion, though crude and incomplete, helps bind him and the other exiles into a fellowship of the heath.

Lear's initial response to Poor Tom ("Has his daughters brought him to this pass?" 3.4.48–49, 62–64, 66–67, 69–72), though affirming Lear's sovereign habit of empathy, does indeed neglect the beggar as an *other*; and this self-indulgence seems an empathetic response to the beggar's initial self-pitying speeches (45–47, 50–61). Then comes Lear's jolting sense of responsibility for "begetting" (congenitally and morally) his unkind daughters:

> Is it the fashion that discarded fathers
> Should have thus little mercy on their flesh?
> Judicious punishment! 'Twas this flesh begot
> Those pelican daughters.
>   (3.4.71–74)

This self-judgment begins to draw Lear out of himself, leading him to elicit the beggar's identity as an other: "What hast *thou* been?" (83). Then, in a lengthy confession of sins, Tom responds to Lear in kind: whereas his first catalogue was self-pitying, blaming his vexations on the "foul fiend" (45–62), this one is self judging, listing his vices to forswear them, urging others to avoid sin and "defy" the fiend. Most readers have viewed this extraordinarily long and colorful catalogue of sins, like the pretense of demon-possession, as part of a tour-de-force performance, a disclosure purely theatrical, having nothing to do with Edgar's real life, his moral and psychological self. But consider what a deeper dimension the play assumes if we take the list, at least in part, as Edgar's genuine confession. Has Edgar (like Prince Hal or, more to the point, like the promiscuous Gloucester) led a self-indulgent life of privilege? This reading would give considerably more weight to Edmund's resentment of his "legitimate" half brother. Tom's lengthy self indictment provokes Lear's most self judging remark: "Thou art the thing itself. . . . / Off, off, you lendings!" (100–108). These initial interactions of king and beggar suggest neither mere insanity nor mere selfishness but a significant give-and-take, a complex form of compassion, which deepens in the next sequence.

Gloucester's sudden appearance, provoking Edgar to imagine a cruel fiend who "hurts the poor creature of earth," stresses anew humankind's vulnerability to abuse. In this sequence, however, Gloucester's capacity to reject his child, and the group's capacity to reject Poor Tom, is abated, especially through the influence of Lear's "madness." As Lear continues his "other-directed" frame of mind ("What's he?"), the group erupts into a torrent of identity questions, emphasizing both their unbonded strangeness and their anxious desire to relate:

> *Lear.* What's he?
> *Kent.* Who's there? What is't you seek?
> *Gloucester.* What are you there? Your names?
> (3.4.125–27)

Fearful of being identified by his father, Edgar in his role-playing relapses into self-pity, listing Tom's disgusting habits and society's efforts to punish and marginalize him (128–39):

> Poor Tom . . . that in the fury of his heart, when the foul fiend rages, eats cow dung for salads, that eats the dead rat and the ditch dog, drinks the green mantle of the standing pool; who is whipped from tithing to tithing and stock-punished and imprisoned.
> (3.4.128–34)

Edgar's shift from impersonal to personal pronoun ("that . . . that . . . who . . .") enforces his identity-shift from a bestial predator on vile lower beings to a human who is himself despised by those pious betters who "tithe." Gloucester, one of the self-righteous, would deny the beggar their fellowship ("What, hath your grace no better company?"), and he ignores the beggar's cry, "Poor Tom's a-cold." But Lear refuses refuge without his new acquaintance, insisting that Tom be included in Gloucester's charity: "Come, let's in all"; "With him! I will keep still with my philosopher" (3.4.178–80).

A major sign of Lear's compassion is his addressing the almost-naked, ranting beggar as "noble philosopher" and "learned Theban." Lear's conceit is more than insane confusion, or a selfish enhancing of his own status by raising Tom's. Playing on a Boethian subtext, Shakespeare revises the dream-vision of Lady Philosophy's splendor and measured eloquence into the vulgar reality of a mad-dog Cynic: Lear has good grounds for comparing Tom with the legendary Diogenes (whose contempt for proud artifice led him to wear a blanket and speak bluntly) and his follower Crates (who threw his wealth into the sea and sharply criticized lustful hearts).[32] This demeaning vision of "Philosophy" likewise plays on an Erasmian subtext, reflecting Renaissance sages' praise of folly.[33] It is not just Tom's poverty but his confessional candor, comparable to the Cynics' self-annihilative zeal, that impresses the guilty Lear. His madness thus seems increasingly purposive, and far from passive.

While Lear admires such aggressive, even abusive, self-stripping, his calling Tom "philosopher" also has a constructive purpose: Lear, as part of his subconscious conflictual motives in act 3, seeks to establish the beggar's dignity and worth, making him acceptable to Gloucester and the others, as well as to the beggar himself. Gloucester, while trying to ingratiate himself to Lear in self-pitying terms, treats Tom as a disposable nothing (3.4.140–79); and though Kent-as-Caius assists in persuading Gloucester to accept the beggar, he too (Edgar later recalls) "having seen me in my worst estate, / Shunned my abhorred society" (5.3.213–14). In reaction to their snubbing, Lear addresses the Bethlehem pauper as his better, someone in touch with life's deepest truths. His attributing worth and wisdom to the beggar, a central instance of "reason in madness," carries both symbolic import and characterological impact: it helps Edgar to sever himself from victimization fantasies, and it challenges the caste-bound mindset of Lear's former courtiers. Though Lear does not offer money or clothing (a flaw to Marxist critics),[34] his wish to extend sapient fellowship to Tom serves as catalyst for Gloucester's later generosity (4.1.31–76).

Such charitable communality is hard-won, especially for Tom, who concludes the scene with the bitter vision of a hero who uses the grandiosity of his proud height, his "dark tower," to devour others:

> Child Rowland to the dark tower came;
> His word was still, "Fie, foh, and fum,
> I smell the blood of a British man."
>   (3.4.181–83)

He is a "child" not just as a candidate for knighthood but, like the protagonists of *King Lear*, as the privileged person who is in fact immature, self-obsessed, and fearfully primitive.

In scene 6 Lear at first seeks to consummate the vengeful fantasy that began scenes 2 and 4: "To have a thousand with red burning spits / Come hizzing in upon 'em" (3.6.15–16). Lear begins to arraign his daughters as demons, a psychic hell which Tom fears: "Frateretto calls me ..."; "The foul fiend bites my back" (3.6.6, 16). But as in scenes 2 and 4, Lear's empathetic impulse gains ascendancy. He empowers the wretched exiles as justicers, and they play along, comforting and enabling him to voice rage without acting on it. Lear's fantasy-trial ends not with an auto-da-fé of burning witches but with images that gently domesticate their identity as he guiltily displaces them in the dock: "The little dogs and all, / Tray, Blanch, and Sweetheart, see, they bark at me" (3.6.61–62); yet he still evades culpability by projecting his power-hunger on others: "Is there any cause in nature that makes these proud hearts?" (3.6.76–77).

To assist Lear's fantasy and "working-through," Edgar—as if sensing his psychic impact on Lear through transference—abandons his demon-obsessed role: "Let us deal justly" (3.6.40). He sings a ballad to solace Lear "Sleepest or wakest thou, jolly shepherd? . . ." (3.6.41–44) and answers Lear's desperate sadness with a lengthy exorcism of dogs, thus dispelling his own vicious familiars and self-abusive impulses. Lear is enabled to lull his tempestuous conscience ("Make no noise"), veil his pride ("Draw the curtains"), and defer his narcissistic appetites ("We'll go to supper i' the morning" (3.6.82–83). Lear's and Gloucester's judgmental proceedings thus turn back upon themselves. Their attempts to enforce trials of others are transformed into a process of self-discovery through the nurture of exiles and servants, who comfort Lear and carry him from danger, defend Gloucester and tend his wounds—enabling both fathers to turn inward and confront conscience.

Edgar-as-Tom is often described as choric and functional, without Lear's psychic depth, self-consciousness, and capacity for self-discovery; but minimizing Edgar's character, which is richly complex as he undergoes profound psychic change, eviscerates a major component of the play. Near the heart of *King Lear* is the deep psychological exchange transacted between Lear and the protagonists of the mirror plot. The form of *King Lear* cannot be understood without acknowledging the importance of the actions of Gloucester and his sons, both as a suggestive analogue for Lear and his daughters, and as a central factor in Lear's self-discovery. Lear approaches his true self through the otherness of Tom's naked misery and then through Gloucester's blind misery; both humbling confrontations prepare Lear for the deeper epiphanal awareness of Cordelia. Lear's anagnorisis must, to some extent, privilege Edgar and Gloucester: through their experience of the same ultimate death-terror and shame of mortality, they assume a depth and presence that informs Lear's acknowledgment of them.

Enthusiastic Gloucester, like other counselors (Polonius in *Hamlet*, Gonzalo in *The Tempest*) is more gullible in his proud self-insulation than Lear, more vulnerable to deception and abuse; yet he is also more open to emotional expression. Gloucester is less able than Lear to understand and enunciate, less experienced in the self-control, judgment, and authority that one hopes to find in sovereignty; but he is also less hampered by skeptical questioning and detachment, more spontaneously open to love.

The polar opposite foil for Lear is Edgar (and Edmund), whose penetrating intelligence is evident in his quick wit and ironic aphorisms, his clev-
erness in role-playing, surviving, and eventually conquering; but, traumatized
by his brother's treachery and his father's easy abandonment of their bond,
Edgar distances himself from all emotional bonds—a condition which makes
him extremely similar to both Prince Hal and Hamlet. Traumatized brilliance
helps to explain his long delay in revealing his identity to his father, his persistent losing himself in volatile role-playing, his brutal remark to his dying
brother ("The dark and vicious place where thee he got . . . ," 5.3.175–76).
Edgar's consummate defensiveness makes him as much an avoider of love as
Lear; and his half-feigned madness, his half-feigned demon-possession, and
his genuine impoverishment and humiliation make him an extraordinarily
complex and appropriate embodiment of the "otherness" that Lear must
centrally acknowledge. Finally, in the extravagance of Lear's "madness"—
subjected to the anguish of all passions and all conscientious awareness at
once—his agon surpasses that of both Gloucester and Edgar, revealing a poignant childishness inextricably mixed with a truly sovereign sympathy that
begins to reconstitute human bonds in the poverty of the heath.

In contrast to Macbeth, who in his central sequence tries to "cancel and
tear to pieces" the "great bond" of universal siblinghood by butchering his former best friend,[35] Lear in the cycle of act 3 affirms a radical community of
spirit. His sympathetic self-stripping attracts faithful servants who mirror that
sense of relatedness, drawn to foolish fellowship with an outcast king. Amid
such sensitive souls Lear experiences an inner storm of guilt and charity—more
painful than the whirlwind of suffering by which Job perceived the face and voice
of God. To enforce a skeptical reading of Lear's experience, Elton cites polar
opposite Renaissance views of storm: old-fashioned naifs identify the thunder
with divine providence, newfangled skeptics demystify it.[36] But surely a sophisticated mean (Erasmus, Montaigne) is closest to Shakespeare's view. Elton also
neglects Renaissance use of paradox in tempest allusions and the metaphoric
"inner storm" of madness to awaken God's voice within, conscience.[37]

Again the cycle ends with a choric reflection by one at the wheel's nadir.
After surviving act 3's stormy cycle, beggared Edgar, like Kent in the stocks,
is detached and hopeful:

> To be worst,
> The lowest and most dejected thing of fortune,
> Stands still in esperance, lives not in fear.
> The lamentable change is from the best,
> The worst returns to laughter.
>   (4.1.1–7)

That Edgar's resilience is met by Gloucester's despair (Fortune having whirled them contrarily in act 3) underscores the wheel's mysterious interconnectedness, irony, and paradox as they begin the final two-act cycle of reunion.

Seeing Cordelia: Restoring Id by Introjection

In acts 4–5 Lear's development again inverts Macbeth's. Macbeth precipitously initiates his final murderous cycle by seeking out the witches (forcing a false epiphany), but he absents himself from the slaughter of innocents and is also absent as Macduff's English pilgrimage achieves, with Malcolm, the true epiphanic moment (4.3). (We are not moved by Malcolm's ritual temptation, an archaic remnant from chronicle history which most directors cut, but by the poignant moment when Macduff learns of his family's massacre, a revelation that is axis for the cycle of acts 4–5 in that it fixes the resolve of Macduff, Malcolm, the Scottish and English forces, and the audience.) Lear, absent for much of act 4 as Gloucester's Dover journey wavers from suicide to pilgrimage, appears belatedly for reunion with Gloucester and epiphanic reconciliation with Cordelia. Again the illuminative encounter in the last scene of act 4 is pivotal, the dynamic and defining axis for the final two-act cycle.

Though the outer storm has abated, the inward fiery wheeling of shame and love intensifies as in acts 4–5 Lear incurs humiliating divestiture at the self's most primal stage. In this final cycle the king, like Gloucester, returns to a childlike state of physical and emotional vulnerability, an introjective dependence which vacillates between frustrated despair and ecstatic renewal of bonds. Gloucester in act 4 is a barometer of Lear's direction, but Lear is far prouder, more resistant to recovering childlikeness. His intense dependency-love for Cordelia alternates with cruelty toward others: mockery of Gloucester's (and love's) blindness, an urge to kill the sons-in-law who threaten his sole claim to nurturant love, boasts of slaying Cordelia's executioner and of former battle prowess, spasmodic fury at being distracted from watching her body. These impulses characterize Lear's regression to the primal core of selfhood, the id, and its experience of the most deeply nurturant parental love, usually expressed by the mother. This final sequence activates the memory of absolute affection, so travestied in the opening ritual by presumptions of kingly worth: "Which of you doth love us most?"

In *King Lear* the psychic functions in the three cycles of action parallel the main bondings of human identity, though in reverse order: in acts 1–2, bonds with parental authority (adult-heterosocial strivings to consolidate gender and power); in act 3, homosocial bonds (sibling-love, or envious rivalries); and in acts 4–5, infant bonds (especially mother love). In this final two-act cycle the dominant relational mechanism is *introjection*, the most primitive and powerful ego-function, especially in response to the death of a beloved nurturer.[38]

In acts 4–5 the introjective principle is reformed as Gloucester rebukes his blindness as a "superfluous and lust-dieted man" (4.1.66) and his cannibalistic rage when Edgar was the "food of thy abused father's wrath" (4.1.21–22). Now, wishing Tom the "bounty and the benison of heaven" (4.6.223–29), the changed Gloucester unknowingly lavishes wealth and affection on his child. In turn, he accepts generosity from the poor (from servants, from the good old man, and from Edgar-as-Tom), helping him become, like Lear, a "child-changed father," impassioned by good and evil children, but also restored to childlikeness. Thus Gloucester is fully attuned and receptive to Lear's "mad" reflections: "Thou know'st the first time we smell the air / We wawl and cry." Edgar, "pregnant to good pity," reinforces the primal affection, gaining, as in Macbeth's insight, the Godlike simplicity of "a naked new-born babe" (1.7.21). In acts 4–5 Macbeth destroys children, Lear and Gloucester die for love of them.

Lear, however, proudly resists this deepest bond and its reduction to vulnerable simplicity. He crowns himself with rank, poisonous weeds that infest the "sustaining corn" (4.4.6); he accuses women of "riotous appetite" (4.6.123); and he runs from Cordelia, becoming almost infantile (4.6.202–3). He must be captured by love. The filial two-act cycle turns on his reunion with Cordelia (4.7), the most moving epiphany and the focal point of Lear's deepest shame; and the cycle concludes with the traumatic stripping away of her life, for which Lear is partly responsible, and the horror of his powerlessness to revive her. As Cavell notes, Lear in these acts operates at a peak of defensive denial,[39] despite the transparency of Cordelia's affection: she is the only epiphanal figure without any duplicity. In act 4 he evades guilt by proclaiming universal absolution from moral law, but then flees Cordelia. In act 5 he refuses to confront the wicked daughters, then denies Cordelia's death. That she must invade England stresses Cordelia's aggressive charity and Lear's active evasion. Lear's love-test, his ardent avoiding of love, and his shameful joyous reunion all imply the main theme, the valuation of love (what Augustine calls "love of love," *amor amoris*).[40] Lear's best self is shaped by Cordelia's presence; healthy love, including self-love, must be learned.

The revelation of Cordelia again uses supernatural terms ("Thou art a soul in bliss") and a provocative image of Fortune's wheeling that moves deeper than the cycles of courtly power in acts 1–2, deeper than the whirling of the mind in stormy madness in act 3:

> ... I am bound
> Upon a wheel of fire.
> (4.7.47–48)

Assisted by Elton's glossary of analogues for the fire-wheel,[41] one perceives three levels of meaning—each deriving from varied mythic sources. As a Wheel of Hell (Ixion's wheel or Dante's complex vision in the *Inferno* of circles within circles, all turning around Satan's paralyzing fury) it springs from Lear's proud, willful rage at his failure to command Cordelia's love. As a Wheel of Purgatory it is Lear's penitent shame ("mine own tears do scald like molten lead"), causing him to avoid her presence. As a Wheel of Heaven (a fiery "wheel of the sun") it is Lear's illumination through love. All three levels of passion's cyclic burning focus on Cordelia, the "revealed heart."[42] With her tearful joy, the rage and shame dissolve, leaving love dominion.

Cordelia's forgiving love is the axis of acts 4–5; her death, the only means of complete communion, is the cycle's fitting end.[43] This paradox is the most complex element of Shakespeare's retelling of the *Everyman* morality, where Good Deeds' accompanying Everyman into the grave comforts the audience in the hope of activating their own goodness. Cordelia is a suggestive realization of Charity or Good Deeds, her generosity inspiring but also reflecting her father's sovereign instinct for charity (his prayer for the poor, his empathy for the Fool and Tom): she is indeed his "child" (though, like Marina in *Pericles*, she has also become her father's mother). At first Cordelia's preceding Lear into the grave gives no comfort; and the moral lesson (that Everyman can keep only what he gives away) seems insufficiently realized in Lear's experience. But as he stands immersed in affection for a child whose virtue surpasses the Cynics, sustaining him with faithful bonding and kind deeds, Lear at her death extends and consummates the epiphanic attentiveness of the earlier reunion scene. Not only is he distracted from mortal fears, but his mysterious final words (in the folio version) suggest that Lear sees—internalizes, becomes one with—her parting spirit.[44]

Like Lear, we perceive Cordelia's immortal spirit only through epiphanic awareness, for this theatrical production subjects the audience to psychological stripping similar to his. Kiefer observes that *King Lear*—unlike *Julius Caesar*, *Hamlet*, *Macbeth*, and *Antony and Cleopatra*—has no outward manifestation of the supernatural: "no evidence of magic, no witchcraft, no portents ... no ghosts or other spirits, and no miracles."[45] Kiefer, however, does not acknowledge the many *immanent* manifestations of the supernatural in *King Lear*: the genuinely "fiendish" behavior of Goneril, Regan, Edmund, Cornwall; the "spirit" of naked Tom and the "magic" of Edgar's artful performance and language; the "miracle" of Gloucester's revivification in faith; the absoluteness of Cordelia's "bond" and the persistence of her spiritual presence even after death. *King Lear* is charged with the supernaturalism of human figures who reflect or deflect God's image, engaged in paradoxical cycles of action which suggest providential order.[46]

Each manifestation of spirit—Goneril's fiendish power-hunger, Tom's resistance of fiends and quest for charity, above all, Cordelia's appearance as a "soul in bliss" (4.7.47), a gracious, forgiving "spirit" (4.7.50)—serves as axis in a cycle of humiliating divestiture and self-exposure for Lear. Each shameful vision of an Other promotes deepening levels of self-awareness. The encounter with Goneril, focusing the initial cycle, dismantles the superego's contrived image of parental-kingly-Godlike authority. The meeting with Poor Tom focuses the middle cycle, an interplay of ego with its doubles in a quest for philosophical insight. The reunion with Cordelia focuses the final cycle, exposing yearnings of the childlike id for absolute love, the nexus for Lear's "wheel of fire."

In Ezekiel's spectacular vision of God's providential working, "like a wheel inside a wheel" (or "wheels within wheels")[47] each multidimensional "wheel" revolves around the spiritual power and radiance of an animal-human-angelic "beast," which in its composite and dynamic form reflects the Creator's nature. This complex revelation supersedes those fatalistic emblems which show Fortune, or Death, at the wheel's center.[48] So too, mature Shakespearean dramaturgy consists of reiterated cycles of action, each revolving around an epiphanic encounter with a natural-supernatural figure whose "spirit . . . was in the wheel."

As in the prophet's vision, *King Lear* also portrays "wheels within wheels": subsumed in the three great turnings of Lear's fortune are other characters' revolutions of selfhood, each shaping his/her own cycle by choosing an authority-figure as the axis defining the wheel's process. Oswald, Edmund, and the soldier who kills Cordelia adopt the rising arc of the new power clique; Kent, the Fool, Edgar, and Cordelia submit to Lear's and Gloucester's falling arc and, in so doing, attain the freedom of moral solidarity and purpose:

> [O]f a number of spheres turning about the same centre, the innermost one approaches the simplicity of middleness and is a sort of pivot for the rest . . . ; that which is furthest separated from the principal mind is entangled in the tighter meshes of fate.[49]

Lear, rather than Macbeth, pushes toward the inmost simplicity of the "principal mind," that is, conscience, the voice and vision of God-likeness.

In the last two-act cycle of *King Lear*, the inward pilgrimage of act 4, culminating in reunion with Cordelia, is countered by the arc of warfare in act 5, culminating in the vision of her dead body. At the end of this final cycle Edmund's choric reflection on Fortune is quite different in tone from the remarks of Kent and Edgar when each touched bottom to conclude the play's first two cycles of action: "The wheel is come full circle; I am here" (5.3.174). Giving no credence to spiritual reality, Edmund lacks the optimism that Kent finds *because* of his shaming in the stocks ("A good man's fortune may grow out at heels, . . . Nothing almost sees miracles / But misery," 2.2.164, 172–73) and that Edgar finds in nakedness and contemnation: "The worst returns to laughter" (4.1.1–9). In striking contrast, Edmund's remark is resoundingly final, not only because he is dying but because he views the wheel of human being reductively, as a cycle of materialistic self-assertion. His "I am" is swallowed by "here," the lowly dust at the wheel's bottom, where he began. Equally ironic and reductive is Edmund's boast of conquering the hearts of Goneril and Regan ("all three / Now marry in an instant"), for none of them has enjoyed truly companionate marriage, the consummation of *oneself as another*. The Fool, who at first seemed to affirm Edmund's materialistic egotism when he advised hitching one's cycle only to the "great wheels" that move upward (2.4.70–73), ignores his own opportunistic maxim by following Lear into the storm. His foolish loyalty epitomizes *King Lear's* paradoxical cycles. As in Boethius's *Consolation* and Dante's *Commedia*, the way up may be achieved by enduring the way down.

Lear, Gloucester, Edgar, Kent, and Cordelia engage in cycles of abasement that ultimately exalt: "the last shall be first." Edgar, in assuming the humblest human form, the Bethlehem beggar, learns the agony of spinning privilege into poverty, and vice versa; and, like Boethius, he learns self-reflection, that he must "on himself turn back the light of his inward vision, / Bending and forcing his far-reaching movements / Into a circle."[50] This self identity is achieved by social awareness and bonding, the cycle of "good pity" (4.6.220) which restores the gratitude of children to parents and of parents to the Creator, "the love common to all things":

> . . . they seek to be bound by their end, the good,
> Since in no other way could they endure,
> If the causes that gave them being did not flow back
> Under the power of returning love.[51]

Vincenzo Cioffari notes that Aquinas, Dante, Boccaccio, and Petrarch conceived God as the "*causa per se* of our Fortune" ("the love that moves the spheres"), and viewed human will as a subordinate cause.[52] The ending of *King Lear* (both quarto and folio) suggests that the wheel of Lear's destiny, not just the resolutional cycle of acts 4–5 but the drama as a whole, is moved by love. It is a force much larger than Lear himself, as shown by the many who extend it so assiduously on his behalf (Cordelia, Kent, Albany, Gloucester, Edgar, the King of France, gentlemen, servants) and by Lear's persistent failure to receive and reciprocate it with grace. The authenticity of the play's final psychological triumph stresses Lear's residual inadequacies when he finally engages wholeheartedly in this mysterious force.

For Shakespeare the fundamental cause of "fortune" is not philosophical attraction to the idea of the Good but creaturely fellow-feeling, which draws the comedies and romances to a final communal celebration, and which the tragedies affirm as the best resource for confronting death. Such bonding redefines the cycles of historical change and the wheels of our inner being. Edgar, the heir apparent, is the best final *sprecher*, and the best candidate for sovereignty, not only by his former exposure to aloneness, nakedness, and death-terror but also by his modest admission of partial detachment from the "wheel of fire"—the burning of shame and love which so consumed his father, then still more terribly his godfather Lear. Humbled by their vision and passion, he does not presume to "see so much" or "live so long."

Notes

1. In "The Uniqueness of *King Lear*," *ShJE* (1984): 44–61, E. A. J. Honigmann calls *Lear* an "Oedipus-Everyman play," in which "a sinner who becomes a thinker . . . suffers rather than initiates action" (47). To this universal sufferance-myth one might add the stories of Job and Prometheus, who also figure as prominent analogues for Lear. Yet all of these, except Job, actively initiate and sustain their own suffering—and none more than Lear.

2. Bradley, "Construction in Shakespeare's Tragedies," in *Shakespearean Tragedy*; Jones, *Scenic Form in Shakespeare*, 152–94.

3. Snyder, *The Comic Matrix of Shakespeare's Tragedies*, 137–79; Stephen Booth, *King Lear, Macbeth, Indefinition and Tragedy* (New Haven: Yale University Press, 1983), chap. 1.

4. Ernest Becker, *The Denial of Death* (New York: Free Press, 1973), 36–46, 115–23.

5. Elton, *King Lear and the Gods*, 63–71; Harry Berger, Jr., "*King Lear*: The Lear Family Romance," *Centennial Review* 23 (1979): 348–76.

6. For discussion of act divisions in the folio *Lear*, see Jones, *Scenic Form in Shakespeare*, 160; G. Taylor, "The Structure of Performance," 48–50; Jewkes, *Act Division in Elizabethan and Jacobean Plays*, 35–40.

7. George W. Williams, by examining "twenty-one specific petitions . . . to the gods, to the heaven(s), and to Nature or Fortune," discovers a more optimistic dialogue with divinity than that described by William R. Elton, Susan Snyder, and others ("Petitionary Prayer in *King Lear*," *SAQ* 85 (1986): 360–73.

8. Gary Taylor, *To Analyze Delight: A Hedonist Criticism of Shakespeare* (Newark: University of Delaware Press, 1985), 162–236.

9. Heilman, *This Great Stage*; Mack, *Everybody's Shakespeare: Reflections Chiefly on the Tragedies* (Lincoln: University of Nebraska Press, 1993), 172–75.

10. See, for example, Soellner, *Shakespeare's Patterns of Self-Knowledge*; Paul Jorgensen, *Lear's Self-Discovery* (Berkeley and Los Angeles: University of California Press, 1981).

11. Lawrence Josephs, *Character Structure and the Organization of the Self* (New York: Columbia University Press, 1992), chap. 5 ("The Archaic Relational Matrix").

12. See Frederick Kiefer, *Fortune and Elizabethan Tragedy* (San Marino, CA: Huntington Library, 1983), 296. See the comments on Fortune by Kent (2.2.176, 5.3.282–83), the Fool (2.4.70–73; 3.2.76), Edgar (3.6.101–114; 4.1–12; 5.2.9–11), Cordelia (5.3.3–6), Lear (5.3.16–19), and Edmund (5.3.29–34). Cf. Vincenzo Cioffari, "Fortune, Fate, and Chance," in *Dictionary of the History of Ideas*, 2:225–36, and *Fortune and Fate from Democritus to St. Thomas Aquinas* (New York. Privately Printed, 1935); Rolf Soellner, "*King Lear* and the Magic of the Wheel," *SQ* 35 (1984): 274–89; Howard R. Patch, *The Goddess Fortuna in Medieval Literature* (Cambridge: Harvard University Press, 1927); Raymond Chapman, "The Wheel of Fortune in Shakespeare's Historical Plays," *RES* 1 (1950): 1–7; Russell A. Fraser, *Shakespeare's Poetics in Relation to King Lear* (London: Routledge and Kegan Paul, 1962), 46–60; Samuel C. Chew, *The Pilgrimage of Life* (New Haven: Yale University Press, 1962), 22–69; Elton, *King Lear and the Gods*; Northrop Frye, *Fools of Time*, 13–14, 88–95, 116; Leo Salingar, *Shakespeare and the Traditions of Comedy* (Cambridge: Cambridge University Press, 1974),129–74.

13. Elton, *King Lear and the Gods*, 63–71.

14. See Bibliography, 5H, "Repetition Compulsion."

15. Mark Rose, *Shakespearean Design*, 13–15, 35–39, 43–44, 126, 151, 179 n. 21.

16. For discussion of Lady Macbeth's demonism, see W. Moelwyn Merchant, "'His Fiend-like Queen,'" *ShS* 19 (1966): 75–94.

17. Inga-Stina Ewbank traces the sterility wish in *Lear* and *Macbeth* to *Medea*, "The Fiend-like Queen: A Note on 'Macbeth' and Seneca's 'Medea,'" *ShS* 19 (1966): 82–94.

18. Cf. 1.4.170, 268, 274–88, 2.4.129–31, 172–73, 278–85, 3.2.7–9.

19. See Bibliography, 5I, "Sublimation."

20. On the universal psychological content of Lear's love-test, see Alan Dundes, "'To Love My Father All': A Psychoanalytic Study of the Folktale Source of *King Lear*," *Southern Folklore Quarterly* 40 (1976): 353–66.

21. See Ricoeur, *Oneself as Another*, 336–39.

22. Boethius, "The Consolation of Philosophy," trans. S. J. Tester, in *The Theological Tractates and The Consolation of Philosophy* ed. E. H. Warmington (Cambridge: Harvard University Press and London: William Heinemann 1978), 325–31.

23. That Lear in his central cycle induces his own madness in self-exile on a stormy heath, while Macbeth deceitfully hosts an inaugural banquet, epitomizes their contrary developments.

24. For the iconographic linking of fortune with tempest, apparently as synonyms (both driven by time, temporality), see Edgar Wind, *Giorgione's "Tempesta" with Comments on Giorgione's Poetic Allegories* (Oxford: Clarendon Press, 1969); Kiefer, *Fortune and Elizabethan Tragedy*, 287.

25. See Stephen Greenblatt, "Shakespeare and the Exorcists," in *Shakespearean Negotiations* (Berkeley: University of California Press, 1988), 94–128; John L.

Murphy, *Darkness and Devils: Exorcism in King Lear* (Athens: Ohio State University Press, 1984), chap. 7.

26. Nicholas Grene, *Shakespeare's Tragic Imagination* (New York: St. Martin's Press, 1992), 178.

27. William Gulstad, "Mock-Trial or Witch-Trial in *King Lear?*" *N&Q* 239 (4) (1994): 494–97.

28. See Bibliography, 5G, "Projection and Projective Identification."

29. Berger, "The Lear Family Romance," 356–64; Alexander Leggatt, *King Lear* (New York: Harvester Press, 1988), 33, 79–81; Jonathan Dollimore, *Radical Tragedy: Religion, Ideology and Power in the Drama of Shakespeare and His Contemporaries* (Chicago: Chicago University Press, 1984), 189–203; and Sears Jayne, "Charity in *King Lear.*" *SQ* 15 (1964): 277–88, who finds "no compensating love anywhere in the world of this play" (285). A more balanced view is Kent Cartwright's tracing of the audience's alternating engagement with and detachment from Lear, in *Shakespearean Tragedy and Its Double: The Rhythms of Audience Response* (University Park: Pennsylvania State University, 1991), 181–226, esp. 202–16.

30. For St. Augustine, sane self-love reflects Creator love (*De moribus ecclesiae* 25.46–29.61; *De trinitate* 8–15). See Bibliography, 5D, "Narcissism and Self-love."

31. Berger, "The Lear Family Romance," 367–76.

32. On the Cynic philosophers' wise madness in connection with Poor Tom, see E. M. M. Taylor, "Lear's Philosopher," *SQ* 6 (1955): 364–65; Soellner, *Shakespeare's Patterns of Self-Knowledge*, 300–302; Jane Donawerth, "Diogenes the Cynic and Lear's Definition of Man, *King Lear* III.iv.101–109," *ELN* (Sept. 1977): 10–14; F. G. Butler, "Who Are *King Lear's* Philosophers? An Answer, with Some Help from Erasmus," *ES* 67 (1986): 511–24; Steven Doloff, "'Let me talk with this philosopher': The Alexander/Diogenes Paradigm in *King Lear,*" *HLQ* 54 (1991): 253–55. Cf. John Leon Lievsay, "Some Renaissance Views of Diogenes the Cynic," *Joseph Quincy Adams Memorial Studies*, ed. J. G. McManaway, G. E. Dawson, and E. E. Willoughby (Washington, D.C.: Folger Library, 1948), 447–55. In Elton's more pessimistic reading, Lear's "philosopher" visually parodies Stoic denial of passion, and asking him the cause of thunder undermines belief in providence (97–98, 197–213).

33. For Erasmus's and Montaigne's satire of presumption and praise of folly (exemplified on the heath and in Lear's "sermon" to Gloucester in act 4), see Peter McNamara, "*King Lear* and Comic Acceptance," *Erasmus Review* 1 (1971): 95–105; Elton, *King Lear and the Gods*, 192–94, 231–33, 259; Soellner, *Shakespeare's Patterns of Self-Knowledge*, 296–97, 314; and Leo Salingar, "*King Lear*, Montaigne and Harsnett," in *Dramatic Form in Shakespeare and the Jacobeans* (Cambridge: Cambridge University Press, 1986), 107–39.

34. Dieter Mehl's critique of Lear's largely unrealized prayer for the poor ("Lear and the 'Poor Naked Wretches,'" *Deutsche Shakespeare Gesellschaft West* [1975]: 154–62) is made a crux in Dollimore's Marxist reading (*Radical Tragedy*). Cf. Dollimore, "Shakespeare, Cultural Materialism and the New Historicism," in *Political Shakespeare*, ed. Jonathan Dollimore and Alan Sinfield (Manchester: Manchester University Press, 1985), 2–17.

35. Interpretations of Macbeth's "great bond" include his complicity with witches, his friendship with Banquo, the general bond of universal siblinghood, and, for Garry Wills, the baptismal bond with God (*Witches and Jesuits: Shakespeare's Macbeth* [New York: Oxford University Press, 1995], 59–61).

36. Elton, *King Lear and the Gods*, 197–212.

37. See Josephine W. Bennett, "The Storm Within: The Madness of Lear," *SQ* 13 (1962): 137–55,

38. On the establishing of self-identity in reaction to the death of a beloved nurturer, see Bibliography, 5C, "Introjection, Internalization, Identification."

39. Stanley Cavell, "The Avoidance of Love: A Reading of *King Lear*," in *Must We Mean What We Say? A Book of Essays* (New York: Scribner's, 1969), 267–353.

40. See Augustine, *De trinitate*. On Cordelia's aggressive charity, see Berger, "The Lear Family Romance," 374.

41. Elton, *King Lear and the Gods*, 135–36, 175 and n. 234–38, 258, 326.

42. Murray J. Levith, *What's in Shakespeare's Names* (New Haven, CT: Archon Books, 1978), 57.

43. Compare the *liebestod* of Pyramus and Thisbe, Romeo and Juliet, and especially Antony and Cleopatra, whose communion in the final scene of act 4 is axis for the final two-act cycle.

44. The optimistic potential of Lear's final words (in the folio) is noted by Elton in *King Lear and the Gods*, 258 n.; Thomas Clayton, in *The Division of the Kingdoms*, 121–41; Doebler, in "Rooted Sorrow," 168–69. Cf. Williams, "Petitionary Prayer," 371.

45. Kiefer, *Fortune and Elizabethan Tragedy*, 295.

46. In its cycles of action that revolve around immanent epiphanies, and in the development of these axial visions from lovelessness to love, Shakespeare's *King Lear* forms an intriguing analogue with Dante's spiritual pilgrimage: from frustration in the *Vita Nuova* (12.26–34), where Dante is excluded from the circle of Love, to the joyous end of the *Paradiso*, where, in the presence of God, Dante's desire is made perfect, "like a wheel in even revolution":

> Ma gia volgeva il mio disiro e 'l *velle,*
> Si come rota ch' igualuieute e mossa,
> L'Amor che move il sole e l' altre stelle.
> (33.143–45).

Dante Alighieri, *La Divina Commedia*, ed. C. H. Grandgent (Boston: D.C. Heath, 1933), 972 n. 144: "The circle, being the perfect figure, is an emblem of perfection; and circular motion symbolizes full and faultless activity" (St. Thomas, *In Librum B. Dionysii D Divinis Nominibus*, caput iv, Lectio 7).

47. "They foure had one forme, . . . and their worke was as one whele in *another* whele. . . . Whether their spirit led them, they went . . . & when they were lifted vp from the earth, the wheles were lifted vp besides them: for the spirit of the beastes [*the cherubim*] was in the wheles" (Ezekiel 1:16, 20–21; see 10:9–13, 16–17).

48. Soellner, "*King Lear* and the Magic of the Wheel," *SQ* 35 (1984): 283–84.

49. Boethius, *The Theological Tractates and The Consolation of Philosophy*, 361–63.

50. Ibid., 297; and see 273.

51. Ibid., 375.

52. Cioffari, "Fortune, Fate, and Chance."

MILLICENT BELL

Naked Lear

RuPaul, the well-known female impersonator, is fond of remarking, "you're born naked, and the rest is drag." It is a view that expresses the skepticism about selfhood that Shakespeare dramatized in *King Lear*. That the play's imagery of clothing is conspicuous has been noticed, but not what it signifies. It has not been recognized how this imagery enforces the implication that most of the human qualities that make up personhood are things put on or taken off. RuPaul would say this especially about our identities as male or female. But might it not be a metaphoric idea that applies to all the aspects of ourselves? This is what Lear realizes when he contemplates Edgar as a nearly naked Bedlam beggar. Half in madness, half in a brilliant skeptical rage, he says, "Is man no more than this? Consider him well. Thou ow'st the worm no silk, the beast no hide, the sheep no wool, the cat no perfume. Ha? Here's three on's us are sophisticated; thou art the thing itself." Despite the efforts to restrain him made by Kent and the Fool, Lear tries to tear off his own bedraggled royal robes, and cries, "Off, off, you lendings: come, unbutton here." He goes on to say, "Unaccommodated man is no more but such a poor, bare, forked animal as thou art."

Shut out into the storm by Goneril and Regan, Lear is also expressing his realization that he is not the only one who suffers hunger and cold and exposure. No longer kept oblivious of others' misery by his own privileged

From *Raritan* 23, no. 4 (Spring 2004): 55–70. Copyright © 2004 by *Raritan*.

comfort, he pities the "poor naked wretches, whereso'er [they] are, / That bide the pelting of this pitiless storm," and tells himself, "O, I have ta'en / Too little care of this." But this awakening of humane conscience is prompted by conditions that are themselves symbolic as well as matters of fact. The times were unstable. It had come about that one could prosper or lose all, overnight. And one could *be*, as a consequence, a different man or woman as readily as one could change one's clothing. In Poor Tom o' Bedlam, Edgar personates the vagrant reduced to physical near-nakedness who has also been stripped of his former identity. A storm of change had, through the 1590s, broken up the stability of rural life in England, sending thousands of real Poor Toms out upon the roads, wandering from the deserted villages where their ancestors had had an immemorial place. Their rags were not only the literal consequence of their poverty but could stand for the intangible shreds and shards of former selfhoods. It was a time, also, that gave opportunity to the new rich who made fortunes out of food crop shortages, and, in the dynamic politics of the moment, such a person might make it to the center of things in London and strut in the peacock costumes of the older nobility at court, his previous character forgotten. The threat to conventional conceptions of class and rank made by such self-making swaggerers was felt by the state, and the wearing of certain fabrics of luxury—imported satins and velvets—was restricted. Elizabethan-Jacobean "sumptuary laws" were passed to keep the lower ranks from dressing out of their class. In *King Lear*, Kent says of the upstart steward, Oswald, "nature disclaims in thee—a tailor made thee"—that is, made the person he has become by dressing up a person that "nature" had no role in creating—though he had previously been no more than a "three-suited . . . worsted-stocking knave," limited by ordinance to three suits a year and plain woolen stockings instead of silk.

Dress had never been more metaphysical than it was in the courts of Elizabeth and James I. It is pertinent to the idea of personality as a change of clothes that it was in the late sixteenth century when the word *fashion* acquired the modern meaning of a temporarily favored style of clothing— "the mode of dress . . . adopted in society for the time being," as the *Oxford English Dictionary* states—when to say that something is "in fashion" became a way of saying that it might soon be "out of fashion." What dress signified was similarly changeable. A modern audience will miss the topicality of Lear's odd remark to Edgar in his beggar's rags, "I do not like the fashion of your garments. You will say they are Persian attire, but let them be changed." A Persian embassy had arrived in London early in the reign of James I; there was a "fashion" for Persian silk fabrics and even costume, marking the beginning of the English assimilation of exotic identities. Sir Robert Shirley, who had gone to Persia with the Earl of Essex in 1598, would be painted some years later by Van Dyke in Persian robes of embroidered silk that pictorially declared the subsequent character he achieved as an international diplomat with special Persian connections. Life itself, in the years when Shakespeare wrote, illustrated the malleability of personal being.

There has been controversy about the existence of persistent character in Shakespeare's plays since the time of Thomas Rymer, who, at the end of the seventeenth century, attacked the unclassical inconsistency of Shakespeare's characterization while Dryden defended it, as would the Romantics, who found in the very contradictions and irreducibility of his characters the highest achievement of Shakespearean art. Today, the debate continues, though the issue is not so much a question of critical valuation as a difference about what Shakespeare meant by character. It is still maintained that he was the great inventor of personal interiority as something impossible to give full outward expression to, yet present—as illustrated by Hamlet, when he mocks his mother's reference to how he "seems" in his black mourning clothes, and tells her, "I have that within which passeth show." On the other hand, a good argument is made by a modern school of "cultural materialists" who think Hamlet refers to a vacancy, something that cannot be shown because it does not exist. The latter view is, perhaps, supported by the traditions of ancient and Renaissance skepticism that deny the existence of a constant self, of a spiritual continuity linking all our acts and appearances.

There is no place, in such a view, for any essential, God-implanted and ineradicable soul that has been individuated by divine intention. And the distinction between a clothed and naked human condition that I am identifying in *King Lear* is not a representation of that old duality of outer and inner, the visible and the invisible, matter and spirit, or body and soul, to be found in religious tradition and in philosophy from Plato to Descartes. An alternate tradition was available for a definition of what it is to be human. There existed, from earliest times, a skeptical view that dispensed with dualism or lurked behind the argument that sustained it, as Descartes would illustrate a short while after Shakespeare's own time. This view denied the existence of invisible spiritual essence or said, at least, that we cannot know anything certain about it. Such disbelief that jostled belief was widely available and widely felt in the sixteenth and seventeenth centuries, and penetrated religion itself. The fact that doubt was present where faith was most intense—that faith was necessary where doubt was most threatening—is one of the paradoxes of the age of intensified belief in divine mystery we call the Protestant Reformation. Both the reformers and their Catholic opponents embraced a fideism that acknowledged the inadequacy of unaided human reason, embracing doubt as the very source of faith. We have only begun to realize how pervasive was this countertradition of skepticism that included uncertainty about the existence of essential selves. The clothing of self that covers Lear's naked forked animal is nothing less than the whole of acquired personal being hung upon the mere scaffold of the body, the material "thing itself."

However Shakespeare assimilated it, whether from reading Sextus Empiricus, the author of an ancient Greek manual of skepticism rediscovered and translated into English in the sixteenth century, or from the skeptical essays of a near-contemporary, Michel de Montaigne, or from the general uncertainty of life that permeated the culture of the times, skepticism emerges in *King Lear* and elsewhere in Shakespeare's plays. This is so even though he probably would not have denied the traditional view about souls any more than Montaigne would have allowed himself to do. Lear's declaration about "lendings" is a philosophical statement (with a postmodern skeptical ring) of the way personal identity is something borrowed, something acquired from the outside. What is there to begin with is something rudimentary and impersonal and material.

One should note, perhaps, that Montaigne undertakes to show, in the most famous of his essays, the "Apologie de Raimond Sabond," that man's supposed superiority to the rest of animal nature is without basis, though these "other" animals are without the immortal souls that have been said to be our special distinction. He illustrates, with numerous examples, the modest claims to superiority of Hamlet's "paragon of animals" who is also the "quintessence of dust." So, in *King Lear* the equalizing comparison of human to animal is as frequent a part of the play's language as the reference to clothing. "Die for adultery?" says Lear in his mock trial of his wicked daughters, "the wren goes to't, and the small gilded fly / Does lecher in my sight … the fitchew, nor the soiled horse, goes to't / with a more riotous appetite." The animal comparison serves also, in Montaigne, to reinforce skepticism about the reliability of human perceptions and the vaunted power of that faculty of reason by which we think ourselves so privileged by God. Our only remedy is submission to faith in truths we cannot confidently reach unaided. Gloucester's deprecation of human vision should be recognized as a skeptical statement of the source of faith in this admission of inadequacy:

> I stumbled when I saw. Full oft 'tis seen
> Our means secure us and our mere defects
> Prove our commodities.

It is in this way, exactly, that Montaigne not only reminds mankind of its deficient powers, but says that our very weaknesses serve to prepare us for the realization that reliance on God is our only hope of attaining truth. Montaigne wrote: "The weaknesse of our judgment helps us more than our strength to compasse the same, and our blindness more than our clear-sighted eyes." Such an embracing of human fallibility as a *resource* of faith is a standard component of the fideism that seems wedded to Renaissance skepticism.

Lear's "Is man no more than this?" speech happens to be taken directly from Montaigne, whose essays repeatedly challenge the idea of fixed, intrinsic individuality. Written in 1605 or 1606, *King Lear* picks up the clothes image from Montaigne's words in John Florio's English translation of the *Essays*, published in 1603: "Man is the onely forsaken and out-cast creature, naked on the bare earth . . . having nothing to cover and arme himself withal but the spoile of others; whereas Nature hath clad and mantled all other creatures, some with huskes . . . with wool . . . with hides . . . and with silke." But elsewhere in the play, Shakespeare associates clothing with those donated and removable elements out of which the self may be said to be constructed. Everything starts with Lear's resolution to "*divest*," or undress, himself of "rule, interest of territory, cares of state." Montaigne had praised the Emperor Charles V, who "resigned his meanes, his greatness and Kingdome to his Sonne" when he found his strength waning. "He had the discretion to know," Montaigne wrote, that "reason commanded us to strip or shift ourselves when our clothes trouble and are too heavy for us, and it is high time to go to bed, when our legs faile us." Such a stripping-down by aged wisdom in the expectation of death may have been Lear's original intention. In the words of Job paraphrased by RuPaul, "Naked came I out of my mother's womb and naked shall I return thither." Dying, at the end, Lear repeats his earlier words on the heath, and begs those who stand beside him, "pray you, undo this button."

Lear, of course, has been slow to recognize what he has done by his abdication, how he has surrendered more than he intended, nothing less than that self-defining consciousness that makes him know who he is by knowing, in some measure, his place in the structure of human relationships and identities. Like criminalized and disinherited Edgar, the once-king becomes the "thing itself." Lear's royal authority and dignity are gone; his paternity has become meaningless. As he strips himself literally, the beggar who moans "Tom's a-cold" because of his nakedness is joined to the reduced king. They have become representations of "unaccommodated" man. Lear is referred to by others as "the old man" rather than as king. To the raging elements on the heath he cries, "Here I stand your slave, / A poor, infirm, weak and despised old man." But earlier, he had already lost his sense of who he was, and says, in a declaration too readily seen as madness,

Does any here know me? Why, this is not Lear.
Does Lear walk thus? Speak thus? Where are his eyes?

> Either his notion weakens, or his discernings are
> lethargied—Ha! Sleeping or waking? Sure 'tis not
> so. Who is it that can tell me who I am?

Reminding Regan that his lost dignities are like a fine lady's dress, not "needed" as covering but rather signification of what she is, he says, "O, reason not the need!" He had argued for the importance of retaining that sense of his kingly being she would deny him, forgetting that he had already "divested" himself of these voluntarily. He has forgotten that he acted to Cordelia, a fine lady, so as to "dismantle [Florio's word] / So many folds of favor," as though her cloak or mantle and everything beneath were lifted from her back. She had ceased to be his daughter and a princess, and was banished. When she returns after so much transpires, it is in the altered dress of military armor; she must become an invader of her own country in order to be recognized as a good daughter and the rightful heir of her father, the rightful king.

In a play, of course, costume is sometimes the disguise of a disguiser, doubling its function as a dramatic fiction, a misrepresentation of the person of the actor. The actor who continues to be recognized by the audience as the character met before now is dressed so that he appears as someone else to those on stage. *King Lear*'s two disguised comrades in suffering, Edgar and Kent, go undetected by those around them, however plain it is to us that they are only pretending to be new arrivals to the dramatic scene. But Shakespeare, by the vigor and meaning given these new appearances, forces even the theater spectator to put aside his knowledge of their "real" identity. Disguise has expanded the dramatis personae to include two new characters. The new "clothing" of Edgar and Kent has become transformative. Kent, a senior earl and the king's chief adviser, becomes a rough, plain-speaking serving-man whose renunciation of courtly being and style is a significant changeover. He is someone whose personhood is reduced to a minimum dictated by his honesty. Edgar, the heir of the Earl of Gloucester, is metamorphosed into a ragged vagrant whose condition as Poor Tom precipitates the vision of absolute nakedness in Lear.

Edgar deceives his father even in the latter's blindness, when he cannot perceive what the son he has lost now wears. He adopts disguises of voice, even talking dialect as a West Country yokel in the fourth act. When he approaches the time when he must finally revert to his original self, he describes a discarded self to Gloucester as the horned devil left on the crest of the Dover cliff from which Gloucester thinks he has tumbled. In the end he recovers his previous being in his duel with his brother Edmund. They look alike in their armor, reminding us that one must displace the other, both having a claim to that identity Edgar declares when he calls himself "thy father's son." Edmund has plotted to assume their father's title as Earl of Gloucester, and is called so by Goneril and Regan, who give him a self that cannot be sustained. That transferable self must be recovered by Edgar in the end. In his death struggle with Edmund, he begins as a visored knight who says, "My name is lost." But it is to this brother—whom he must destroy in order to be the man he previously was—that he finally tells his name.

Disguise is usually a device of comedy. It is present only in this one of Shakespeare's major tragedies though common in his comedies and romances. Edgar as the disguised mad beggar may have been played on the Elizabethan stage with something of a comic vivacity as he moaned and cried in his misery. The title page of the earliest edition of the play, the 1608 First Quarto, gives him equal billing with Lear. It reads, "M. William Shak-speare: His True Chronicle Historie of the life and death of King Lear and his three daughters. With the unfortunate life of Edgar, sonne and heire to the Earle of Gloster, and his sullen and assumed humor of Tom of Bedlam." That "sullen and assumed humor" had clearly had a theatrical success the printer wanted possible buyers to recall. We probably don't sufficiently realize how frequently madness was comic on Shakespeare's stage, especially when it was feigned. Hamlet's "antic" humor was meant to provoke laughter.

In comedy such transformations are reversible; the original person returns, casting off the deceptive appearances temporarily assumed or imposed and reuniting the recovered self with those from whom it has been estranged. Yet even in comedy it is always just conceivable that recovery of the lost self will not take place. In the tragic metamorphic universe of *King Lear* recovery is achieved doubtfully or with great difficulty. The true madness from which Lear suffers is that devastating loss represented by the statement "He is not himself," which we utter when a previously sane personality we have known crumbles. Even Hamlet's madness is only uncertainly a pretense, and once, at least, he concedes that he has sometimes been veritably mad. The dangerousness even of Edgar's comic-seeming disguise as a madman is illustrated by the fact that it lasts too long and has become too real. His belated disclosure of his true identity to a father who has long repented and suffered comes when it can do no good to Gloucester, and it actually brings about his death. Its effect can no longer be called either tragic or comic as Gloucester's "flawed heart / Alack, too weak the conflict to support, / 'Twixt two extremes of passion, joy and grief, / Burst smilingly."

Even in comedy, of course, the efficacy of stage disguise sometimes suggests a real alterity otherwise unacknowledged. I come back, again, to RuPaul, who as a man impersonating a woman reminds us of the conditions of Elizabethan stage production, in which gender is something enacted. Such a theatrical practice had a complex connection with theater history that went back well before the special conventions of the Elizabethan-Jacobean stage and the social atmosphere of those years. But, certainly, in Shakespeare's time, the way men could represent women on the stage invoked all the ambiguities that such impersonation might bring to mind. Shakespeare does not, in *King Lear*, use this illustration of the idea of "drag" in its original sense of simulated gender. It is in his comedies that the ambiguity of sexuality represented by male actors appearing as women, or even as women disguised again as men, enforces a special vision of metamorphic gender, and reminds us how much depends—save for the poor forked animal with its differentiating features— upon roles and appearances. In a play such as *Twelfth Night*, Viola's sexual metamorphosis is a further underscoring of the way sexual character, assumed to be so integral and irremovable a part of oneself, might shift or prove other than what the naked body exhibits in its denuded state. Gender becomes a sort of costume, completely credible in its term on the stage, and one of the ways in which the transformative nature of the self may be illustrated.

Transformative change was also credible to Shakespeare's audience as something effected against one's will by the force of magic, which might actually change one from what one was, or make one love or hate the wrong person, as in *A Midsummer Night's Dream*. The mythical tales of men or women transformed into animals by supernatural agency remain a part of folk memory deeply planted in the human consciousness, suggesting a threatening possibility lurking beneath the comic surface of Bottom's metamorphosis into an ass. In *King Lear*, the frequency with which human beings are compared to animals reminds the imagination of this mythic threat.

Edgar's transformation into Poor Tom appears—even if deceptively—as a case of demonic possession, a state that might be a demonstration of how occult powers really may rob one of one's original being and put a usurper in its place. It is probably significant that it is in *King Lear* that Shakespeare's interest in debate about the possibility of such a process surfaces in his reference to a current trial of Catholic exorcists. Mad Tom claims to have suffered from demon torturers who bear comical names—Smulkin, Hobbididence, Mahu, Modo, and Flibbertigibbet—borrowed from the fiends referred to in the trial, and Shakespeare, it is confidently supposed, got them out of a popular polemic against the claims of the exorcists, Samuel Harsnett's *A Declaration of Egregious Popish Impostures*, published in 1603.

But the ambiguities of identity represented by Poor Tom do not end with his account of his sufferings at the hands of these devils who have not, of course, really tortured the Edgar who has disappeared into his disguise. Edgar's sufferings from want and weather may be real, though he is a disguised man. So may be his inner grief and even the madness that could well have overtaken the distressed outcast he has really become; a case, as I have said, like that of Hamlet, whose assumed madness becomes indistinguishable from the frantic despair to which he has been driven. And yet, again, Edgar's suffering and madness may also be as much a fraud as the possession the exorcists claimed to cure. The playwright gives the idea of deception another turn of the screw by making Poor Tom a stock figure for fraud, a "Bedlam beggar." If he appears to be a waif of misfortune, a human castaway, he also poses as one of those well-known cheats who *disguised* themselves as madmen escaped from London's famous Bethlehem Hospital for the insane. They were wont to display painted sores and false mutilations to go with their raving behavior, compelling charity even from those not much better off than themselves, as they traveled from one poor farm or village to another. As Edgar says,

> I will preserve myself, and am bethought
> To take the basest and the poorest shape
> That ever penury in contempt of man
> Brought near to beast . . .
> . . . .
> The country gives me proof and precedent
> Of Bedlam beggars, who, with roaring voices,
> Strike in their numbed and mortified bare arms
> Pins, wooden pricks, nails, sprigs of rosemary;
> And with this horrible object, from low farms,
> Poor pelting villages, sheepcotes and mills,
> Sometimes with lunatic bans, sometimes with prayers
> Enforce their charity.

His disguise is the disguise of a disguiser whose rags and sores are costume.

And yet, that he must function—to Lear, if not to his own father— as the representative of unaccommodated man may explain the otherwise inexplicable way in which he refrains so long from revealing his true identity. Shakespeare gives Edgar's transformed and reduced reality a past out of Elizabethan-Jacobean experience. Leaving behind the mythic ancient world of Lear and his court, his replacement, Poor Tom, describes himself as having once been a well-dressed Elizabethan upper servant whom misfortune has reduced: "Poor Tom, that eats the swimming frog, the toad, the tadpole, the wall-neat and the water—; that in the fury of his heart, when the foul fiend rages, eats cow-dung for salads, swallows the old rat and the ditch-dog; drinks the green mantle of the standing pool; who is whipped from tithing to tithing"—that is, from parish to parish, as the royal statute against vagabonds enjoined—"and stocked, punished and imprisoned—who hath had three suits to his back, six shirts to body," a direct reference to the limited sufficiency of dress that this fictional former status allowed. And now the "naked man," as Lear calls him, has lost even that meager made-up selfhood.

Kent, the play's other disguised character, is banished from the royal court that gave meaning to his life in the fixed relation of courtier to monarch. His title and his former dignity and relation to the throne have fallen away, and he enters a world where order has fallen into disarray. He has, as he says, "razed his likeness" in becoming a nondescript serving man. Lear asks this new person "What art thou?" and the answer comes, "A man, sir"—that is, without differentiating role or even name, someone "unaccommodated," almost, like Edgar, to the point of becoming the "thing itself." Lear seeks a social definition for this new person by asking "What is your trade?" and Kent replies, "I do profess to be no less than I seem"—rejecting any suggestion that "a man" is not sufficient description of him. He claims to be no less than the reduced humanity he exhibits. His list of his capacities is slyly minimal: "to serve him truly that will put me in trust, to love him that is honest, to converse with him that is wise and says little, to fear judgment, to fight when I cannot choose—and to eat no fish," the last being a joking play on "profess," which can refer to religious affiliation and here means that he is not a secret Catholic. Again, Lear asks, "What art thou?" to which Kent merely says, "A very honest-hearted fellow and as poor as the King"—qualities that are *dis*-qualifications for most social roles in the world to which he once belonged. His anonymity is evasive: "That which ordinary men are fit for I am qualified in"—no more.

It is understandable that Kent, who has embraced this reduction, is furiously contemptuous of Oswald, whom he spots as a self-making schemer who has striven to escape his identity as a servant in a great house, someone like the imagined earlier Poor Tom. As I have noted, Kent recognizes Oswald as "a knave, a rascal, an eater of broken meats; a base, proud, shallow, beggarly, three-suited-hundred-pound, filthy, worsted-stocking knave." Once limited by the sumptuary laws and accustomed to eat leftovers from his master's table like a dog, he aspires to change himself. Perhaps he even already has made himself a gentleman by purchasing, for a hundred pounds, one of the knighthoods King James was selling for that price. There is a social-satirical comedy in the contest between Kent and Oswald, between the aristocrat become a nameless man and the menial climbing out of his class.

Kent's minimalism is also one of language, which can, as he employs it, no longer make the claims to meaning that can only be identified as pretension. He tells Cornwall, "'Tis my occupation to be plain." Cornwall is right in saying that this apparent renunciation of "style" may be only another disguise, a pretended frankness that is a form of insincerity:

> This is some fellow
> Who, having been praised for bluntness, doth affect
> A saucy roughness, and constrains the garb
> Quite from his nature. He cannot flatter, he;
> An honest mind and plain, he must speak truth;
> And they will take it, so; if not, he's plain.
> These kind of knaves I know, which in this plainness
> Harbour more craft and more corrupter ends
> Than twenty silly-ducking observants
> That stretch their duties nicely.

That the utterly wicked Cornwall says these lines does not diminish their strength. Kent is not a liar, but it is true that he is hiding his former identity. Kent's honest ruffian impersonation is as much a disguise as Edgar's role of naked beggar, and as suspect as well. We must remember that "honesty" is the disguise of Iago.

And though we are not likely to validate Iago's claim of being the same kind of honest plain-speaker as Kent, there is something arguable in his contempt for Othello's contrasting style of speech. He calls it "bombast circumstance." Suspending our sympathy for Othello may permit us to see his point; Othello's high poetry is an inflation that can be allied even to the banal and meretricious style employed by Goneril and Regan in their early declarations of devotion to Lear. This style may appear at first to be only the device of hyperbole by which love often expresses itself, though its hypocrisy is soon disclosed, and they drop it quickly enough. But Cordelia can offer as an alternative only a rhetoric of silence. Her answer of "Nothing," to Lear's demand that she declare how much she loves him, has a strange correspondence to Iago's final words. When he is asked his reasons for doing what he has done he can only say, "Demand me nothing. What you know you know. From this time forth I never will speak word." Neither love nor hate can discover an appropriate language of sincerity.

"Nothing" resonates in *King Lear*. It is the word with which the stripped Lear is identified because he has lost all his selfhoods. The Fool observes, "I had rather be any kind o' thing than a fool, and yet I would not be thee, nuncle. Thou hast pared thy wit o' both sides and left nothing i' the middle.... Now thou art an O without a figure; I am better than thou art now. I am a fool, thou art nothing." Beneath the mantle of social roles, which he has lost, the poor, forked animal, Shakespeare's language suggests, is a mere lay figure, or nothing. The rest is drag. The reiteration of "nothing" elsewhere in the play serves to remind us also of the nothingness out of which God was supposed to have made everything that is. An atheistic giveaway in Shakespeare's day was the denial of Creation as the Old Testament describes it. Lear says "nothing will come of nothing"—a translation of the ancient materialist *ex nihilo nihil fit*—when Cordelia offers no other response than "nothing" to his demand for a declaration of love. Later, the Fool remarks to Lear, "Can you make no use of nothing, Nuncle?" and Lear responds with the ex nihilo a second time: "Why no boy; nothing can be made of nothing."

But the doctrine that God had created the world out of no prior stuff has always been a prop of the idea that all that is and all that happens is the result of His will. It was also a demonstration of the truth of miracles—that what God could perform transcended any conception we might have of natural law. It had been formulated by the Fourth Lateran Council in 1215 (and was to be reaffirmed by the Vatican in 1870). The materialist idea that nothing comes of nothing was a heresy for Protestants too. The ex nihilo view was called by Calvin a "filthie error." There were few who admitted believing it. Even Montaigne was unable to bring his skepticism to this extreme. The brilliant English mathematician, Thomas Harriot, was *reputed* to uphold it. When he died of a cancer that had begun as a small spot on his nose, a contemporary quipped, "a nihilum killed him at last." But his patron, Raleigh, was warned during his treason trial not to borrow this dangerous view, and Raleigh would deny his adherence to it in the *History of the World*, later written in prison. Lear's declaration would have been felt to be skeptical heresy.

Aristotle had used ex nihilo to support the idea of the eternity of the world. Its denial allows the Christian to believe that time is not infinite but once had a distinct beginning—Creation—as it will have a stop at the Apocalypse. So with the individual life. Birth and death were themselves governed, for the believer, by God's will to start and terminate human existence in its earthly form. If these beginnings and terminations seem without meaning, and time stretches incomprehensibly backward and forward, only a stoic acceptance of the mystery of our arrival and departure sustains life. This is the burden of Edgar's famous remark to Gloucester, "Men must endure / Their going hence even as their coming hither / Ripeness is all." Or, as Hamlet says, "The readiness is all." And perhaps the open structure of *King Lear*, as a play, reflects a human story that has no comprehensible start or finish but is part of a continuum represented by the endlessness of chronicle, as in the oldest sources of the play in which we are told that Cordelia and Lear survive and that, after years, new insurrections by a new generation arise. Perhaps the causes of such initiating events as Lear's preposterous abdication and his rejection of Cordelia are not really important, and modern psychological explanations of his behavior—or of that of his difficult daughters—may be misplaced. And the "sense of an ending," which gives significance to narratives, is gone; the play seems to stop several times before it finally ends. Its structural refusal to close down seems to express a skeptical dismissal of revelation, a weary inconclusiveness in which Lear and Cordelia die along with all the evil characters, without any special illumination. Shakespeare seems to deny the possibility of revelation when Gloucester, recognizing Lear by his voice, says, "O ruined piece of nature, this great world / Shall so wear out to naught"—again invoking the reiterated ex nihilo to which both world and human identity are reduced. When Lear enters bearing the dead Cordelia, Kent asks, "Is this the promised end?" And Edgar asks, "Or image of that horror?" All has transpired in a world without end, and perhaps without final meaning despite the Biblical promise in which belief still lingers.

R. A. FOAKES

Performance and Text:
King Lear

Performance criticism of Shakespeare's plays has been haunted by two anxieties in particular. One is theoretical, and, as formulated by W. B. Worthen, concerns "the legislative power of the authorial work."[1] He is troubled by criticism that uses performance as "an interpretive institution for the recuperation of Shakespearean authority" or as a realization of the text so that "performance becomes merely another way of reading."[2] He thinks of performance as not bound by the text, but as "operating in a given social and historical horizon," and as producing meanings "intertextually in ways that deconstruct notions of intention, authority, presence."[3] Every performance transforms "the text into something else, . . . something concrete that is not captive to the designs of the text."[4] The second anxiety relates more to practice, to what Anthony Dawson sees as an impasse between literary and performance criticism.[5] This anxiety informs Harry Berger's attempt to bridge theatrical and textual analysis by the notion of an "imaginary audition," while concerned that "the literary model of stage-centered reading perforce shuttles back and forth between two incompatible modes of interpretation, reading and playgoing."[6] The problem would seem to be that on the one hand performance criticism may collapse back into another mode of critical reading and support of the authority of the text, while on the other hand it may become a description or celebration of

From *Medieval and Renaissance Drama in England* 17 (2005): 86–98. Copyright © 2005 by R. A. Foakes.

151

ways in which a play by Shakespeare has been adapted or reworked on stage in order to produce new meanings.

I have no solution to offer, but I would like to draw attention to a feature of Shakespeare's dramaturgy that offers authorial guidance without imposing authorial control. In staging a play choices have to be made that limit interpretive possibilities, while at the same time they may produce new meanings, usually by contextualizing the action in relation to contemporary issues. There are various ways in which this can be done. For instance, at the center of *King Lear* is the storm scene in which the old king encounters Edgar, who has transformed himself into the beggar Poor Tom by discarding his clothes:

> My face I'll grime with filth,
> Blanket my loins, elf all my hair in knots,
> And with presented nakedness outface
> The winds and persecutions of the sky.
>   (2.2.180)

Identifying with this poor naked wretch, Lear cries, "Off, off you lendings: come, unbutton here" (3.4.106). Playing the king in the 1998 production by Richard Eyre at the Royal National Theatre in London, Ian Holm literally stripped off his clothes and appeared naked, or virtually so. When the televised version of this production was shown in Los Angeles, Holm was interviewed for the *Los Angeles Times*, and remarked how excited he was that Shakespeare's original intention had been restored in this scene. The director and cast were presumably using an edition that retained here a stage direction introduced by Nicholas Rowe in 1709, "Tearing off his clothes." There is no stage direction at this point in the 1608 Quarto or 1623 Folio texts of the play, and it was, in fact, stage practice until the early twentieth century to have Kent and the Fool prevent Lear from disrobing.

Shakespeare's intentions for staging are not often apparent, and at many points, as in this example from *King Lear*, are finally unknowable. So in this scene one actor playing Lear may strip naked onstage, whereas another may remain regally clothed. Some performance critics have claimed that "Shakespeare controls not only what we hear but what we see,"[7] but in truth Shakespeare leaves a great deal of freedom to the director, actors, and stage designer who control what we see, and in their cutting, rearrangement, or alterations to the text, they exercise much control over what we hear also. In the end they have to settle for one way of staging each part of the action. The reader is free to imagine at leisure various ways of playing a scene, but the director and the actors have to convert the text into an acting script and decide on a particular way of presenting any incident in the action.

In the case of *King Lear* the choices to be made are affected by the existence of two texts, the Quarto (1608) and the Folio (1623). Many think, as I do, that the later one, the Folio text, includes revisions by Shakespeare, and some of these, like the change in the presentation of Cordelia in 4.4 (see below, p. 156–57) relate directly to the main argument of this essay. The Folio text has been used to script many productions in recent times, but almost all of them retain the mock trial sequence in 3.6, which is found only in the Quarto. The choices directors make are rarely governed by a strict adherence to either of the texts of the play. Furthermore, however scrupulous a production may aim to be in remaining faithful to the text(s), it will inevitably reflect the times in which it is staged. The aura of royalty and kingly power manifested in *King Lear* has lost its appeal in the twentieth century, while most people are anxious about three problems that immediately affect society, namely, the swelling numbers of homeless people living on the streets; the aging of the population and the burdens this brings; and the decay of the traditional nuclear family evidenced in broken marriages and single-parent arrangements. These matters have influenced recent productions of the play, and help to account for its popularity in recent times.

Stage productions are thus affected by the conditions of the day, not only in such matters as costume and hairstyle (so that photographs of productions tend soon to look old-fashioned), but more importantly in relation to current social and political issues. Rowe's direction to Lear to tear off his clothes suited Ian Holm since his Lear appeared as a widowed middle-class domestic tyrant who was temporarily joining the homeless in order to feel what wretches feel. Directors have to make many decisions that stress some and shut out others of the possible nuances the reader can dwell upon. If Lear does tear off his clothes at 3.4.107, he may be seen as no more than a "poor, bare, forked animal," in a symbolic reduction of the king to "nothing"; if, on the other hand, in accordance with eighteenth- and nineteenth-century stage tradition, Lear remains robed as a king, the visual irony of his reappearance in 4.6 is enhanced when he appears crowned with weeds (as Cordelia reports in 4.4), his robes perhaps in tatters, but still crying "I am the king himself" and "every inch a king." In Eyre's production, the director preferred to disregard the concern of the play with royal prerogatives and rule, by treating Lear as an autocratic old man of some wealth and status who was dealing primarily with a dysfunctional family. In the opening scene Gloucester, Kent, and Lear, all bearded, all dressed in black, looked pretty much alike, and there was hardly any sense of hierarchy or royalty.

In the theatre directors like to achieve an overall style that will give visual coherence to a production and stamp their mark upon it. *King Lear* is not set in a specific historical time, but seems to invoke an ancient pre-Christian world in the opening scene, in which Lear swears by Hecate, Apollo, and Jupiter. A long tradition of giving the play a visual setting that suggested such a world reached its culmination in Michael Elliott's production for Granada Television in 1983, with Laurence Olivier in the title role. Richard Eyre's production, by contrast, began in no particular age in what appeared to be a drawing room in a large, fairly modern house. Other ways of pressing home a contemporary relevance include bringing on Lear in a wheelchair (Brian Cox, National Theatre, 1990), costuming Lear as an eastern European general in a uniform covered with medals (Donald Sinden, Royal Shakespeare Theatre, 1976), and presenting him as a stuffy old country gentleman (Tom Wilkinson, Royal Court Theatre, 1993).

A director also has to make decisions about matters for which the early texts provide little or no guidance. For instance, no exit is marked for Edmund in the opening scene. He can be sent off on the entry of Lear at line 32, but if, as in Eyre's and some other productions, he remains visible onstage, he may at some points exchange "most speaking looks" with Goneril and/or Regan, and so prepare the audience for his later involvement with both sisters. The Fool has no entry before 1.4, but in that scene seems to know all that has happened at the beginning of the play. His presence would be inappropriate in Ian Holm's drawing room, but can be effective if he is seen lurking in a crowded court in 1.1., as in Michael Elliott's television production. Lear talks of being attended by a hundred knights when he sets off for Goneril's house (1.1.133–36), but how many are seen onstage? Four are needed to carry out Lear's orders in 1.4, but there are no more entries for knights after Lear comes on with "a Knight" at 2.2.192. Nor does the text indicate how far Goneril's complaints about Lear's followers as "Men so disordered, so debauched and bold" (1.4.233) are justified. Peter Brooks's 1962 production for the Royal Shakespeare Theatre and later film version (1970) proved sensational and influential in having a crowd of knights wreck Goneril's dining hall, so providing a plausible basis for her hostility to her father.

Directors may also cut and paste or reshape the text by changing the sequence of scenes, or, for example, by moving the Fool's prophecy at the end of 3.2 so that it follows Lear's exit line at 2.2.475, when he rushes out into the storm. This transposition works quite well, since the Fool has not spoken for 150 lines in 2.2, yet Lear's last words are addressed to him, "O fool, I shall go mad." An interval may be inserted here to allow Lear a respite before his rages in the storm scenes. Directors also may feel the need, as it were, to trademark their production by making it different, as in the *King Lear* in Kathakali mode staged at the Lyceum in London in 1990,[8] and the cross-gendered version produced in New York in the same year by Lee Breuer, with a female Lear, Albany, and Cornwall, and Edmund played as a "sulky seductress."[9] Productions also have to be selective in characterization. Lears may range anywhere in the spectrum between a grand tyrant, as in Trevor Nunn's staging with Eric Porter in the title role, which began with "the great sword, the golden map, the hieratic throne. Here was majesty incarnate,"[10] and a "fidgety, unlovable father with delusions of grandeur," weak in body and voice, as played by James Earl Jones.[11] The Fool may be young or old, and has been convincingly played by women actors, as by Emma Thompson in Kenneth Branagh's Renaissance Theatre account of the play (1990). Goneril and Regan may be presented as mature women with a genuine grievance against their father's tyranny, as embodiments of evil, or somewhere in-between these extremes. Cordelia can be played as testy, like her father, in the opening scene, and as a kind of Joan of Arc warrior when she returns in act 4 (at the head of a French army in the Folio), or in a range of more passive and gentler configurations. The text allows similar latitude in characterizing Edgar as something between a wimp and an emerging hero, and Edmund as in the range between a calculating villain and an abused son who is conditioned by and sees through the hypocrisies of his society.

All these changing aspects of the performance of *King Lear* may stimulate viewers by producing "meanings which have to do with the precise specificity of location, history, and audience," and that recognize some potential, some nuance appropriate to the moment. At the same time, they inevitably limit the play to a particular stage embodiment. Yet every production, whatever its style, and however ideologically driven, establishes what reading cannot do, namely visual significances in the action. Critical accounts of the play are likely to dwell on the play's characters and on language, verbal meanings, and cross-connections. Much performance criticism has not moved far beyond an idealized description of how Shakespeare's plays may seek to "control and shape what an audience hears, sees, and experiences moment by moment in the theater."[12] Editors, too, are mostly concerned with possible ways of interpreting the text, and with its intricacies of relationships and values. In the theater, however, an audience goes to see a play and engage directly with the living interactions of the characters as people and as bodies. They are caught up in a shifting spectacle in which lines are spoken in rapid succession and resist analysis, while visual impressions have an immediate potency. I am thinking not of factitious visual aspects such as scenery or costume, though these have their importance, but of something more fundamental that has to do with the action played out on the stage.

Understanding of the play in performance I believe is generated through a dynamic relationship between the action witnessed and the words heard spoken, a relationship that can often, especially in key scenes, be very complex.[13] I would like to focus attention on this relationship by considering aspects of the action of *King Lear* involving Cordelia and Edgar. These characters have been interpreted by commentators on the text in various ways. Moralistic critics, for instance, have treated the play as a conflict between good and evil, seeing Cordelia as noble and saintlike, with Edgar as a moral parallel to her. Such a view is not "wrong," but is very limited to a simplifying perspective, and it does not take into account the interaction between verbal meanings and the emotional resonances of the action onstage. In the opening scene Cordelia's behavior gives the audience a range of conflicting signals. She refuses to play her part in an official court ceremony (though this can, as in Richard Eyre's production, be reduced to an informal scene, so ignoring her role as a princess and daughter of a king). She willfully disobeys the monarch, her father. She breaks silence to utter "untender" speeches in a public gathering, admitting love for him only according to her "bond," which makes it sound like a legal requirement, and finally she pours scorn on her sisters. So there are elements of obstinacy and self-will in what she says and does. Yet onstage this is not how the scene plays, for what we see is a young girl oppressed by a largely hostile family and forced on a whim of her father's to defend herself. The action staged in effect works against some of the primary meanings of the dialogue.

Cordelia's responses to Lear's demand that she express her love for him, beginning with the one word, "Nothing," are both harsh and just, offensive in relation to him as her parent and as king, if laudable as a refusal to lie. She is Lear's favorite child, which makes her reaction the more bitter to him, but at the same time he treats her as a chattel, a property to be given in marriage to the highest bidder, and her actions deprive her of a dowry. To the audience she is visibly isolated in court, with only Kent as a lone supporter, so that she appears as an underdog, whose only way of defining herself, of standing out against a patriarchal society that denies her individuality, is to act as she does. So her offense in performance tends to seem much slighter than the offense Lear and her sisters give to her. The scene can, of course, be played with varying emphases, as for example with Lear playing a game that Cordelia refuses to join (Granada TV, 1983), or with Cordelia showing an immediate toughness in opposition (Richard Eyre, 1998). However it is done, there is a tension if not a contradiction between the words spoken on the one hand, and on the other hand, the stage action and group dynamics of the characters. Directors and actors can exploit this tension by choosing some point, as it were, on a sliding scale in the way the interaction between Lear and Cordelia is presented, and I think it is this tension that generates the possibility of a multiple range of meanings that, as they accumulate in the staging of the play, contribute toward a sense of depth and complexity.

When Cordelia returns in act 4 she enters, according to the Folio version, with soldiers, leading an invading army as queen of France. Her tender concern for her father is combined with an urge to claim his "right" and put him back on a throne he no longer wants. In one aspect a sort of healing nurse, in another she is a determined warrior who may appropriately be costumed in armor. Again there is a discordance between the meaning of the words spoken, notably in her echo of the words of Christ at Luke 2.49, "O dear father, / It is thy business that I go about," and what the scene shows. This tension is continued in 4.7, when he wakes from sleep in her presence. He imagines he is in France, which suggests that the Gentleman and attendants in the scene, Cordelia herself also, show French emblems or colors. Cordelia's care for Lear and tenderness toward him ensure a flow of feeling in her favor, yet even as she ministers to her father, the moment he awakes she addresses him as king: "How does my royal lord? How fares your majesty?" He has come to acknowledge that he is feeble in body and mind, a "foolish fond old man" whose only concern now is to "forget and forgive," but this is not what she has in mind as she leads him off saying "Will't please your highness walk?" Her actions are those of a loving daughter caring for her father, but her words and bearing are also those of a princess determined to restore King Lear to his throne. The disjunctions between her actions, as she kneels to him and seeks his benediction, his bewildered anxiety to renounce the past, and her apparent determination to restore him to majesty complicate the scene.

Cordelia's last speaking appearance, as Edmund's prisoner, unites her with her father in a physical embrace. Here, in 5.3, surrounded by enemies, Lear's vision of them as birds singing in a cage and outliving "pacts and sects of great ones" is at once absurd (as we know they must die), self-centered (in his desire to possess her), pathetic (as he stares in love now at a face he swore he would never see again), and renunciatory (as a final distancing of himself from power). In a way he realizes the hope he expressed in the opening scene of coming to rely on his daughter's "kind nursery" (1.1.125). His words now, however, seek to absorb her into his private world, withdrawn, no longer concerned for others; in relinquishing his royalty, Lear has given up, and no longer rails against injustice. The decline in him is registered in the way he makes her an objectification of his desire for love as the daughter who, though married to the king of France, seems virginal, and can serve as surrogate nurse, mother, wife, and daughter all rolled into one. Lear has no more thought of her as a person in her own right than he did when he cast her out.

Here, too, however, the implications of what is said are qualified by what is seen in performance. Edmund, who has signaled that Lear and Cordelia can expect no mercy from him (5.1.66–69), enters in 5.3 "in conquest with drum and colours" (Folio stage direction) with prisoners we know cannot expect to live. Just as audience response in the opening scene is affected by the extent to which Cordelia appears to be oppressed and bullied by the court, so here in act 5 the pathos of an old man, "fourscore and upward," and his daughter, a king and queen both stripped of their dignity and reduced to impotence, and furthermore subjected to the brusque, even brutal, handling of their captors, gives the action its dominant emotional resonance. Feeling muffles interpretation, for the spectacle of Lear and Cordelia clinging bodily to one another as all they have left, and humiliated beyond their due and beyond expectation, demands our compassion. Cordelia is "cast down," distressed for Lear as "oppressed king" (5.3.5), whereas Lear speaks as though prison will provide the pleasures of retirement, gossiping about "court news." Her concern is still for him as monarch, while he has abandoned power and kingship. Lear had said he would never see her again (1.1.265–66), and now in 5.3 there is a sense in which he looks at her but does not see her except as a projection of his own fantasies. If he stands onstage united bodily with her, his words mark a mental distance from her. Instead of playing king, he would imagine them as becoming "God's spies," in effect playing God in understanding "the mystery of things," the mystery perhaps of the existence of wickedness that, according to 2 Thessalonians 2.7, will be destroyed by God. In the theater his words themselves remain mysterious, and the interactions between spectacle and words again complicate the resonances of this scene, which is at once deeply affecting and deeply disturbing.

Maynard Mack asserted, wrongly I believe, that we notice in performance "all that we have learned from reading and discussion." He gave primacy to reading, complaining that "directorial theatre" in productions on the modern stage is "reductive in practice."[14] Well, productions of *King Lear* are bound to emphasize one particular mode of interpretation, and may well cut or reshape the play to fit, but it makes more sense to turn Mack's assertion round and say, with Harry Berger, Jr., "What we learn from reading and discussion includes what we notice in performance."[15] Mack shifts into high gear, leaving performance out of account, in configuring the play as a universal morality about "man's terrestrial pilgrimage."[16] Berger considers "text against performance" from a different perspective in a concern about "the interaction of the characters and the community of the play," or the "common ethos informing the behaviour of all the characters," which he aligns with Stanley Cavell's idea of "the avoidance of love."[17] He is interested, that is to say, in the purposes of the characters and the ways in which we assess them psychologically and morally: "in the struggle of interpretation, we define the character's personhood over against our own."[18] He focuses on the text, on the ironies by which a character, so to speak, "intends to communicate one message, but his language, speaking through him and in spite of his effort to control it, conveys another which he didn't intend." This is an awkward formulation, for if we cannot be sure of Shakespeare's intentions, how is it possible to think of a character as autonomous and having intentions? It may be true that Shakespeare establishes through multiple textual meanings complexity of character and "encourages us to assign responsibility"; more dubiously Berger adds "it does not encourage us to confuse this with assigning guilt."[19] A notable example occurs at the beginning of the play, when Gloucester introduces his bastard son Edmund to Kent with words that say more than he notices: "Though this knave came something saucily into the world before he was sent for, yet was his mother fair, there was good sport at his making, and the whoreson must be acknowledged." Gloucester's relish of the "sport" and his jokiness reveal the absence of any shame or moral awareness of his act of adultery. Edmund does not comment, except through bodily stance and facial expression, and we are left to speculate whether he has suffered public humiliations in this way before; Gloucester's lack of feeling may well help to account for Edmund's callousness to him later. But Gloucester's intentions remain uncertain, a matter of the reader's or actor's interpretation—is he oblivious to the way Edmund may feel, simply unthinking, shameless, or is he merely talking in the customary way of men about the court?

The messages characters communicate are conveyed not merely through language (Berger's main concern), but through their visual and bodily interactions with others onstage, and through feeling or the absence of feeling. In concentrating mainly on the text, Berger has a hard time explaining why he finds the most compelling readings of the character of Edgar to be those that stress "his cruelty, his retaliatory impulse, his shame and guilt."[20] Edgar certainly has some of the most unpleasant lines in the play:

> The gods are just, and of our pleasant vices
> Make instruments to plague us.
> The dark and vicious place where thee he got
> Cost him his eyes.
>   (5.3.168)

Edgar's moralizing here and elsewhere is often taken at face value, as though he has an unquestionable right to pass judgment on others (Berger goes on to say "he has assumed the saviour's mantle and feels capable of pronouncing judgment"). Some productions have even given him a crown of thorns when he becomes Poor Tom, so linking him with Christ, as though his endurance of banishment and poverty has earned for him the authority to speak in this way. If Edgar is perceived as a force for good opposing evil in the play, then this simple moral assessment may seem adequate, but Berger had reason to be bothered by him, for when closely examined, his words bite more disturbingly. The "dark and vicious place" is in one sense the vagina or womb of Edmund's mother. In attributing viciousness to the place rather than to the person (his father?), Edgar appears to share the misogynistic attitude to women expressed by Lear in his madness, "there's hell, there's darkness, there is the sulphurous pit" (4.6.123–24). Also, if Gloucester's blinding can be attributed to his vice, might we ask what viciousness in Edgar brought about his exile and misery?

"The place where thee he got" also refers literally to the location, and how can Edgar know whether it was "dark and vicious"? "There was good sport at his making" is Gloucester's version, but Edgar takes a stern moral line, interpreting adultery as the cause of his father's blinding, when we have seen him as the victim of the cruelty of Goneril, Regan, and Cornwall, who punished him for what was to them treachery at a time when he was trying to do good, to help Lear. As self-appointed judge, Edgar speaks as though he knows the mind of God, and interprets the blinding as a punishment for sin. His interpretation has been accepted by many, in part because it seems symbolically appropriate in relation to an old tradition of punishing adulterers by the loss of the sight that first stimulated their lust, and in part because it makes some sense of Edgar's claim that "the gods are just," a claim contradicted by the death of Cordelia and the play as a whole.

However, in those scenes where Edgar's words are most disturbing when subjected to close analysis, the visual context and the nature of the action, as in the case of Cordelia, tend in performance to qualify if not disarm the critic. The lines cited are spoken over the dying Edmund after the duel between the brothers, and in context feed into Edmund's recognition that "The wheel is come full circle." The machinations of Goneril and Regan have been exposed, Regan has just been poisoned, and the "desperate" Goneril has made her final exit. Fortune's wheel has come full circle for all three, and Edgar's lines remind us that Gloucester too has met with a kind of poetic justice. The lines thus support the mood of the moment, a certain exhilaration in the physical overthrow of Edmund, a sense that Edgar as Abel has overcome Edmund as Cain, that good has triumphed over evil, a sense shortly to be disrupted by the entrance of Lear with Cordelia in his arms. In witnessing the action we do not have time to pause over Edgar's words as exposing character or motives. In the immediate context they may be heard rather as a plangent cry, both celebratory and anguished, that justice has, for the moment, been done—but at great cost. Even so, there is something unsettling about Edgar's judgmental words to his father.

At Albany's request Edgar goes on to explain how, in his disguise as Poor Tom, he came to know the "miseries" endured by his father,

Led him, begged for his, saved him from despair,
Never—O fault!—revealed myself unto him
Until some half-hour past . . .
   (5.3.19)

Here in the Folio text (the Quarto has "father" in place of "fault"), Edgar
again gives mixed signals. He acknowledges his fault in not revealing himself, while claiming to have saved Gloucester from despair. The idea of
despair invokes Christian values in what is generally a pagan play; Edgar
speaks as if he has saved his father from losing faith in the gods and from
thoughts of suicide. What then are we to make of his first encounter with
the newly blinded Gloucester, who is stumbling along led by another old
man? Gloucester speaks words to his guide that may be heard by Edgar, who
is onstage when they enter:

   O dear son Edgar
The food of thy abused father's wrath,
Might I but live to see thee in my touch
I'd say I had eyes again.
   (4.1.23–26)

These lines are spoken just as the Old Man notices the presence of Poor
Tom, and just before Edgar's aside, "Who is't can say I am at the worst?"
   Does Edgar pass up an opportunity to reveal himself to his father when
he takes charge of him at this point? Apparently, yes. But Gloucester comes
onstage led by a stranger, and there is a reason why Edgar, a banished man,
his picture "circulated through all the kingdom" (2.1.82), might not make
himself known. Furthermore the visual and emotional focus of the scene is
on Gloucester's bleeding eyes, and Edgar's words direct attention to this horrible spectacle. A director who wishes to show "cruelty" in Edgar might place
him where he clearly hears his father's cry to him, but an audience is likely to
attend to the overwhelming pathos of a blind and bleeding old earl.
   Yet it is possible that Edgar becomes aware that he may have been
responsible for the "despair" he associates with his father. Even when he acts
as guide he maintains a certain distance, what Stanley Cavell sees as an avoidance of recognition because he is ashamed and "cannot bear the fact that his
father is incapable, impotent, maimed. He wants his father still to be a father,
powerful, so that *he* can remain a child."[21] It could also be that in action Edgar
enjoys having a power over his father, as when he tricks him into throwing
himself off a nonexistent cliff in 4.6. Shakespeare draws attention to Edgar's

deception, as he takes on the traditional role of the devil in tempting his father to suicide, pretending to be "some fiend" (4.6.72). There is something disturbing about Edgar's aside, "Why I do trifle thus with his despair / Is done to cure it" (4.6.33); we might well ask whether it would it not have been simpler for him to stop playing Poor Tom and reveal himself as Edgar. Cavell thinks Edgar has a capacity for cruelty that "shows how radically implicated good is in evil."[22] The action onstage, however, does not invite such moral schematization. What is disturbing about Edgar arises from the disjunctions spectators may perceive between his words and his actions, between a concern for principle that makes him judgmental to the extent of playing God, and the feelings of love or compassion that mark his intentions as good.

I think Shakespeare had a superb instinct for opening up a range of the emotional possibilities in his plays, possibilities that in performance are more prominent than issues of judgment, morality, or consistency of characterization. As I suggested earlier, the words spoken in the dialogue often function as a kind of counterpoint to what is shown onstage, and meanings may be generated through choices made in staging the interaction between the verbal and the visual. Still disguised as Poor Tom when he approaches Dover with his father in 4.6, Edgar speaks blank verse again, in "better phrase" than previously, as Gloucester notices; Edgar lies yet speaks truth too in saying "You're much deceived." Edgar continues to deceive his father at the end of the scene, when speaking in his own voice he answers Gloucester's question, "Now good sir, what are you?" by saying

> A most poor man, made tame to fortune's blows,
> Who, by the art of known and feeling sorrows,
> Am pregnant to good pity.
>   (4.6.217–19)

Edgar has just applauded Gloucester's rejection of suicide, "Well pray you, father," but still his good pity falls short of revealing himself. However, his words about compassion are spoken just as Oswald enters like a bounty hunter to seize as a "proclaimed prize" the old "traitor," and so immediately precede Edgar's fight with Oswald to protect his father. In the Royal Shakespeare Theater production by Adrian Noble (1993), Edgar savagely blinded Oswald, grinding his staff into his eyes as if to revenge the blinding of his father.[23] This display of cruelty exaggerated the disjunction between Edgar's talk of good pity and his violence in killing Oswald, but did not seem implausible. The effect of emphasizing a gap between his words and the action onstage contributed to a sense of the complexity of Edgar and the way circumstances keep on revealing the inadequacy of his stated principles.

At the same time, the emotional focus maintains sympathy for him, since Oswald draws his sword with intent to kill. So on "well pray you, father," does Gloucester fail to recognize his son's voice, or is Edgar still teasingly not revealing himself fully? It is sadly ironic that when Edgar does eventually say what he feels, he has to report the death of his father, brought on by the revelation so long postponed.

It seems obvious enough to say that watching a performance of a play like *King Lear* offers a different experience from reading the text. Much less obvious are the ways in which the significances generated in performance differ from and relate to the meanings that can be teased out from the language in reading the play. The immediate emotional power of the work as staged, or what might be called the affective resonances of the action, may at critical moments run counter to the verbal meanings of what is said by the characters. As the examples of Cordelia and Edgar show, the visual context of what happens onstage enriches our sense of the complexity of these characters as we are made aware of the disjunctions between their words and actions. Directors and actors may use various means to accentuate or diminish the spectator's sense of these disjunctions. Making Edgar brutally grind out the eyes of Oswald is one way of accentuating a sense of cruelty. If Shakespeare was himself responsible for changes in the Folio text, he introduced the military display in 4.4 when Cordelia enters "with drum and soldiers" (F) in contrast to the Quarto, where she comes on with a doctor and attendants. In these and the other instances I have considered there is a spectrum of possible stagings that may permit directors and actors to choose from a range of different emphases, and the stage images and action have an unstable relationship with the dialogue. Directors and actors are always finding new ways of playing scenes, and it seems that we can never exhaust the significance of Shakespeare's great plays, significances that lie not simply in the language or the performance, but in the varying possibilities for interpretation generated by the gaps, discrepancies, and contrasts between the emotional register of what is seen and the verbal meanings of what is said.[24] This may explain why it is that seeing a new performance of a play can be so rewarding in making us aware of new aspects of the shifting relationships between words and action.

Notes

1. W. B. Worthen, *Shakespeare and the Authority of Performance* (Cambridge: Cambridge University Press, 1997), 155.

2. Ibid., 163, 178.

3. Ibid., 180, 190.

4. Ibid., 180.

5. Anthony B. Dawson, "The Impasse over the Stage," *ELR* 21 (1991): 309–27; he argues that performance and reading yield incommensurate values.

6. Harry T. Berger, Jr., *Imaginary Audition* (Berkeley and Los Angeles: University of California Press, 1989), 140.

7. Barbara Hodgdon, "Shakespeare's Directorial Eye," in *Shakespeare's More than Words can Witness: Essays on Visual and Nonverbal Enactment in the Plays* (Lewisburg, PA: Bucknell University Press, 1980), 115–29, citing 115; compare W. B. Worthen, *Shakespeare and the Authority of Performance* (Cambridge: Cambridge University Press, 1997), 6.

8. Described by Worthen, 34–37.

9. See Amy S. Green, *The Revisionist Stage. American Directors Reinvent the Classics* (Cambridge: Cambridge University Press, 1994), 103–14.

10. Robert Speaight, "Shakespeare in Britain," *SQ* 19 (1968): 368–70.

11. Herbert R. Coursen, Jr., "The New York Shakespeare Festival," *SQ* 24 (1973): 424–27.

12. Jean Howard, *Shakespeare's Art of Orchestration* (Urbana: University of Illinois Press, 1984), 2; see also Worthen, 155.

13. David Young proposed something similar in claiming that each play has "some kind of profound and productive tension between dramatic action and expressive language," but in his comments on plays he was concerned with psychological intensity (in *King Lear*), language and themes in a conventional way.

14. Maynard Mack, *King Lear in our Time* (Berkeley and Los Angeles: University of California Press, 1965), 4, 40.

15. Harry Berger, Jr., "Text against Performance: The Gloucester Family Romance," in *Shakespeare's Rough Magic: Renaissance Essays in Honor of C. L. Barber* (Newark, N.J.: University of Delaware Press, 1985), 224.

16. Mack, 117.

17. Stanley Cavell, "Disowning Knowledge" in *Six Plays by Shakespeare* (Place: Cambridge University Press, 1987), 56.

18. Berger, 227.

19. Ibid., 212.

20. Ibid., 223.

21. Cavell, 56.

22. Ibid., 55.

23. Reported by Peter Holland in his review in *Shakespeare Survey* 47 (1994): 202.

24. Shakespeare exploits discrepancies of this kind for comic effect in his consciously hypocritical villains like Richard III and Iago, whose lies are finally penetrated by the foolish Roderigo: "your words and performances are no kin together" (*Othello*, 4.2.184). Such examples illustrate one way in which Shakespeare deliberately uses the kinds of discrepancy I have considered.

Chronology

1564	William Shakespeare christened at Stratford-on-Avon April 26.
1582	Marries Anne Hathaway in November.
1583	Daughter Susanna born, baptized on May 26.
1585	Twins Hamnet and Judith born, baptized on February 2.
1587	Shakespeare goes to London, without family.
1589–90	*Henry VI, Part 1* written.
1590–91	*Henry VI, Part 2* and *Henry VI, Part 3* written.
1592–93	*Richard III* and *The Two Gentlemen of Verona* written.
1593	Publication of *Venus and Adonis*, dedicated to the Earl of Southampton; the *Sonnets* probably begun.
1593	*The Comedy of Errors* written.
1593–94	Publication of *The Rape of Lucrece*, also dedicated to the Earl of Southampton. *Titus Andronicus* and *The Taming of the Shrew* written.
1594–95	*Love's Labour's Lost*, *King John*, and *Richard II* written.
1595–96	*Romeo and Juliet* and *A Midsummer Night's Dream* written.
1596	Son Hamnet dies.

1596–97	*The Merchant of Venice* and *Henry IV, Part 1* written; purchases New Place in Stratford.
1597–98	*The Merry Wives of Windsor* and *Henry IV, Part 2* written.
1598–99	*Much Ado About Nothing* written.
1599	*Henry V, Julius Caesar,* and *As You Like It* written.
1600–01	*Hamlet* written.
1601	*The Phoenix and the Turtle* written; father dies.
1601–02	*Twelfth Night* and *Troilus and Cressida* written.
1602–03	*All's Well That Ends Well* written.
1603	Shakespeare's company becomes the King's Men.
1604	*Measure for Measure* and *Othello* written.
1605	*King Lear* written.
1606	*Macbeth* and *Antony and Cleopatra* written.
1607	Marriage of daughter Susanna on June 5.
1607–08	*Coriolanus, Timon of Athens*, and *Pericles* written.
1608	Mother dies.
1609	Publication, probably unauthorized, of the quarto edition of the *Sonnets*.
1609–10	*Cymbeline* written.
1610–11	*The Winter's Tale* written.
1611	*The Tempest* written. Shakespeare returns to Stratford, where he will live until his death.
1612	*A Funeral Elegy* written.
1612–13	*Henry VIII* written; The Globe Theatre destroyed by fire.
1613	*The Two Noble Kinsmen* written (with John Fletcher).
1616	Daughter Judith marries on February 10; Shakespeare dies April 23.
1623	Publication of the First Folio edition of Shakespeare's plays.

Contributors

HAROLD BLOOM is Sterling Professor of the Humanities at Yale University. Educated at Cornell and Yale universities, he is the author of more than 30 books, including *Shelley's Mythmaking* (1959), *The Visionary Company* (1961), *Blake's Apocalypse* (1963), *Yeats* (1970), *The Anxiety of Influence* (1973), *A Map of Misreading* (1975), *Kabbalah and Criticism* (1975), *Agon: Toward a Theory of Revisionism* (1982), *The American Religion* (1992), *The Western Canon* (1994), *Omens of Millennium: The Gnosis of Angels, Dreams, and Resurrection* (1996), *Shakespeare: The Invention of the Human* (1998), *How to Read and Why* (2000), *Genius: A Mosaic of One Hundred Exemplary Creative Minds* (2002), *Hamlet: Poem Unlimited* (2003), *Where Shall Wisdom Be Found?* (2004), and *Jesus and Yahweh: The Names Divine* (2005). In addition, he is the author of hundreds of articles, reviews, and editorial introductions. In 1999, Professor Bloom received the American Academy of Arts and Letters' Gold Medal for Criticism. He has also received the International Prize of Catalonia, the Alfonso Reyes Prize of Mexico, and the Hans Christian Andersen Bicentennial Prize of Denmark.

NORTHROP FRYE was University Professor at the University of Toronto and also a professor of English at Victoria College at the University of Toronto for many years. He wrote numerous books, including the seminal work *Anatomy of Criticism*.

ARTHUR KIRSCH is a professor emeritus at the University of Virginia. He is the author of *The Passions of Shakespeare's Tragic Heroes* and *Shakespeare and the Experience of Love*, and the editor of several other titles.

167

DAVID BEVINGTON is a professor emeritus at the University of Chicago, where he also is chairman of theater and performance studies. He is the editor of Bantam Books' 29-volume paperback edition of all of Shakespeare's works, editor of *The Complete Works of Shakespeare* for Longman, and author of *Shakespeare: The Seven Ages of Human Experience* and other titles.

PAUL A. CANTOR is a professor at the University of Virginia. He is the author of *Shakespeare's Rome: Republic and Empire*, the *Hamlet* volume in the Cambridge Landmarks of World Literature series, and other works on Shakespeare as well.

RALPH BERRY has taught at the University of Manitoba at Winnipeg, York University, and the University of Ottawa. Among his many books are *Shakespeare in Performance: Castings and Metamorphoses*, *Changing Styles in Shakespeare*, and *Shakespeare and Social Class*.

FRANK KERMODE is a retired professor who taught at Columbia University. He is the author of many books, including *The Age of Shakespeare* and *Shakespeare, Spenser, Donne*.

ROBERT LANIER REID is a professor at Emory & Henry College, where he also has been chairman of the English department. In addition to his *Shakespeare's Tragic Form*, he has published articles on Shakespeare, Spenser, and Renaissance psychology in various journals and lectured widely on Shakespeare, Spenser, and Renaissance literature.

MILLICENT BELL is a professor emerita at Boston University. She is the author of *Shakespeare's Tragic Skepticism* and other titles, and she also is a translator.

R. A. FOAKES is a professor emeritus at the University of California, Los Angeles. He is the editor of many volumes of Shakespeare plays. His publications also include *Shakespeare and Violence*, *Coleridge's Criticism of Shakespeare*, and many other titles.

Bibliography

Anderson, Peter S. "The Fragile World of Lear." In *Drama in the Renaissance: Comparative and Critical Essays*, edited by Clifford Davidson, C. J. Gianakaris, and John H. Stroupe, pp. 178–91. New York: AMS, 1986.

Berger, Harry, Jr. "Text against Performance: The Gloucester Family Romance." In *Shakespeare's "Rough Magic": Renaissance Essays in Honor of C. L. Barber*, edited by Peter Erickson and Coppélia Kahn, pp. 210–29. Newark; London: University of Delaware Press; Associated University Presses, 1985.

Bevington, David. *This Wide and Universal Theater: Shakespeare in Performance Then and Now*. Chicago: University of Chicago Press, 2007.

Bradley, A. C. *Shakespearean Tragedy: Lectures on* Hamlet, Othello, King Lear, Macbeth. Basingstoke, England; New York: Palgrave Macmillan, 2007.

Chakravorty, Jagannath. *King Lear, Shakespeare's Existentialist Hero*. Calcutta: published for Shakespeare Society of Eastern India by Avantgarde Press, 1990.

Cookson, Linda, and Bryan Loughrey, eds. *Critical Essays on* King Lear, *William Shakespeare*. Harlow, Essex, England: Longman, 1988.

Danson, Lawrence, ed. *On* King Lear. Princeton, N.J.: Princeton University Press, 1981.

Davidson, Clifford. "The History of *King Lear* and the Problem of Belief." *Christianity and Literature* 45, nos. 3–4 (Spring–Summer 1996): 285–301.

Davis, Nick. *Stories of Chaos: Reason and Its Displacement in Early Modern English Narrative*. Aldershot, England; Brookfield, Vt.: Ashgate, 1999.

Foakes, R. A. "King Lear: Monarch or Senior Citizen?" In *Elizabethan Theater: Essays in Honor of S. Schoenbaum*, edited by R. B. Parker and S. P. Zitner, pp. 271–89. Newark; London: University of Delaware Press; Associated University Presses, 1996.

169

Garber, Marjorie. *Shakespeare and Modern Culture*. New York: Pantheon, 2008.

Goodland, Katharine. *Female Mourning in Medieval and Renaissance English Drama: From the Raising of Lazarus to* King Lear. Aldershot, Hants, England; Burlington, Vt.: Ashgate, 2005.

Greenblatt, Stephen. "The Cultivation of Anxiety: *King Lear* and His Heirs." *Raritan* 2, no. 1 (Summer 1982): 92–114.

Guilfoyle, Cherrell. *Shakespeare's Play within Play: Medieval Imagery and Scenic Form in* Hamlet, Othello, *and* King Lear. Kalamazoo: Western Michigan University, Medieval Institute Publications, 1990.

Halio, Jay L. King Lear: *A Guide to the Play*. Westport, Conn.: Greenwood Press, 2001.

Hays, Michael L. *Shakespearean Tragedy as Chivalric Romance: Rethinking* Macbeth, Hamlet, Othello, *and* King Lear. Cambridge, U.K.; Rochester, N.Y.: D.S. Brewer, 2003.

Holland, Peter. "Evading *King Lear*." *Poetica* 33 (1990): 46–62.

Honigmann, E.A.J. *Myriad-Minded Shakespeare: Essays on the Tragedies, Problem Comedies and Shakespeare the Man*. Basingstoke, England; New York: Macmillan; St. Martin's, 1997.

Hopkins, Lisa. *Shakespeare on the Edge: Border-Crossing in the Tragedies and the Henriad*. Aldershot, Hampshire, England; Burlington, Vt.: Ashgate, 2005.

Ioppolo, Grace, ed. *A Routledge Literary Sourcebook on William Shakespeare's* King Lear. London; New York: Routledge, 2003.

Kahan, Jeffrey, ed. King Lear: *New Critical Essays*. New York: Routledge, 2008.

Kahn, Paul W. *Law and Love: The Trials of King Lear*. New Haven, Conn.: Yale University Press, 2000.

Kronenfeld, Judy. King Lear *and the Naked Truth: Rethinking the Language of Religion and Resistance*. Durham, N.C.: Duke University Press, 1998.

Leggatt, Alexander. *King Lear*. New York; London: Harvester/Wheatsheaf, 1988.

———. *Shakespeare's Tragedies: Violation and Identity*. Cambridge, England: Cambridge University Press, 2005.

Marks, Robert Gordon. *Cordelia, King Lear and His Fool: A Bold, Fresh Look at the Greatest of Shakespeare's Plays—*King Lear. Harbord, NSW: House of Cordelia, 1995.

McCallum, Alistair. King Lear: *A Guide*. Chicago: Ivan R. Dee, 2001.

McDonald, Mark A. *Shakespeare's* King Lear *with* The Tempest: *The Discovery of Nature and the Recovery of Classical Natural Right*. Dallas: University Press of America, 2004.

McGinn, Colin. *Shakespeare's Philosophy: Discovering the Meaning Behind the Plays*. New York: HarperCollins, 2006.

Miola, Robert S. "New Comedy in *King Lear*." *Philological Quarterly* 73, no. 3 (Summer 1994): 329–46.

Muir, Kenneth, ed. King Lear: *Critical Essays*. New York: Garland, 1984.

Neely, Carol Thomas. *Distracted Subjects: Madness and Gender in Shakespeare and Early Modern Culture*. Ithaca, N.Y.: Cornell University Press, 2004.

Nordlund, Marcus. *Shakespeare and the Nature of Love: Literature, Culture, Evolution*. Evanston, Ill.: Northwestern University Press, 2007.

Ogden, James, and Arthur H. Scouten, eds. Lear *from Study to Stage: Essays in Criticism*. Madison, N.J.: Fairleigh Dickinson University Press; London/Cranbury, N.J.: Associated University Presses, 1997.

Paris, Bernard J. *Bargains with Fate: Psychological Crises and Conflicts in Shakespeare and His Plays*. New Brunswick, N.J.: Transaction Publishers, 2009.

Rosen, Alan. *Dislocating the End: Climax, Closure and the Invention of Genre*. New York: Peter Lang, 2001.

Sadowski, Piotr. *Dynamism of Character in Shakespeare's Mature Tragedies*. Newark: University of Delaware Press; London; Cranbury, N.J.: Associated University Presses, 2003.

Snyder, Susan. *Shakespeare: A Wayward Journey*. Newark; London, England: University of Delaware Press; Associated University Presses, 2002.

Taylor, Gary, and Michael J. Warren, ed. *The Division of the Kingdoms: Shakespeare's Two Versions of* King Lear. Oxford: Oxford University Press, 1983.

Thompson, Ann. *King Lear*. Atlantic Highlands, N.J.: Humanities Press International, 1988.

Weiss, Wolfgang. *King Lear*. Bochum, Ger.: Kamp, 2004.

Wise, Inge, and Maggie Mills, eds. *Psychoanalytic Ideas and Shakespeare*. London: Karnac, 2006.

Wittreich, Joseph. *"Image of that horror": History, Prophecy, and Apocalypse in* King Lear. San Marino, Calif.: Huntington Library, 1984.

Woodford, Donna. *Understanding* King Lear: *A Student Casebook to Issues, Sources, and Historical Documents*. Westport, Conn.: Greenwood Press, 2004.

Zak, William F. *Sovereign Shame: A Study of* King Lear. Lewisburg, Pa.: Bucknell University Press; Cranbury, N.J.: Associated University Presses, 1984.

Zimmerman, Susan, ed. *Shakespeare's Tragedies*. New York: St. Martin's, 1998.

Acknowledgments

Northrop Frye, "*King Lear*." From *Northrop Frye on Shakespeare*, edited by Robert Sandler. Copyright © 1986 by Fitzhenry and Whiteside.

Arthur Kirsch, "The Essential Landscape of *King Lear*." From *Shakespeare Quarterly* 39, no. 2 (Summer 1988): 154–70. Copyright © 1986 by the Folger Shakespeare Library.

David Bevington, "'Is This the Promised End?' Death and Dying in *King Lear*." From *Proceedings of the American Philosophical Society* 133, no. 3 (September 1989): 404–15. Copyright © 1989 by The American Philosophical Society.

Paul A. Cantor, "*King Lear*: The Tragic Disjunction of Wisdom and Power." From *Shakespeare's Political Pageant: Essays in Literature and Politics*, edited by Joseph Alulis and Vickie Sullivan. Copyright © 1996 by Rowman and Littlefield.

Ralph Berry, "Lear's System." From *Tragic Instance: The Sequence of Shakespeare's Tragedies*. Published by the University of Delaware Press. Copyright © 1999 by Associated University Presses.

Frank Kermode, "*King Lear*." From *Shakespeare's Language*. Published by Farrar, Straus and Giroux. Copyright © 2000 by Frank Kermode.

Robert Lanier Reid, "Lear's Three Shamings." From *Shakespeare's Tragic Form: Spirit in the Wheel*. Published by the University of Delaware Press. Copyright © 2000 by Associated University Presses.

173

Millicent Bell, "Naked Lear." From *Raritan* 23, no. 4 (Spring 2004): 55–70. Copyright © 2004 by *Raritan*.

R. A. Foakes, "Performance and Text: *King Lear*." From *Medieval and Renaissance Drama in England* 17 (2005): 86–98. Published by Associated University Press. Copyright © 2005 by R. A. Foakes. Reprinted with permission.

Index

abdication, 117, 141

actors and acting, 152, 155, 163

"addition," 99–100, 100–101

afterlife, 55–56, 62, 63–64

aging, 24–25, 41–42, 57–64, 78–79, 83n21, 95

Albany (*King Lear*)
    division of Lear's kingdom and, 90, 91, 92
    as fool, 21
    morality and, 22–23
    time and, 25
    use of language and, 105–106

allusions, biblical, 27, 48–49, 106, 110, 130

anger *See* rage

Apocalypse, the, 35–36, 64, 98, 148

"Apologie of *Raymond Sebond*" (Montaigne), 35, 140

asides, Cordelia (*King Lear*) and, 93

audiences
    characterization and, 14–16
    Cordelia (*King Lear*) and, 49, 93–94
    nature and, 18
    stage performances and, 155, 157–158

Bell, Millicent, 137–149

Berger, Harry, 151, 158–159, 159–160

Berry, Ralph, 85–96

Bevington, David, 53–65

Bible, the, 33–36

biblical allusions, 27, 48–49, 106, 110, 112n11, 130

blindness, 23, 76–77, 107–108
    See also Gloucester (*King Lear*)

Bloom, Harold, 1–12

Bottom (*A Midsummer Night's Dream*), 29

Bradley, A. C., 82n14, 82n16, 85–86, 92, 94, 113

Breuer, Lee, 154–155

Brook, Peter, 93–94, 105, 154

Burgundy (*King Lear*), 90, 91, 95

Cantor, Paul A., 67–83

Cavell, Stanley, 158, 161, 162

characterization
    Cordelia (*King Lear*) and, 43, 92–94
    identity and, 139
    Lear (*King Lear*) and, 67–68, 74–77, 82n14, 85–86
    oppositions and, 37
    protagonists and, 114–115
    stage performances and, 155, 163

Christ figures, Cordelia (*King Lear*) and, 94, 95

Christianity, 14, 47–48, 48–50, 148

chronology, 165–166

Cleopatra (*Antony and Cleopatra*), 102

clothing
  human nature and, 141
  identity and, 137, 138–139
  Lear (*King Lear*) and, 100
  social order and, 145–146
  stage performances and, 152, 153

comedy, 14, 143–144

conclusion, of *King Lear*, 10–11, 28–29
  death and endings, 33, 42, 61–64, 109–111
  justice and, 109
  youth and age, 83n21

contemporary issues, stage performances and, 153

Cordelia (*King Lear*)
  biblical allusions and, 27, 106
  conclusion and, 28–29
  death and endings, 45, 62, 63
  death of, 33, 40, 41–44, 109
  division of Lear's kingdom and, 91–92, 92–94
  family relationships, 89
  Fool (*King Lear*) and, 4, 38
  id and, 127–132
  love and, 20–21, 47–48
  political authority and, 77–78
  reunion scene and, 72–73
  stage performances and, 156–158, 163
  use of language and, 99
  variant texts and, 153

Cornwall (*King Lear*), 90, 91, 92, 147

costumes *See* clothing

Creeth, Edmund, 65n5

cruelty, 105, 106–107, 108–109, 162

Cymbeline, 53–54

Dante Alighieri, 135n46

Dawson, Anthony, 151

death and endings
  aging and, 42

Cordelia (*King Lear*) and, 40, 41–44, 45
  Ecclesiastes and, 36
  human nature, 114
  "'Is This the Promised End?' Death and Dying in *King Lear*" (Bevington), 53–65
  Lear (*King Lear*) and, 39
  Michel de Montaigne and, 44–45
  morality plays and, 40
  nihilism and, 148–149
  providence and, 33
  Richard II and, 36–37

disguises, identity and, 142–146

Don John (*Much Ado about Nothing*), 6

Donne, John, 112n10

Dover, division of Lear's kingdom and, 90, 92

Duke (*Measure for Measure*), 61, 63

Ecclesiastes, 33–36, 36–37, 39

Eden, 16–17

Edgar (*King Lear*)
  characterization of, 2, 23, 40, 106–107, 122
  death and endings, 61–62
  disguises and, 142–143, 144–146
  identity and, 20, 125, 126
  madness and, 144–145
  nature and, 20
  oppositions and, 38, 39
  political authority and, 79–80, 132
  stage performances and, 159–163
  use of language and, 105
  See also Poor Tom (*King Lear*)

Edmund (*King Lear*)
  fate and, 131
  Freudian psychology and, 1
  Harold Bloom on, 3, 6–10, 11–12
  identity and, 142–143
  Lear's opinion of, 72
  nature and, 17, 19, 24
  Northrop Frye and, 14–15

political authority and, 79
stage performances and, 154,
    157–158, 159, 160
use of language and, 101, 109–
    110
ego, Poor Tom (*King Lear*) and,
    119–127
Elliott, Michael, 154
Elton, William R., 4, 6
Everyman, 129
Eyre, Richard, 152, 153, 154

Falstaff, 4, 5
family relationships
    aging and, 41–42
    death and endings, 53–54, 57
    generational conflicts and, 24–25
    Lear (*King Lear*) and, 15, 89
    love and, 20–21, 127–128
    nature and, 82n13
    power and, 59
fashion, 138–139
fate
    Cordelia (*King Lear*) and, 128–
        129
    Edgar (*King Lear*) and, 126–127
    love and, 131–132
    morality and, 22–23
    plot structure and, 116–117,
        130–131
    stage performances and, 160
Faulconbridge (*King John*), 6
Feste (*Twelfth Night*), 5–6
Foakes, R. A., 151–164
Folio text *See* texts, variant
Fool (*King Lear*)
    aging and, 41, 42
    Cordelia (*King Lear*) and, 43
    death and endings, 58
    fate and, 131
    fools and, 27–28
    Harold Bloom on, 3–6, 11, 12
    nature and, 21
    oppositions and, 37–38
    prophesy and, 27

social order and, 100
stage performances and, 154
use of language and, 102
foolishness, 21–23, 86–87
fortune, 29–30
    See also fate
Fortune and Elizabethan Tragedy
    (Kiefer), 116–117
France (*King Lear*), 48, 90–91, 95
freedom, 1–2
Freud, Sigmund, 1, 8, 42–44, 45–46
Frye, Northrop, 3, 13–30

gender roles, 118, 143–144, 154–155
generational conflicts, 24–25
geographical divisions, of Lear's
    kingdom, 89–92
Gloucester (*King Lear*)
    death and endings, 61
    division of Lear's kingdom and,
        90, 92
    Edgar (*King Lear*) and, 123, 124,
        143
    Edmund (*King Lear*) and, 8
    morality and, 23
    oppositions and, 38–39
    paternal love and, 128
    political authority and, 119–120
    self-discovery and, 125
    stage performances and, 159,
        160–161
    use of language and, 98, 101,
        104–105, 107–108, 109–110
gods, 18, 21, 54, 55, 58–59, 60
Goneril (*King Lear*)
    Edmund (*King Lear*) and, 7–8,
        9, 10
    family relationships, 89
    morality and, 22
    nature and, 18
    Northrop Frye and, 15
    opening scene and, 87–88, 88–89
    superego and, 116–119
    use of language and, 99
good and evil, 28–29

Hamlet, 29, 33, 103, 139
heart, 32–33, 34
Henry V, 76
historical background, *King Lear* and, 13–14
history plays, 24
Holm, Ian, 152, 153
Horatio (*Hamlet*), 4
human nature
    death and endings, 114
    identity and, 139–140
    King Lear and, 31–32
    love and, 127–128
    moderation and, 80–81
    nakedness and, 137–138
    oppositions and, 114–115
    political authority and, 73–74
    suffering and, 97–98
    wisdom and power, 70–71, 71–72

Iago (*Othello*), 6, 8–9, 147
id, Cordelia (*King Lear*) and, 127–132
identity
    clothing and, 137, 138–139
    disguises and, 142–147
    Edgar (*King Lear*) and, 122–123
    human nature and, 139–140
    Kent (*King Lear*) and, 146–147
    kingship and, 25–26, 117
    "nothing" and, 20
    political authority and, 87–89, 118–119
    psychological theories and, 116
    use of language and, 102
illegitimacy, Edmund (*King Lear*) and, 6
inheritance, 87–89
introjection, 128
"'Is This the Promised End?' Death and Dying in *King Lear*" (Bevington), 53–65

Jaffa, Harry, 69, 81–82n6
Job, Book of, 109

Johnson, Samuel, 42, 49
justice
    conclusion and, 109
    Ecclesiastes and, 34–35
    Lear's madness and, 124–125
    political authority and, 71, 73–74, 78, 79
    stage performances and, 160
    use of language and, 103–104

Kent (*King Lear*), 21, 92, 94
    disguises and, 146–147
    Oswald (*King Lear*) and, 15–16
    prophesy and, 26–27
    use of language and, 101–102
Kermode, Frank, 97–112
Kiefer, Frederick, 116–117, 129–130
King Lear (character) *See* Lear (*King Lear*)
"King Lear" (Frye), 13–30
"King Lear" (Kermode), 97–112
"*King Lear:* The Tragic Disjunction of Wisdom and Power" (Cantor), 67–83
King Leir (chronicle play), 46, 47–48
kingship
    characterizations and, 115
    division of Lear's kingdom and, 89–92
    Ecclesiastes and, 34, 35
    identity and, 20, 25–26, 141–142
    Lear's character and, 117
    Macbeth and, 115–116
    nature and, 19
    Richard II and, 37
    stage performances and, 153, 158
    wisdom and power, 57–58, 68, 69–70, 76–77, 78
    See also political authority
Kirsch, Arthur, 31–52
Kübler-Ross, Elisabeth, 56, 57

Lady Macbeth (*Macbeth*), 117–118
language, use of, 32–33, 97–112, 146–147, 162, 164n24

late romance plays, 53–56
Lear (*King Lear*)
    characterization of, 114–115
    death and endings, 10–11, 57–64
    Edmund (*King Lear*) and, 7
    identity and, 25–26
    kingship and, 47
    love and, 11–12, 21
    nature and, 17–18, 19–20
    oppositions and, 39
    paternal love and, 128
    Poor Tom (*King Lear*) and, 28,
        124
    stage performances and, 156, 157,
        158
    as tragic hero, 69–81
    use of language and, 103–104,
        107–108
"Lear's System" (Berry), 85–96
"Lear's Three Shamings" (Reid),
    113–135
Leontes (*The Winter's Tale*), 53
love
    additions and, 100–101
    Cordelia (*King Lear*) and, 20–21,
        44, 45
    desire for power and, 86
    Edmund (*King Lear*) and, 7, 8, 10
    fate and, 131–132
    Harold Bloom on, 11–12
    hearts and, 32–33
    human nature and, 127–128
    inheritance and, 87–89
    paternal love, 7, 15, 128, 129
    self-love and, 121–122
    wisdom and power, 72–73
Luke, Helen, 62–63

Macbeth, 115–118, 119, 120, 121,
    127
Mack, Maynard, 158
madness, 26, 29, 30, 32, 114
    comedy and, 143
    death and endings, 40, 60–61
    Edgar (*King Lear*) and, 144–145

ego and, 119–127
Fool (*King Lear*) and, 4, 5
justice and, 124–125
use of language and, 98, 103–104,
    108
wisdom and power, 70–71
Marina (*Pericles*), 40–41
Marlowe, Christopher, 9
Marx, Groucho, 68
Marxism, 31
A Midsummer Night's Dream, 29
moderation, political authority and,
    80–81
Montaigne, Michel de, 35, 44–45,
    140–141, 148
morality
    Cordelia (*King Lear*) and, 129
    death and endings, 64
    Edgar (*King Lear*) and, 159–160
    fate and, 22–23
    Lear's madness and, 121, 124
    nature and, 17, 18
    stage performances and, 156
    wisdom and power, 73
morality plays, 40, 49, 59–60, 65n5,
    129
motherhood, 118

"Naked Lear" (Bell), 137–149
nakedness, human nature and,
    137–138
nature
    Albany (*King Lear*) and, 105–106
    family relationships and, 82n13
    Fool (*King Lear*), 21
    Northrop Frye and, 16–20
    social order and, 24
    use of language and, 112n9
    See also human nature
nihilism, 148
    See also nothing
Noble, Adrian, 162
nothing
    Cordelia (*King Lear*) and, 99
    Ecclesiastes and, 34, 36

Northrop Frye and, 20–21
use of language and, 101, 102,
    147–148
Nowottny, Winifred, 86

"Of Judging of Others Death"
    (Montaigne), 44–45
Old Age (Luke), 62–63
Olson, Elder, 86
oppositions
    Cordelia (*King Lear*) and, 48
    death and endings, 36–37, 60
    Gloucester (*King Lear*) and,
        38–39
    human nature and, 114–115
    Lear (*King Lear*) and, 39–40
    nothing and, 102
    use of language and, 101–102
Orwell, George, 85
Oswald (*King Lear*)
    clothing and, 138, 146
    Edgar (*King Lear*) and, 162–163
    Kent (*King Lear*) and, 15, 26–27,
        101, 102
Othello (*Othello*), 147

paganism, 11
paradoxes *See* oppositions
paternal love, 7, 15, 128, 129
patience, 107, 108
Pattison, E. Mansell, 56–57
"Performance and Text: *King Lear*"
    (Foakes), 151–164
performances *See* stage performances
Pericles, 53, 109
Pericles (*Pericles*), 40–41, 53
philosophy, 123–124, 139–140
plot structure, 113, 115–116, 116–
    117, 148–149
political authority
    Cordelia (*King Lear*) and, 92–94,
        94–95, 156, 157
    division of Lear's kingdom and,
        89–92
    human nature and, 73–74

identity and, 87–89, 118–119
Lear (*King Lear*) and, 69, 81–
    82n6
loss of, 119–120
rage and, 76
wisdom and power, 70–81
political ideology, *King Lear* and, 31
Poor Tom (*King Lear*)
    clothing and, 145–146
    ego and, 119–127
    identity and, 26, 137, 138
    nature and, 18, 19, 20
    prophesy and, 27–28
    the supernatural and, 144
    use of language and, 98, 103, 104
    See also Edgar (*King Lear*)
Posthumus Leonatus (*Cymbeline*),
    53–54, 55
power
    Edgar (*King Lear*) and, 79–80,
        161–162
    Edmund (*King Lear*) and, 8–9
    family relationships and, 59
    "*King Lear*: The Tragic
        Disjunction of Wisdom and
        Power" (Cantor), 67–83
    kingship and, 57–58
    Regan (*King Lear*) and, 88
    See also political authority
pride, 75, 76, 77, 127
projection, ego and, 121
prophesy, 19, 26–27, 30
Prospero (*The Tempest*), 54
providence, 33
psychological stages, death and
    endings, 56–57
psychological theories
    Cordelia (*King Lear*) and, 127–132
    Goneril (*King Lear*) and, 116–119
    Poor Tom (*King Lear*) and,
        119–127
    Sigmund Freud and, 1, 8, 42–44,
        45–46

Quarto text *See* texts, variant

rage, 39, 44, 58–59, 74–75, 76, 103
Regan (*King Lear*)
    Edmund (*King Lear*) and, 8, 9, 10
    family relationships, 89
    Northrop Frye and, 15
    opening scene and, 88, 89
    political authority and, 95
    use of language and, 99, 102–103
Reid, Robert Lanier, 113–135
Richard II, 36–37, 46–47
Romeo (*Romeo and Juliet*), 22
RuPaul, 137, 143–144

self-love, 121–122, 125
self-pity, 121, 122
setting, 13–14, 153–154
skepticism, 139, 140
social order, 16–17, 131, 138, 145–146
sources, for *King Lear*, 13, 14, 33–35, 42, 46
stage directions, 152, 154, 163
stage performances
    Cordelia (*King Lear*) and, 94, 156–158, 163
    disguises and, 143–144
    Edgar (*King Lear*) and, 143, 159–163
    gender roles and, 143–144
    "Performance and Text: *King Lear*" (Foakes), 151–164
    Peter Brook and, 93–94, 105
storms, 126, 154
sublimation, Goneril (*King Lear*) and, 118–119
sumptuary laws, 138
superego, Goneril (*King Lear*) and, 116–119
supernatural, the, 120–121, 129–130, 144

Tate, Nahum, 42
The Tempest, 53, 54
texts, variant
    Albany (*King Lear*) and, 106
    stage directions and, 163
    stage performances and, 153, 161
    storm scene and, 152
    use of language and, 97, 104, 111n1, 112n5
textual authority, "Performance and Text: *King Lear*" (Foakes), 151–164
"The Emotional Landscape of *King Lear*" (Kirsch), 31–52
theology, 2–3, 11, 14, 16–17, 22, 148
time, pace of action and, 23–24, 25
Tom o'Bedlam (ballad), 28
Touchstone (*As You Like It*), 5–6
tragedy, 14, 29–30, 67–68, 69
tragic heroes, Lear as, 67–81, 82n14, 82n16
Twelfth Night, 144

vanity, 34, 36, 44
Viola (*Twelfth Night*), 144
violence, political authority and, 79, 80

Welsford, Enid, 100
wheels, fate and, 128–129, 130, 131–132
The Winter's Tale, 53, 54
wisdom, power and, 67–83
witchcraft, 120–121
word usage *See* language, use of
Worthen, W. B., 151

Yahweh, 3, 7, 11, 12
Young, David, 164n13